To, Leon,

Thank you and For w...
for The King & His Joy,
Wishing you Peace,
and Happiness.
    Be Blessed.

In His Love &
By His Grace.
    RAJ.
    09-2012.

Rec'v— 9/13/12
    Leon!

Endorsements

I highly recommend Christians everywhere to take time and read this powerful, confrontational, and yet soul mending new book by Raj Vemuri. From Dr. Vemuri's vast educational experience, combined with his inspiring life story of converting to Christianity from Hinduism, Dr. Vemuri deals with real day to day issues Christians face in their walk with God.

Almost every topic I have dealt with in over 20 years of pastoral ministry is dealt with and answered in this book. I pray that this new book finds its way into the hands and hearts of Pastors and Christians everywhere.

Rev. & Dr. Richard N. Ledford, II
Sr. Pastor Restoration Place, Tallahassee, FL.

Raj Vemuri is a man of God who seeks to honor the Lord through his life and testimony. A learned man with triple doctorate degrees, he is a humble servant, which is a rare combination of character traits. He is a gifted writer who distinguished himself through his first book, *From Hinduism to Christ*. He feels the calling to write, which is evident in every page of his book.

The present book takes a different turn, addressing many practical issues of the Christian walk and presenting numerous insights for personal edification and spiritual maturity. The title, as well as the content of each chapter, is thought provoking and enlightening. I believe this book will prove to be a great aid in life's journey for one and all around the world and perpetuate the teaching ministry of Dr. Raj.

Rev. Moses Kumar, PhD
Author, Bishop, Counselor, Pastor, and Speaker
President, Hyderabad Bible College
Hyderabad, India

I have been working with Christian leaders (authors, counselors, evangelists, ministers, pastors, teachers, etc.) for over forty-five years, and I must say that Dr. Raj Vemuri is a soaring eagle. The deep insight that he shares in this book is unsurpassed, and I know that it will bless you beyond measure.

Richard G. Arno, PhD
Author and Founder
National Christian Counselors Association
Sarasota, Florida

It is with great honor and respect that I have for my friend and fellow servant of our Lord Jesus Christ, Raj Vemuri. I feel that I can call him a friend due to the fact that a friend will not always tell you just what you want to hear but sometimes what you need to hear. As a brother in the Lord, Raj and I often have opportunities to sit down and discuss his heartfelt passion about the Kingdom of God. Having known him for the past 6 plus years, it has been my shared delight to converse many times about the Word of God.

Raj Vemuri is probably one of the most learned men that I know, with his wealth of knowledge and insight of other religions in contrast to the one true God. From the time we met I knew that there was something very special about him. After reading his first book, 'FROM HINDUISM TO CHRIST', it confirmed those thoughts. He is a man on a mission and that mission is to share God's truth with everyone he encounters and through this form of media, he would be able to touch people's lives all over the world.

Wade Mike
A genuine and humble man of God whom I have utmost respect.
A true disciple of Jesus Christ.

"Must Jesus bear the cross alone, And all the world go free? No, there's a cross for everyone, And there's a cross for me" [Thomas Shepherd]. John 3:16 says, "For God so loved the world," not the church and not religion, but the world, "that He gave His only begotten Son that whosoever believeth in Him should not perish but have everlasting life."

Rev. Raj Vemuri is a dear friend, brother, scholar, devoted husband, devoted father, but most importantly, he is a believer. It is our prayer and belief that once you have finished reading this book, your life will never be the same.

We all have a cross to bear and a crown to wear, and this book will help us apply godly principles and wisdom to our life's many challenges. Thank you, brother Raj, for getting our attention and stirring up the gift that is within us.

Rev. Isaac Randolph, III
Senior Pastor, Deliverance By Faith Ministries
Tallahassee, FL

May the clarity of thought, excellence of research, presentation of experience, and love of the Lord Jesus Christ bless you as you learn from noted author, Raj Vemuri.

JoAnne Arnett.
President: Center For Biblical Studies, Tallahassee, FL.

BEAR YOUR CROSS AND WEAR YOUR CROWN

Applying Godly Principles To Life's Challenges

"Deny yourself, pick up your cross, and follow Me."—Jesus

REV. RAJA SEKHAR VEMURI, Ph.D., Th.D.

WestBow
PRESS

Copyright © 2012 by Rev. Raja Sekhar Vemuri, Ph.D., Th.D.

All rights reserved. No part of this book may be used or reproduced by any means, graphic, electronic, or mechanical, including photocopying, recording, taping or by any information storage retrieval system without the written permission of the publisher except in the case of brief quotations embodied in critical articles and reviews.

Scripture taken from the New King James Version. Copyright 1979, 1980, 1982 by Thomas Nelson, inc. Used by permission. All rights reserved.

WestBow Press books may be ordered through booksellers or by contacting:

WestBow Press
A Division of Thomas Nelson
1663 Liberty Drive
Bloomington, IN 47403
www.westbowpress.com
1-(866) 928-1240

Because of the dynamic nature of the Internet, any web addresses or links contained in this book may have changed since publication and may no longer be valid. The views expressed in this work are solely those of the author and do not necessarily reflect the views of the publisher, and the publisher hereby disclaims any responsibility for them.

Any people depicted in stock imagery provided by Thinkstock are models, and such images are being used for illustrative purposes only.

Certain stock imagery © Thinkstock.

ISBN: 978-1-4497-4255-3 (hc)
ISBN: 978-1-4497-4254-6 (sc)
ISBN: 978-1-4497-4253-9 (e)

Library of Congress Control Number: 2012904197

Printed in the United States of America

WestBow Press rev. date: 05/04/2012

Contents

Some Key Scriptures xv
Acknowledgments xix
A Special Note xxi
Preface xxiii
Introduction xxix

Chapter 1: Balance: Are We Losing It?
   Matters That Need Immediate Attention
   Introduction 1
   Attitude—Positive/Good or Negative/Bad? 2
   Negative (or Bad) Attitude 6
   Positive (or Good) Attitude 8
   Conscience—Clear or Compromised? 9
   Defiled (or Guilty) Conscience 12
   Pure (or Clear) Conscience 13
   Seared Conscience 14
   Weak (or Uninstructed) Conscience 15
   Roving Eyes 16
   Gossip—Talebearing 19
   Judging Others—Casting Stones 24
   Emotions—Feelings, Reactions, Etc. 28
   Self-Esteem—Self-Worth, Etc. 31
   Thoughts—Adaptive or Maladaptive 34
   Time—Misuse and Wasting 37
   Tongue—Loose and Untamed 39
   Conclusion 41

Chapter 2: Prayer Life
Are Your Prayers Being Answered?
Introduction 42
Different Types of Prayers 46
Common Reasons for Unanswered Prayers 46
Does God Answer Prayer? 49
Intercessory Prayer 50
Fasting 53
Prayer and Fasting 54
Conclusion 54

Chapter 3: Self-Deception
Being a False Witness
Introduction 55
Fear of Rejection 58
Misrepresentation 60
Making Empty Promises and Breaking Promises 64
Talk Is Cheap (But Not Free) 66
The Bottom Line 67
Conclusion 67

Chapter 4: Establishing a Comfort Zone
Creating Our Own Safety Zone
Introduction 69
Choosing Our Inner Circle 69
Not Open and Willing to Invite Others;
Not Open and Willing to Join Others 70
Open and Willing to Learn; Open and Willing to Teach 71
Learning to Be Humble 72
Learning to Practice Humility 75
Conclusion 78

Chapter 5: Tithing
Robbing God or Ourselves?
Introduction 83
Giving Conveniently 87

Giving Grudgingly..88
Giving Sacrificially...89
Giving Cheerfully and Joyfully 93
Conclusion 95

Chapter 6: God, Our Heavenly Father
Who He Is and How We See Him
Introduction 97
The Names of God 100
God of Convenience..103
God Who Forgives...107
God Who is Just 109
Heavenly Father—God Who Forgives and Judges..................111
God in the Old Testament 112
God in the New Testament 112
Conclusion 112

Chapter 7: Equal Opportunity Destroyers
Areas That Can Bring Us Down
Introduction 114
Anger—Explosive and Impulsive 115
Impatience..117
Selfishness/Self-centeredness 119
Ingratitude and Lack of Appreciation..............................123
Expectations—Awards and Rewards 126
Food—Overeating and Wasting; Gluttony 128
Greed—Materialism 131
Jealousy—Envy...134
Lust—Actions, Deeds, Desires, Motives, Etc. 137
Pride—Self-Righteousness 141
Conclusion 145

Chapter 8: Personality
Self-Identity: Who Am I?
Introduction—What Is Personality?.................................146
Why Study Personality? 150

    DSM-IV-TR 151
    The Biblical View of Personality 154
    Conclusion 155

Chapter 9: Psychology: Can It Be Trusted?
    A False Gospel
    Psychobabble 156
    Introduction 156
    How Psychology Sees Mankind 158
    How God Sees Mankind...161
    Conclusion 163
    Myths of Psychology 163
    Introduction 163
    Conclusion 178

Chapter 10: Integration
    Merging Psychology and Theology
    Introduction 180
    Psychology versus Christianity 180
    Psychology versus the Church 182
    Psychology versus the Bible 185
    The Danger of Integration 188
    Conclusion 188
    Christian Counseling..*190*
    Introduction 190
    Biblical Foundation for Counseling 191
    God's Way for Lasting Change..192
    The Change Process, Utilizing God's Power 196
    Conclusion 197

Chapter 11: The Accountability Factor
    Sin and Its Consequences
    Introduction 199
    Sowing and Reaping 201
    Our Treasure and Our Heart...205
    Conclusion 207

Chapter 12: The Best Things in Life are Still Free
    Areas to Focus On
- Introduction 208
- Compassion 209
- Encouragement..209
- Faith 211
- Forgiveness 212
- Grace 214
- Hope 215
- Listening...216
- Love..219
- Mercy 221
- Tolerance 222
- Understanding 225
- Conclusion 227

Chapter 13: The Conclusion
    Telling Yourself the Truth
- Introduction 229
- Examining Our Heart..231
- Examining Our Thoughts......................................232
- Ready and Willing to Serve God and Others 235
- Conclusion 236

Salvation 241
- Introduction 241
- The Four Spiritual Laws 244
- A Model Salvation Prayer......................................245

A Final Note...247
Bibliography...249
Reference from the Holy Bible 257
My Testimony 263
About the Author 267

To my wife, Vicki, who has shown
love, support, understanding, patience,
tolerance, and has been a good
role model. What she has done
for me cannot easily be put into words.
I am blessed to be married to a
woman who loves the Lord.

To my daughter, Danielle, who has
been a true blessing as well as
an inspiration. She has touched
my life in more ways than I can
express. Though she cannot express
herself, she speaks volumes.

Thank you both for making me
a better man of God.
I could not ask for more

Some Key Scriptures

The following Scripture verses from the New King James Version are included as encouragement for you, the reader:

"This poor man cried out, and the Lord heard him, and saved him out of all his troubles" (Psalm 34:6).

"Be still, and know that I am God; I will be exalted among the nations, I will be exalted in the earth" (Psalm 46:10).

"For you formed my inward parts; You covered me in my mother's womb. I will praise You, for I am fearfully and wonderfully made. Marvelous are Your works, and that my soul knows very well" (Psalm 139:13-14).

"Trust in the Lord with all your heart, and lean not on your own understanding; In all your ways acknowledge Him, and He shall direct your paths" (Proverbs 3:5-6).

"Keep your heart with all diligence; for out of it spring the issues of life" (Proverbs 4:23).

"My Son, keep your father's command, and do not forsake the law of your mother. Bind them continually upon your heart, tie them around your neck" (Proverbs 6:20-21).

"Fear not, for I am with you; be not dismayed, for I am your God. I will strengthen you. Yes, I will help you. I will uphold you with My righteous right hand" (Isaiah 41:3).

"Call to Me, and I will answer you, and show you great and mighty things, which you do not know" (Jeremiah 33:3).

"My people are destroyed for lack of knowledge. Because you have rejected knowledge, I also will reject you" (Hosea 4:6).

"Come to Me, all you who labor and are heavy laden, and I will give you rest" (Matthew 11:28).

"Jesus answered and said to him, 'Most assuredly, I say to you, unless one is born again, he cannot see the kingdom of God'" (John 3:3).

"Do not marvel that I said to you, 'You must be born again'" (John 3:7).

"For God so loved the world that He gave His only begotten Son, that whoever believes in Him should not perish but have everlasting life" (John 3:16).

"Jesus said to him, 'I am the way, the truth, and the life. No one comes to the Father except through Me'" (John 14:6).

"Nor is there salvation in any other, for there is no other name under heaven given among men by which we must be saved" (Acts 4:12).

"If you confess with your mouth the Lord Jesus and believe in your heart that God has raised Him from the dead, you will be saved" (Romans 10:9).

"'As I live,' says the Lord, 'every knee shall bow to Me, and every tongue shall confess to God'" (Romans 14:11).

"To the weak I became as weak, that I might win the weak. I have become all things to all men, that I might by all means save some" (1 Corinthians 9:22).

"He who calls you is faithful, who also will do it" (1 Thessalonians 5:24).

"Behold, I am coming quickly! Blessed is he who keeps the words of the prophecy of this book" (Revelation 22:7).

Acknowledgments

I would like to acknowledge the following individuals for their contribution in more ways than one.

My wife, Vicki, who supported me with her diligent prayers, words of wisdom, and understanding:

My daughter, Danielle, who cannot express herself verbally and yet has inspired me immensely.

My Pastor friends: Rev. Moses Kumar, Pastor Ward Bradley, Rev. Isaac Randolph, Rev. Terry Fitzgerald, and Rev. & Dr. Richard Ledford. Thank you for your prayers, encouragement, and words of wisdom.

My Christian brothers and sisters: Cliff, Wade Mike, Officer Kevin Guimaraes, Annette, Damien Wilson, Robert Mattox, Layne Amrozovicz. Thank you all for your encouragement and friendship.

My siblings: Nirmala Kuchibotla, Dr. Radha Vemuri, Sudhakar Vemuri, Swarna Kunapuli, Dr. Ramesh Vemuri, Lakshmi Kuchibotla, and Padma Hari. Thank you for your ongoing support, encouragement, and for standing by me through thick and thin.

My good friends: Dirk Engstrom, Jason West, Steve Bauer, Jerry Ebisuzaki. Thank you for your friendship and for encouraging me to press on.

A special thanks to my editor, Mrs. Shirley G. Spencer, who has done an excellent job. God bless you.

I would like to say a kind word of encouragement to the editorial team at WestBow Press.

Most importantly, to my Lord and Savior, Jesus Christ, who has anointed and blessed me to write this piece of work. It has opened my own eyes and brought a godly change in me.

A Special Note

I have been a born-again (saved) believer since January 13, 1986. The term *born-again* means I have accepted Jesus Christ as my personal Lord and Savior. During these more than twenty-six years, I have seen, heard, read, and observed numerous spiritual struggles in many Christian people's lives, including those who are in leadership positions, such as pastors, deacons, elders, evangelists, missionaries, administrators, bishops, teachers, and so on.

For the past several years, I have felt strongly in my spirit that many believers are grieving the Holy Spirit, and I am no exception. The list of how we are grieving the Holy Spirit is exhaustive; however, I will mention some key areas where we are consistently falling. The list includes, but is not limited to, the following:

1. Not loving God as much as we ought to
2. Not fearing God as much as we ought to
3. Trying to turn God into a God of convenience
4. Not reading the Word (the Bible) daily
5. Not keen on praying for self and for others
6. Giving promises and not keeping them
7. Not tithing regularly
8. Being a false witness
9. Choosing to be selfish and self-centered
10. Not being thankful and appreciative enough
11. Taking God and others for granted
12. Presenting ourselves as holy and righteous
13. Judging others

14. Entertaining and encouraging gossip
15. Not practicing humility and refusing to humble ourselves

The Holy Spirit inspired me to write this book first to myself as an eye-opening process, and I have realized I am not the only one dealing with the issues mentioned above. Nevertheless, it is my understanding that literally tens of thousands of people (possibly more) may be experiencing the same things I have been facing.

Therefore, let us learn to be patient, kind, tolerant, and understanding of one another, and instead of judging one another in an ungodly manner, let us learn to appreciate, respect, and accept each other, despite our disagreements and differences.

Writing this book is my way of confessing to and repenting of those sins for which I have been and am still guilty. God, by His love, mercy, compassion, and forgiveness, has blessed and delivered me. There is genuine joy and peace in my life, and there is rejoicing in heaven for victory of one more soul being delivered from the clutches of the Enemy, Satan.

I would like to share a Scripture verse from the New Testament as I close: "And do not grieve the Holy Spirit of God, by whom you were sealed for the day of redemption" (Ephesians 4:30 NKJV).

Thank you for your understanding, and may God bless you and your family.

RAJ VEMURI

Preface

This book is written to encourage those who struggle daily in their walk with God and to try to meet the spiritual needs of many believers, beginning with myself. My desire is to address and encourage four kinds of Christians, both genuine and those who merely profess Christianity.

The first category includes those who are saved and are doing their best to serve God and others on a day-to-day basis. These are the individuals who are not afraid of confessing, repenting, and turning around if and when the need arises.

I am not inferring that these people are perfect, because no person can claim that distinction except God (Jesus). But these believers are easy to identify because of their transparency, meaning for the most part that "what you see is what you get." One can expect these individuals to be humble. My message to them is, continue the good work, and thank you for making a significant difference in the kingdom.

The second group includes those who are also saved and yet display pride (false pride/self-righteousness) and self-centeredness (selfishness), among other sins. Allow me to say again that sin can be found in any person. The New Testament confirms this fact: "For all have sinned and fall short of the glory of God" (Romans 3:23).

What makes the difference, however, is the variation of sin from one person to another. For example, one man may smoke only one cigarette a day, and someone else may smoke five a day, and another person may smoke ten a day, and so on. All are smoking, and yet they differ from each other in the quantity of cigarettes consumed. Likewise, everyone sins, but some sin much more than others.

Regarding the second category of believers, they can be identified and recognized by their attitudes. They are apt to make such statements as, "Look at the expensive car I am driving"; "I must be doing something right. That is surely why God is blessing me with wealth"; "My great love for God is revealed by my church attendance"; or "I am well-known not only in my hometown but also wherever I go"; and so on.

These people present themselves as holy and righteous when they are actually false witnesses, thus deceiving only themselves. They are quick to judge others, but when the tables are turned, they do not like it and may even ignore the person who is passing the judgment or opinion. My message to these individuals is one of warning: Please be careful how you present yourself, because whatever God gives, He also can take away, and He is known to do just that. In other words, God can undo what He has done. Let us, therefore, confess, repent, and turn around before it is too late.

The third category includes those who say they are saved but are in a backslidden condition. These individuals once served God in love and fear. They tried to live a good and right life as unto the Lord; however, something stressful may have happened in their life. Perhaps they lost a loved one, employment, or a home, or they did not receive a promotion or raise they felt was their right. When adversity struck, they cried out to God and expected Him to alter the situation to suit their needs/desires within a specific time frame.

When God did not answer or respond as they expected, they started blaming God and eventually became insensitive to Him and the Holy Spirit. Slowly and surely, their faith weakened and they became a backslider. These individuals possibly are carrying the heavy burdens of anger, bitterness, and unforgiveness.

The gospel of Luke tells us a story of a son who once walked away from everything and later realized the error of his ways. When he came to his senses, he returned to his father, confessed his sins and repented, and asked his father to forgive him and take him back. And the father forgave his son, restored him, and gave him all he had and more. The parable of the lost son is found in Luke 15:11-32.

God also forgives and is reconciled to us when we confess, repent, and change our ways. In the New Testament, we read, "If we confess our sins, He is faithful and just to forgive us our sins and to cleanse us from all unrighteousness" (1 John 1:9). God looks at the heart (inside) and not on the outward appearance (see 1 Samuel 16:7).

My message to these individuals is a plea for reconciliation: God is not a man that He should lie and fail. He is always right, and He is always right on time with everything and with everyone. He knows everyone's past, present, and future. God loves us, and He only wants the best for us. Therefore, let us repent and return, as did the Prodigal Son, before it is too late. He will always accept us back when we go to Him with a broken heart and a contrite spirit (see Psalm 51:17).

And finally, there are those who profess to be Christians, and yet they do not know the meaning of being born-again or saved. When asked if they are saved, they either do not know what is being asked, or they may answer yes out of obligation. There are several reasons why some people convince themselves they are saved when in fact they are not (at least not according to God's Word). Their explanations may include, but are not limited to, the following: "I was born into a Christian family"; "I go to church regularly"; "My parents are Christians;" and so on.

I have many Catholic and Jewish friends, who I have asked if he or she has been saved. Without exception, they each told me they had never heard the terms *saved* or *born-again*. When I try to share the gospel (especially John 3:3, 7, and 16), they are offended and tell me to mind my own business. My Catholic friends told me they are Christians, are sure of going to heaven, and therefore do not want to hear anything about being saved or born-again.

My Jewish friends tell me they are still waiting for a messiah to come; therefore, they say, John's gospel does not refer to them. They also contend that since they are "God's chosen people," the concept of being saved or born-again does not apply to them. They are convinced that their entrance into heaven is guaranteed; hence, they have no need to be born-again or saved. That's the end of that defense.

In addition to Catholic and Jewish friends, I also have some cohorts from my college years who belong to other traditions, such as Jehovah Witnesses, Mormons, and so on. They too deny the concept of John 3:3, 7, and 16, and yet they have convinced themselves that they too are saved or born-again.

My message to these individuals is to point them to Christ as Savior and Lord: Salvation is an individual and unique experience, which means one's parents or grandparents or any other person cannot pray the sinner's prayer on one's behalf. In order to be saved or born-again, each individual, without exception, must pray his or her own salvation prayer. Every person is expected to confess with his or her mouth and believe in his or her heart that Jesus Christ is Lord and Savior in order to be saved or born-again.

The Bible mentions four different terms relating to salvation, all with the same meaning. In other words, they are interchangeable. These four terms are: *born-again* (John 3:3, 7), *saved* (Romans 10:13), *believer* (1 Thessalonians 1:7), and *children* (or child) *of God* (John 1:12). If you have never confessed your sins and repented before God, you are not saved according to the Word of God.

In order to be saved (or born-again), an individual is required to confess with his mouth and believe in his heart that Jesus died for him. When one accepts Christ as his or her personal Lord and Savior, that person is then *saved* or *born-again* or a *believer* or a *child of God.* Anyone who accepts Jesus Christ as his or her personal Lord and Savior will become a new creature (2 Corinthians 5:17) and can be spiritually related to one another as a brother or sister in the Lord.

There is, however, one other category that the Bible refers to as apostasy, which means to fall or turn away from the faith. In other words, when an individual renounces his or her faith, that person falls into the state of apostasy. Apostasy is not the same as backsliding, as there is always hope for the backslider.

The term *apostasy* is found in the New Testament: "Let no one deceive you by any means; for that day will not come unless the falling away comes first, and the man of sin is revealed, the son of perdition" (2 Thessalonians 2:3). There may be many reasons why one chooses to "fall away" from the faith, but in my opinion, an individual may have his or her conscience "seared" in order to come to the state of apostasy.

When an individual voluntarily renounces his or her faith, it is then over for that person because God gives us free will, and He does not force us to choose Him. I believe during this stage, God will turn the individual over to a "reprobate" mind. The New Testament book of Romans mentions the "reprobate mind," which is surely God's judgment on those who have opted to fall away (see Romans 1:21-32).

My desire or goal is not to judge or stereotype anyone. During the planning and writing of this book, I have kept myself in mind, for I have my share of sins and shortcomings and have been counseled by the Holy Spirit for some time now.

I was led to write this book first for myself and then for those who share similar burdens. As for any other individuals, it is up to them to decide as to the portion of this book that applies to them personally. In other words, the final decision is between each reader and God.

My sincere prayer and desire is that all those who read this book would do so with an open mind, and that each one will learn to be sensitive to the Holy Spirit. This instruction may not apply to those individuals who either do not believe in God or do not want anything to do with God.

I strongly encourage each reader to examine his or her thoughts and, more importantly, his or her heart so that we all can try to maintain a clear conscience before God and each other. The Word of God places heavy emphasis on the heart: "Keep your heart with all diligence, for out of it spring the issues of life" (Proverbs 4:23).

I would like to remind all the readers that this book is specially written for those who call Jesus Christ their personal Lord and Savior. However, I believe it can also benefit those who are open and willing to learn the truth as it relates to God. It also gives each reader an opportunity to examine his or her heart as to his or her standing before God.

I realize I have repeated some information related to salvation, but this was for good reason. I believe we humans are created in God's own image, and He loves us so much that He desires to have fellowship with us all the time (eternally) and does not wish that any should perish (see 2 Peter 3:9).

Wishing you and your family the best.

Happy reading.

Introduction

This book not only explores the very issues we face daily; it also offers encouragement and hope to anyone who is willing to make positive, productive, and permanent changes in his or her life.

Too many individuals grapple with excessive stress, which affects every area of their lives, including emotional, financial, mental, physical, legal, moral, friendships, relationships, and, most importantly, spiritual. Of course, not all stress is detrimental. God allows some degree of anxiety to challenge and motivate us to change and learn from the past so that when we are confronted with it again, we will know what to do and how to respond.

Instead of complaining and finding excuses when trials, tribulations, and persecutions come our way, we should be thankful because God is giving us an opportunity to make necessary corrections and put something right. The Bible declares, "In everything give thanks; for this is the will of God in Christ Jesus for you" (1 Thessalonians 5:18).

I am convinced that our two most important needs are to love and to be loved. And as there are two important needs, there also seems to be two debilitating fears (of course, there are more). One of the most incapacitating fears an individual can develop is the dread of rejection. No one enjoys or anticipates being disdained or disregarded. Rejection can be so unpleasant as to obligate or force an individual to act in a manner that will make others like him.

The other paralyzing fear is anxiety concerning the unknown. God loves us, will not reject us, and will accept anyone who calls upon

Him. Even so, not everyone is willing to open up and share his or her secret struggles as it relates to rejection. I believe this is generally the case because not everyone is capable of speaking the truth, and not everyone is willing to accept the truth, hence the expression, "truth hurts." However, we seldom realize or even acknowledge that lies can hurt even more than speaking the truth. Because of not wanting to offend, we deceive ourselves as well as others.

The tactics we use in the process can include lying, manipulation, control, and such deception. We are often tempted to use these devices to gain acceptance and love from others. But their use often leads to defensive actions where we only tell others what we think they want to hear. As a result, we may compromise our integrity, not to mention the gradual searing of our conscience.

The truth is, God sees everything. He also knows everything. He is all-knowing, ever-present, and all-powerful. He gave us a conscience as a measuring tool or guide to help us keep our lives in alignment with God's principles daily.

God's creation is such that almost every human on Earth has the capacity to learn and understand His awesome creation and love. Anyone who is willing to accept this truth can have an everlasting relationship with God the Father, Jesus Christ the Son, and the Holy Spirit the Comforter who will change one's life forever.

I once heard someone say you cannot give what you do not have. This statement is true. If all we have is confusion, loneliness, and emptiness, how can we pretend to give something we do not possess or even understand? Claiming we can give what we do not have is nothing less than hypocrisy.

Furthermore, when others discover the games we play, they may lose confidence in what we are saying because we have not lived up to the godly standards we profess. Of course, there will always be individuals who test our consistency in either direction: how we portray ourselves in striving to live a godly life or our choosing to play games.

Joy, *peace*, and *happiness* are three words we hear often these days. Though most everyone wants to be happy, not everyone is happy. What seems to be the problem then? First, we must define what we mean by the term *happiness*. Second, we need to realize that happiness means different things to different people, or simply, "To each his own."

The *Oxford American Desk Dictionary and Thesaurus* defines happiness as "feeling or showing pleasure or contentment." Happiness can be attained in two ways: to try to "create" happiness on our own terms or to accept the happiness God "gives" freely. Let me explain how these two types of happiness work and operate.

Man-Created Happiness

When a man tries to create happiness on his own terms, he needs to understand that it can be temporary, obligatory, easily taken away, and often comes with a hefty price tag. Some examples of behaviors or things one might use to find happiness include, career, cars, drinking, drugs, gadgets, home, money, power, sex, shopping, smoking, friendships/relationships, status, toys, and so on.

Everything on this list (drinking, drugs, gadgets, home, illicit sex, shopping, smoking, toys, etc.) is costly. Some are temporary, meaning they will eventually end (career, power, status, etc.). Some can be eliminated either by force (cars, gadgets, money, etc.) or by nature (hurricane, tsunami, tornado, fire, etc.).

And some things in life can be obligatory. When we humans operate out of obligation, we generally do it for two reasons: We are not willing to speak the truth, or the other person is not ready or willing to receive the truth. Think about it: How often do we either lie or exaggerate because we do not want to hurt other people's feelings?

For instance, husbands and wives may say only what their spouses want to hear in an effort to forestall nagging or arguments. Simply to maintain a smooth transition or flow, we may say things to quiet the other person, purely out of obligation.

But truth is so powerful it can stand alone. It does not need a witness. It can and will survive on its own. And truth usually reveals itself sooner or later. That is why the Bible declares: "You shall know the truth, and the truth shall make you free" (John 8:32).

By nature, humans tend to be clever when it comes to hiding the truth. Many of us are afraid to tell the truth for fear of being rejected. Rejection can be devastating, especially when one is trying so hard to be truthful and honest.

Yet, regardless of how and why we try to deceive others and ourselves, God still knows the truth about everyone. In fact, He knows our past, present, and future. We can do nothing to hide from God or from our own conscience, assuming the latter is intact.

God-Given Happiness

God is the only one who can give us true and genuine happiness. The happiness He supplies is permanent, natural, free (no strings attached), and cannot be taken away unless we choose to reject it. Examples include, compassion, faith, forgiveness, grace, love, mercy, patience, understanding, wisdom, and so on. Everything on this list is free, permanent, and natural, meaning, it comes from the heart.

Those of us who call Jesus our Lord and Savior ought to apply God's principles to our lives daily. As we do so, we grow closer to God and become more effective witnesses for Christ. This is especially important to those hurting individuals who may be praying for a godly person to come across their path with some genuine encouragement and compassion.

When people are suffering, they appreciate and more readily receive the genuine. And once they have experienced godly compassion and encouragement, they understand the importance of sharing this gift with others. In the gospel of Matthew, we read: "Freely you have received, freely give" (10:8). God's will is that His children (those who have accepted Christ as Savior) engage in prayer, encouragement, fasting, and intercession for one another.

The purpose of this book is twofold: First, it was written to persuade readers to believe that God has chosen them to receive unlimited blessings from heaven. Second, its purpose is to show them how to receive and claim those blessings and promises.

My desire is that as you study and apply the principles explained in this book, they will initiate positive and productive changes in your life. Others no doubt will be greatly influenced as they witness your godly life as it is brought into compliance with standards backed and supported by the Word of God.

This book will explore many important yet crucial areas of life. For instance, you will find yourself examining your heart and thoughts with regard to grace, forgiveness, love, fear of rejection, failure of modern psychology, psychobabble, accountability, sowing and reaping, tithing, judging others, conscience, emotions, use of time, use of the tongue, friendships, fellowship, giving, pride, self-righteousness, selfishness, self-centeredness, hypocrisy, and many other equally important issues.

Now, let us start this journey by raising the standard of God's Word, which, when applied, can transform every aspect of our lives. The ultimate goal or desire is for us to find true peace and happiness. We need to understand that no man can give that which only God provides.

Therefore, let us pour out all of our heart's desire to the Lord who can bless us with true and genuine peace and happiness, something for which we have been yearning for ages. As you read this book, please meditate on the apostle John's statements: "You shall know the truth, and the truth shall make you free," and "Therefore, if the Son makes you free, you shall be free indeed" (John 8:32, 36).

My sincere prayer is that God will shine His mercy and grace on everyone who comes across this book. I wish all its readers and their families the best. May you find true peace, joy, and happiness. God Bless.

Chapter One

Balance: Are We Losing It?

Matters That Need Immediate Attention

Introduction

Based on my own life experiences, keen observation, reading, listening to sermons, and hearing others talk and share, it is evident to me that many of us struggle in the area of balance. This is especially true as it relates to attitudes, conscience, emotions, gossip, judging others, self-esteem, thoughts, time, the tongue, and what we view. Because these sins occur so frequently (daily), we are unable to be effective witnesses. How can we confront these traits in others when we are guilty of the same faults?

Each of these grievances needs to be examined carefully, and when one or more is identified, we should take immediate steps to bring our actions into alignment with the Word of God, which is the Bible.

I will explain in detail at least ten important areas of our lives that can either make us or break us in terms of how we conduct ourselves with others and, most importantly, how we relate to God, our heavenly Father.

For over fifteen years, I have counseled individuals, marriages, and families from a biblical perspective. I have observed that many people seem to struggle with the issues mentioned above.

Though I considered covering other equally important areas in which many of us fall and fail, I settled on addressing only those with which I have dealt personally or have counseled, encouraged, and advised others.

I sincerely hope and pray that, with God's help and our ability to maintain an open mind, we will make positive and productive changes in our lives so others will be motivated to do what is right before God and others.

Let us begin this chapter with the following important issues.

Attitude—Positive/Good or Negative/Bad?

Attitude is an important character trait, and studying it can help us understand others and ourselves. Attitude is definitely a word we hear often, perhaps even daily.

As we interact and associate with one another directly (in person) and indirectly (via telephone, fax, texting, e-mail, etc.), we discover and understand a lot about each other as it relates to personality. One's personality consists of many characteristics, and attitude plays a key role in how others perceive us.

What exactly is attitude and are there different types? According to the *Oxford Desk Dictionary*, the word *attitude* means "opinion or way of thinking, behavior, reflecting this position, feeling, view."

Merriam Webster's Dictionary defines the word *attitude* as a "mental position or feeling with regard to a fact or state; the position of something in relation to something else." Well-known psychologist Gordon Allport defined attitude as a "like or dislike that influences our behavior toward someone or something" (Allport, 1935).

Other terms often used as synonyms for attitude are: "mental attitude, disposition, position, posture, feeling, mood, sentiment, cognition, temper, perspective, frame of mind, mannerism, view, or orientation" (Robbins, 2011).

More simply put, attitude is our <u>inward disposition</u> toward an object, person, group, event, and/or circumstance. Author James Kalat argues that "our attitude consists of three components: emotional, cognitive, and behavioral" (Kalat, 2005). The emotional component explains how we feel about something. The cognitive component explains what we know or believe. The behavioral component explains what we are likely to do in a given situation or circumstance.

Dr. Kalat further adds that persuasion plays a key role since it attempts to alter or change our behavior and eventually our attitudes (Kalat, 2005). Can one's attitude be measured? Yes, attitude can be judged, using scales also referred to as psychometric assessment tools.

Many scales are available by which one's attitude can be gauged. One such common or well-known assessment tool is the Likert Scale, also known as "Summated Rating Scales" (Dawes and Smith, 1985).

The Likert Scale, named for psychologist Rensis Likert, may have points or numbers ranging from either one to five or from one to seven. Number 1 usually represents "strongly disagree" and number 5 (or 7) represents "strongly agree." Number 3 (or 4) usually denotes a "neutral" stance.

A number is allotted for each question asked, and the total sum of all the numbers (or answers) helps us understand where an individual stands in terms of his or her opinions (or beliefs).

Attitudes can be expressed in many different ways. We tend to select an avenue of expression that suits our personality. For instance, some people reveal attitude with facial expressions, while others reveal it by their tone of voice.

Some display an attitude in their behavior, while others reveal it in the way they perform a task or job. We choose different ways of expressing our attitudes, directly or indirectly and verbally or nonverbally.

What does the Bible say about attitude? God's Word has much to say on the subject. Pastor Tom Moore explains that the "English word *attitude* is translated in the Bible as mind, countenance, and heart" (Moore, 2011).

The apostle Paul gave the best example of an attitude in the New Testament. Scripture verses in the Old Testament also deal with attitude. And, let us not forget that Jesus is and was the ultimate example of someone with a perfect attitude.

When an individual is "saved" or "born-again," he or she becomes a "new creature." The Bible declares that, at that point, "old things have passed away; behold, all things have become new" (2 Corinthians 5:17). And part of becoming a new creature is that one's attitude is to become like that of Jesus. In the New Testament, we read, "Let this mind be in you which was also in Christ Jesus" (Philippians 2:5).

This concept of putting off the old self and developing new attitudes is confirmed by another passage: "That you put off, concerning your former conduct, the old man which grows corrupt according to the deceitful lusts" (Ephesians 4:22).

Let us consider some biblical examples, beginning with Jesus. The Lord was known to maintain a perfect attitude in every situation and at all times. He was optimistic, always obedient to the Father, did His Father's will, and worried about nothing.

Just as Jesus checked with His Father on everything, we too should seek God's guidance and direction about every aspect of our lives. One author explains, "Jesus' attitude was never to become defensive, discouraged, or depressed because His goal was to please the Father rather than to achieve His own agenda" (Houdmann, 2009).

Jesus maintained balance in all aspects of His life. In other words, He did not vacillate from one extreme to the other. For instance, we can act happy when we win the lottery or receive a pay raise or promotion, and so on. Then, just as quickly, we can become sad, depressed, helpless, and so on, when things do not go our way. This would qualify the concept of shifting from "one extreme to the other," where one's emotions, feelings, thoughts, and actions are definitely unbalanced or out of control.

Jesus, on the other hand, set a good example for all of us and established Himself as a positive role model. He showed patience in the face of trials. Where suffering was involved, He maintained hope. When blessings came His way, Jesus practiced humility. And regardless of how badly He was treated, Jesus maintained balance. "When He was reviled, [He] did not revile in return; when He suffered, He did not threaten, but committed Himself to Him who judges righteously" (1 Peter 2:23).

Another excellent biblical example can be found in the life of the apostle Paul. Though he spent a great amount of time in prison, he never showed discouragement. To the contrary, he modeled the attitude we should have under similar circumstances.

Paul encouraged the Philippians and us to "only let your conduct be worthy of the gospel of Christ, so that whether I come and see you or am absent, I may hear of your affairs, that you stand fast in one spirit, with one mind striving together for the faith of the gospel" (Philippians 1:27).

The apostle Paul admonished us to always act, behave, and respond with a Christlike attitude, even when things are not going our way. Later in this same epistle, he writes, "Let this mind be in you which was also in Christ Jesus" (Philippians 2:5).

In his letter to the church in Ephesus, the apostle encourages believers to adopt godly traits: "Therefore be imitators of God as dear children" (Ephesians 5:1).

As stated earlier, attitudes can be either positive (good) or negative (bad). The Bible gives examples of both types for our observation.

Negative (or Bad) Attitude

What is the correlation between negative attitudes and one's relationship with God? Negative attitudes are easy to detect and do not require deep discernment. Some obvious signs of negativity are arrogance, a critical spirit, disrespect, impatience, judgment, pride, rebellion, rudeness, self-centeredness, discourteousness, and such like.

Author Dale Robbins states that "attitudes are inner dispositions of the heart and thoughts . . . they are the hidden intentions which will eventually serve as the basis for our actions" (Robbins, 2011). The book of Proverbs challenges as well as confirms this statement by declaring: "For as he [a person] thinks in his heart, so is he" (Proverbs 23:7).

Note the fact here that no one knows an individual's thoughts except that person and God. Consequently, an inward change must take place, and we must depend on and trust God to help us as we learn to submit and surrender our attitudes to Him.

Negative attitudes affect our relationship with God in several ways:

1. When things are working out for us, we seem to be doing what is right. But when trials, tribulations, and persecutions come and our world begins to shake, we respond by distancing ourselves from God, becoming critical of other Christians, and so on.

    During these difficult times, we need to learn to persevere. In the apostle Paul's letter to the Romans, we read these encouraging words: "And we know that all things work together for good to those who love God, to those who are the called according to His purpose" (Romans 8:28).

2. Negative attitudes can persuade us to turn away from God. In the book of Genesis, we read the following: "The Lord said to Cain, 'Why are you angry? And why has your countenance fallen?'" (4:6). We do not know for sure why God rejected Cain's offering. Possibly, Cain maintained a negative attitude. Regardless of the reason, Cain's offerings fell short of God's standards.

3. Many people are offended when they are confronted about ongoing sins. You may try to intervene because you care and have good intentions, but the wayward one may perceive you as having a "holier-than-thou" attitude.

   This type of intervention may cause the confronted individual to avoid and ignore you at all costs. His or her next step is usually to badmouth you. This in turn results in that person having a strained relationship with God. The Bible declares that no one can hide and escape from the all-seeing eyes of God.

4. Finally, negative attitudes can lead to wrong decisions. The natural tendency for many of us is to want to be like others (keeping up with the Joneses, you know). In the process of striving to be like others, we tend to make wrong choices because we want to "fit in" and be accepted.

In the Old Testament book of 1 Samuel, we read: "Look, you are old, and your sons do not walk in your ways. Now make us a king to judge us like all the nations" (1 Samuel 8:5). The Israelites' request for a king is understandable, but God wanted and expected Israel to be a holy and separate nation, unique from all others (see Leviticus 20:26).

Yet, they wanted a king like other nations, meaning, the reasons and motive for asking for a king (of their choice) was wrong and in direct opposition to God's plan.

When we choose to be like others (especially when our role models are not serving God), we are asking for spiritual troubles. Sometimes, God is known to give us what we ask for in order to teach us a lesson.

Positive (or Good) Attitude

The Bible clearly states that we should always strive to conform our attitude to that of Jesus Christ (Philippians 2:5). Just as we can detect the signs associated with negative attitudes, the same holds true for positive attitudes.

Those who show and maintain positive attitudes are recognized by such character traits as optimism, consideration, encouragement, forgiveness, humility, kindness, love, patience, sympathy, a teachable spirit, and so on. Paul's epistle to the Galatians mentions nine fruits of the Spirit that compare favorably to a positive attitude (read Galatians 5:22-23).

Let us consider some benefits of maintaining a positive attitude:

1. A positive attitude can influence others. The best example may be that of Moses. In Exodus, we read: "And Moses said to the people, 'Do not be afraid. Standstill, and see the salvation of the Lord, which He will accomplish for you today. For the Egyptians, whom you see today, you shall see again no more forever" (Exodus 14:13). When people around Moses felt troubled, Moses called on the Lord to intervene on his behalf, and the Lord answered his prayer. This incident motivated the people to adopt the same attitude as Moses, which was to "stand firm" and trust in God.
2. Positive attitudes can help us overcome trials and tribulations. Sometimes we face tasks that overwhelm and challenge us. In the natural, the prospects may seem more than we can accomplish. However, when we approach the situation with a positive mind-set and give the matter to God, He will guide us every step of the way. The biblical example of Ruth, a woman of God, fits this category (see Ruth 2:6).

Attitude is not a secret that can be kept or hidden. Whether it is negative or positive, a person's attitude can and will reveal itself based on the signs he or she demonstrates and displays, which manifest themselves one way or another. Whether through facial expressions, tone of voice, thoughts, or actions, we are constantly sending messages to others; therefore, it is important that we cultivate and maintain only those attitudes that line up with the Word of God. By doing this, not only are we bettering ourselves, we are also helping others to become good role models.

Conscience—Clear or Compromised?

What is conscience? One author explains it as follows: "If you've ever done someone wrong and then found yourself unable to look that person in the eye, you've experienced the power of human conscience. It has a tremendous power over the spirit to either bring it great strength or to sap it and its power" (Arch, 1999).

The word *conscience* is important, not only from a spiritual viewpoint but also from a legal standpoint. From a spiritual aspect, God has given us a conscience as a measuring tool or guide to help us discern right from wrong. The apostle Paul confirmed this truth when he said, "I myself always strive to have a conscience without offense toward God and men" (Acts 24:16). Everyone, especially a believer, must make sincere efforts to maintain a clear conscience before God.

From a legal standpoint, in a mental insanity case, the courts will examine an individual's mental condition to determine if the perpetrator knows the difference between right and wrong. When it is ruled that the individual cannot make that differentiation, he or she may be declared not guilty by reason of insanity and admitted to an inpatient psychiatric treatment facility as opposed to serving time in jail.

The *Oxford Desk Dictionary* defines *conscience* as "an inner feeling or voice viewed as acting as a guide to the rightness or wrongness of one's behavior" (Spark Publishing, 2007). In other words, it serves as a "moral sense of right and wrong."

There are those who choose to compromise their conscience. Compromise results when a person tries to obtain a clear conscience by putting an end to an immoral or questionable way of life while still enjoying it. But the Bible says, "There is a way that seems right to a man, but its end is the way of death" (Proverbs 14:12; 16:25).

It is important that one tries diligently to maintain a clear conscience at all times. How do we know what we are saying or doing is right or wrong? Who decides what is right or wrong, and how can we be sure of it? What moral guidelines should we follow?

The Bible answers these questions in the New Testament. The apostle James clarified the point when he said, "Therefore, to him who knows to do good and does not do it, to him it is sin" (James 4:17). This simply means, even after determining what is good and bad, choosing to do wrong is considered sin before God.

Several signals let us know when we have a guilty conscience. For instance, suppose I have wronged someone. When I see that person, I may be unable to look him or her in the eye. That is a good indication my conscience is reminding me of the wrong I have done. The Bible makes it clear that God has blessed everyone with this internal "warning device" and expects us to use it as a standard by which to govern our lives (see Acts 24:16).

The apostle Paul describes conscience as a law written in our hearts, and he explains this in Romans. Describing people who are a "law unto themselves," Paul says they "show the work of the law written in their hearts, their conscience also bearing witness, and between themselves their thoughts accusing or else excusing them" (Romans 2:15).

A man or woman of God should do nothing to displease God, our Creator. Jesus is not only our role model; He is also the highest standard by which we should rule our lives. I am not talking about being perfect. Only God bears that distinction, but He expects us to do our best, the best way we know how, at all times possible. Even so, when we fail, He is always there to forgive us (1 John 1:9).

The Bible also mentions a "seared" conscience, which is the result of an individual becoming insensitive or calloused to his or her own wrongdoing. A person with a seared conscience has reached a place where he or she is not bothered by ungodly behavior. This kind of conscience applies to the great apostasy referred to by the apostle Timothy when he said: "Speaking lies in hypocrisy, having their own conscience seared with a hot iron" (1 Timothy 4:2).

The Bible also uses "reprobate mind" to indicate a seared conscience: "And even as they did not like to retain God in their knowledge, God gave them over to a debased [reprobate] mind, to do those things which are not fitting" (Romans 1:28).

Apostasy means to "fall away" from one's faith and belief, and a debased or reprobate mind is a corrupted state to which the Lord Himself can surrender one. Both apostasy and a reprobate mind are closely tied to the conscience being seared. In a nutshell, there is no hope for an individual who persistently lives a life of seared conscience; it could possibly be his or her point of no return.

Besides "clear" and "seared," there are other types of consciences, such as defiled (guilty), pure (clean), and weak (uninstructed). Other terms used as synonyms for a defiled conscience are *corrupted*, *dirty*, *evil*, and such like.

The Old Testament does not mention the word *conscience* precisely, but the concept is obvious. One example among many relates to King David, whom the Bible refers to as a "man after God's own heart." In 2 Samuel 24, we learn that David was smitten in his heart when he failed to trust fully in the power of God. As soon as he sought the Lord's forgiveness, however, his guilt turned to joy (see vv. 10, 14).

Also recall the incident he experienced with Bathsheba (2 Samuel 11). David's lust for this beautiful woman was so strong that he ordered her husband, Uriah, into battle against valiant men, hoping he would die in the fight, and he did. When David realized the severity of what he had done, he went before the Lord, confessed his sins, repented, and asked God to forgive him.

The New Testament contains many more Scripture passages that deal with conscience. Most of them can be found in the writings of the apostle Paul.

I have done some biblical counseling to prison inmates for a few years now, and in all that time, I have yet to meet even one individual who was optimistic about his future. On the contrary, Paul wrote encouraging letters to others while he was in prison. Among his pages of godly instruction and advice, he always focused on doing what is right in order to maintain a clear conscience.

Let me explain other types of conscience, which include defiled (guilty), pure (clear), seared, and weak.

Defiled (or Guilty) Conscience

The term *defiled* means one has an impure, unclean, or corrupted conscience. Not only can a person's conscience be seared, it also can be corrupted, as explained in the book of Titus: "To the pure all things are pure, but to those who are defiled and unbelieving nothing is pure; but even their mind and conscience are defiled" (1:15). This passage goes on to say they profess to know God, but in reality, they do not, which constitutes unbelief. Pastor Steve explains, "When we walk as Christians in unbelief of what God says, it causes our conscience to become defiled" (Steve, 1997).

Some people pretend to be holy and righteous on Sunday but act quite the opposite the rest of the week. This is wrong, and God will judge this kind of defiled conscience. He will see to it that such hypocrisy is exposed sooner or later.

The Word of God firmly declares that no one can hide, run, or escape from God. He knows everything about everyone. We cannot be perfect, but we can all try not to have a defiled conscience.

What then should be our goal? We should have a conscience that is clear and sensitive to every appearance of evil. The apostle Paul obviously had that testimony, for he said, "I tell the truth in Christ, I am not lying, my conscience also bearing me witness in the Holy Spirit" (Romans 9:1).

Pure (or Clear) Conscience

To have a pure or clear conscience means to be free from guilt and corruption. As mentioned above, Paul stressed the importance of maintaining this state of being: "This being so, I myself always strive to have a conscience without offense toward God and men" (Acts 24:16).

One author elaborates on Acts 24:16:

> Not that Paul would never offend God or man through sin (1 John 1:9), but rather, he wanted to always be able to look God "in the eye" and every person "in the eye," knowing that there was nothing between them that had not been confessed and made right (Arch, 1999).

Additional Scripture passages that deal with a clear conscience are Proverbs 3:21-26; 2 Corinthians 1:12; 1 Timothy 1:5; 2 Timothy 1:3; and Hebrews 9:14.

Seared Conscience

Of all the types mentioned, a seared conscience may be the worst. According to the apostle Paul, a conscience can be overridden to the point of becoming ineffective: "Speaking lies in hypocrisy, having their own conscience seared with a hot iron" (1 Timothy 4:2). When a person's conscience is seared, he tends to distance himself from God, giving Satan an opportunity and an open door to suggest actions contrary to God's Word.

During this stage, an individual becomes insensitive to the concepts of right and wrong. Many biblical preachers compare this stage to that of apostasy. This is a serious condition, as the person has no hope whatsoever of returning. The Bible also speaks of the "reprobate mind" as it also relates to no hope of coming back (see Romans 1:28).

How then does one's conscience become seared? It happens when a person sins again and again (habitually) to the degree that his or her conscience is no longer pricked or stirred. People with a seared conscience can be difficult to deal with because they do not care about logic and reasoning. Often they will say and do things that are rude and offensive and think nothing of it. They consider what they say and do as more important than anything or anyone else. It is difficult (but not impossible) to reach those with a seared conscience because their analytical skills are deadened; hence, they are not easy to approach.

As a result of a seared conscience, even some Christians refuse to repent of their wrongdoing. Any counseling and/or preaching of the Word may not affect their spirit because they cannot experience God moving within them.

People can have their conscience seared through a variety of ways. The one path many people follow is lying, which is a serious sin and happens to be one of the seven abominations mentioned in Revelation 21 (see v. 8). Proverbs 6 catalogs seven sins the Lord hates, and a lying tongue is second on the list (see vv. 16-19).

Weak (or Uninstructed) Conscience

Those living a life with a weak conscience are definitely walking a thin line (figuratively speaking). The weak conscience operates in a danger zone in that it is "essentially an uninstructed conscience . . . lacking in a knowledge of the Bible to the point where it is overly sensitive and calls some activities 'sins' which are not wrong according to the teachings of the Bible" (Arch, 1999).

What do I mean by "danger zone"? It means an individual can be spiritually lukewarm for so long, he or she will find it difficult to come back. I sincerely believe there is no such thing as a "gray area." According to the following passages, the Bible strongly opposes such a concept: Hebrew 9:27; Matthew 5:37; Matthew 12:30; and Revelation 3:15-16.

Consider the following nonbiblical examples:

1. A woman is either pregnant or she is not pregnant. There is no such thing as being slightly pregnant or half-pregnant.
2. One is either hungry or not hungry; thirsty or satisfied. There is no such thing as "maybe" hungry or thirsty.
3. When a coin is tossed, it will land on either "heads" or "tails," and that's that.

The gray area is a man-made concept for the sake of convenience. In my opinion, those who put themselves in the gray area are taking huge risks, especially as it relates to spiritual matters.

How then does one develop a weak conscience? One author states, "The Bible does speak of people whose consciences have been weakened through repeated commission of sin. Each time they sinned, their consciences became weaker and weaker. Eventually, their weakened consciences became 'seared with a hot iron,' destroyed altogether through sin" (Online Article, 2011).

Another author states, "What is right or wrong is determined not by what we believe, but by what the Bible teaches. When we bring our judgment into line with what the Bible teaches, our conscience will function as God designed it to function" (Scott, 2010). Very well said; that lines up with the Word of God.

Finally, I would like to encourage every reader to make a habit of examining his or her own thoughts and heart daily. The goal is not to wait so long that you fall victim to a defiled conscience or, worse yet, a seared conscience. The solution is to confess, repent, and make genuine changes before it is too late.

Roving Eyes

Roving eyes! What is this, and why is it so important? Should it matter? When I think of the word *roving*, I am reminded of other terms, such as *wandering*, *unsettled*, and *searching*. What we see and how we see it, meaning, the motives and intentions associated with it, is important in God's sight.

Roving includes what we read, see, and watch by way of television, the Internet, magazines, books, movies, shopping malls, and other avenues. One pastor made a bold and convincing statement when he said, "Roving eyes are connected to a troubled and unsatisfied heart" (Wilkerson, 1988).

King Solomon, who is considered the wisest man who ever lived, gave us a strong directive when he said, "Keep your heart with all diligence, for out of it spring the issues of life" (Proverbs 4:23). Many individuals, both men and women, struggle with the sin of lust, and I was no exception.

Let me gently remind you that lust pertains to much more than things of a sexual nature. Individuals also can lust for nonsexual matters, such as careers, clothing, gadgets, money, power, status, and so on. However, lust often seems to focus most prevalently on things that are sexual in nature.

The Lord wants us to choose wisely what we see and watch. This can range from anything we view on television to what we see inadvertently in shopping malls, at restaurants, movie theaters, stadiums, concerts, bookstores, carnivals, fairs, and trade shows. It can also involve media by which we entertain ourselves, especially in terms of what we view, such as "soft" and hardcore pornography, X-rated and R-rated movies, and so on.

A particular incident comes to my mind: One day, I saw a man of God walking in the mall. When a beautiful woman passed by him, he could not resist the temptation to immediately turn around and watch her until she was out of sight. This behavior qualifies as what the Bible describes as the "lust of the eyes." Jesus said, "Whoever looks at a woman to lust for her has already committed adultery with her in his heart" (Matthew 5:28). This same warning applies to any woman who may be tempted to lust after a man with her eyes.

As for television programs, it does not take a rocket scientist to figure out that filth is aired on most of the channels. A few come to mind that are especially corrupt, including special channels, such as HBO, Showtime, and many of the so-called reality shows. Many households have a television in each room, and every set has cable-operated channels.

Many parents are so busy watching their own shows or doing their own thing that they fail to properly monitor what their children are watching. This neglect gives children plenty of opportunities to watch whatever they want without their parents ever knowing the types of programs they are viewing.

Many channels feature shows that display violence, some degree of nudity, or both, and children usually watch what their parents or other adults are watching. When parents view inappropriate television shows, their children often lose interest in seeing what is wholesome and of value.

Children in general tend to repeat and imitate what they see at home and outside the home, especially when it comes to negative and improper behavior. In addition to television programs, children, adolescents, and teenagers also enjoy playing video games. One particular game among many that gets a lot of attention is "Grand Theft Auto." Games of this sort send strong immoral messages that capture the imagination of impressionable young minds.

Television is becoming more and more corrupt in terms of programs for adult viewing. A few years ago, subjects pertaining to sex were banned for discussion or viewing on television channels. But today countless programs center on such themes as infidelity and/or adultery, having children out of wedlock, the acceptance of homosexuality, and issues relating to sex, including viewing of the sex act itself.

Programs that specifically come to my mind include those targeting woman. These programs present a constant barrage of subliminal messages that desensitize the viewer, thus gaining acceptance. As a result, immoral acts or ways of living are perceived as acceptable. Over time, one may begin to believe that what they are viewing on television is the recognized standard as opposed to what is outlined in the Bible.

As for the Internet, it is becoming more complicated every day. Children these days are so smart that many of them know how to receive and send electronic messages even at the tender age of four or five.

Following the electronic mail stage, many move quickly to other areas of Internet use, such as web surfing, text messaging, and socializing in online chat rooms. Cases have been reported where individuals using Myspace, Facebook, Twitter, and other social media sites have behaved inappropriately and gotten themselves into trouble.

Many computers these days are equipped with an option whereby parents can choose to control what their children watch. However, not every parent is computer literate, and some children take advantage of their parents' ignorance. On the other hand, some parents surf the Web, looking for the wrong kinds of websites, thus being a bad and negative example not only to their children but also to everyone around them.

I once heard someone use the phrases, "Garbage in, Garbage out," and "We are what we eat." I also believe, "We are what we watch." I am not sure if there is any truth in these statements, but I do know God made us in His image, and the Bible says, "Therefore you shall be perfect, just as your Father in heaven is perfect" (Matthew 5:48).

Once again, I would like to remind readers of the importance of dealing with the issue of "roving eyes." Allow only what is clean and pure through the eye-gate. Too many individuals have forfeited their joy, peace, and happiness in their lives and marriages because of the lust of the flesh, which is often exacerbated by the sin of roving eyes. May we determine to end this matter once and for all by asking God for His forgiveness, changing our behavior, and moving ahead.

Gossip—Talebearing

A wise man once said, "Those who gossip *to* you will also gossip *about* you" (unknown source). That statement contains much truth. People who enjoy gossiping look for others to befriend who also enjoy the same activity. But the need to get involved in this type of activity is difficult to break once we open ourselves up to it.

As is the case with most sins, strongholds form that enslave individuals who engage in these types of activities. Gossip helps no one. On the contrary, it carries the potential of destroying the reputations and sometimes the very lives of good people. It also creates an environment of mistrust among those who choose to entertain loose conversation.

God takes gossiping seriously. In fact, He underscores the gravity of this sin by including it as one of the Ten Commandments: "You shall not bear false witness against your neighbor" (Exodus 20:16). Therefore, when we speak about others, it is important that we volunteer only information specifically requested. Even then, we can choose to say nothing. If we feel we must respond, we are told to speak only "the truth in love" (Ephesians 4:15).

Gossiping about others can be cruel and unfair to the person being discussed. That is why it is important to let that person know what was said about him or her and to whom it was said. For example, suppose "John Doe" is caught committing a crime and his accuser relates his opinion regarding the incident, but John Doe offers another explanation. When John Doe appears in court, the judge probably will request to hear both sides of the argument before rendering a judgment on the case. So, you see, even a criminal or wrongdoer is allowed an opportunity to present a defense or relate his side of the story before being judged.

This is not the case, however, when we entertain or choose to participate in gossip. The individuals about whom we are gossiping may not even know they are being discussed. Thus, they are not being given the opportunity to speak out in their own defense about any possible untruths being put forth by their accusers.

Each time we spread rumors or participate in gossip, our action has the potential of not only hurting the person who is the subject of the talk, it may also destroy our own credibility. Once others discover that we spread rumors or participate in backbiting, they will be reluctant to trust us with any information. And once trust is destroyed, it is nearly impossible to restore. Even if we succeed in regaining the confidence of others, it may take us months or even years to do so.

Those who choose to participate in gossip seem to have too much time on their hands thus finding occasions to entertain wrongdoing. Because of loneliness and other factors, widows and widowers can be especially vulnerable to this kind of activity and must be cautious when in conversation about others.

Timothy specifically warns widows against idleness and participating in gossip. In 1 Timothy 5, we read: "Having condemnation because they have cast off their first faith; And besides they learn to be idle, wandering about from house to house, and not only idle but also gossips and busybodies, saying things which they ought not" (vv. 12-13).

An old adage speaks to the issue: "Idle hands are the Devil's workshop." Thus, the solution for not opening ourselves up to rumor mongering is to stay busy doing anything that is productive and beneficial for others and ourselves. In other words, the busier we are, the less time and opportunity we have to gossip.

One can actually use gossiping to gauge where he or she stands spiritually in terms of faith. The closer one is to God, the less he or she will engage in activities that offend Him. God cautions us against allowing the sin of gossiping and spreading rumors to take root in our lives. Gossip usually begins with a simple and short conversation. Then, as people's curiosity is piqued, it quickly moves on to gossip and hearsay and eventually spirals out of control.

The New Testament writer James compares the tongue to a raging fire. Consider the similarities: A fire is ignited with a spark, and then, as the wind fans it, the flames spread quickly, eventually getting out of control and consuming whatever is in their path.

Similarly, when the tongue speaks, the information is conveyed to anyone within hearing distance. Like a wildfire, gossip has the potential of raging out of control and destroying the reputations of godly men or women.

Furthermore, once gossiping is allowed to become a stronghold in one's life, it can produce an addiction. Those who open themselves to gossip are in danger of becoming unable to break free from this compulsive behavior. Those who are under its control are obsessed with knowing everything about everyone around them, and they eagerly anticipate hearing any tidbit of information about others they can share or embellish. They also seem to have a way of seeking out comrades who share the same need for spreading hearsay.

God sternly warns His people about becoming false witnesses against anyone. Several Bible passages underscore how seriously God views this issue. In the book of Leviticus, we read, "You shall not go about as a talebearer among your people; nor shall you take a stand against the life of your neighbor: I am the Lord" (19:16).

The book of Proverbs says much about the sin of gossiping. In chapter 11, we read, "A talebearer reveals secrets, but he who is of a faithful spirit conceals a matter" (v. 13). In chapter 13, we read, "He who guards his mouth preserves his life, but he who opens wide his lips shall have destruction" (v. 3).

In Proverbs 18, we read, "The words of a talebearer are like tasty trifles, and they go down into the inmost body" (v. 8). In chapter 26, we find this warning: "He who passes by and meddles in a quarrel not his own is like one who takes a dog by the ears" (v. 17). And finally, chapter 26 includes the following truth: "Where there is no wood, the fire goes out; and where there is no talebearer, strife ceases" (v. 20).

Both men and women can choose to participate in gossip, though women are accused more often of participating in this wrongdoing. Regardless of who is involved, God takes everything into account for He is all-knowing. When we badmouth someone and spread rumors, especially when they are lies, God, in His justice, will protect the victim, and we will be required to give account to God for every idle word we speak.

At the same time, God knows how to teach us lessons, and He is in control. For instance, He might put our blessings on hold, or He could allow someone else to gossip about us, thus bringing about a situation whereby we are required to confess what we have done and ask the forgiveness of the person wronged by our speech.

When a person gossips, he tends to convince himself that he is speaking to only one person. But often this is not the case. At the outset, he has no idea how many people eventually will become involved. Initially, he may have spoken to one person, but that one person will repeat the conversation to another person or persons. Finally, a host of individuals are involved, creating a tangled web that grows larger and more complex as time goes by.

Let us examine some additional Bible passages that address this issue. In the book of Matthew, we read Jesus' words: "Judge not, that you be not judged" (7:1). And in the apostle Paul's letter to the Romans, we read: "Being filled with all unrighteousness, sexual immorality, wickedness, covetousness, maliciousness; full of envy, murder, strife, deceit, evil-mindedness, *they are whisperers*" (1:29, emphasis added).

A close examination of these verses further underscores the seriousness with which God views the sin of gossiping. When we reject Him and His Word, He allows us to be ruled by our own evil nature, thus falling into the trap of repeated sinful behavior.

What can be done about this sin? Our first step toward preventing gossip is to examine our own hearts and thoughts before the Lord every minute of every day. We must learn to exercise self-control, which happens to be one of the nine fruits of the Spirit (see Galatians 5:22-23). If we say nothing malicious to or about anyone, there is then no chance for gossip to begin.

Another wise decision is to refuse to purchase or read magazines or gossip columns or to view television programs that focus on such activities. The Bible sternly warns us to "abstain from every form of evil" (1 Thessalonians 5:22). In effect, we are to refuse to read gossip magazines. Retailers often place these types of publications strategically at the checkout area of the local grocery store in an effort to arouse our curiosity and tempt us to buy them so we can learn the latest smut on celebrities.

Another prudent move is to interrupt or promptly put an end to gossip when it comes by way of another person who is "just wanting to share." In an honest but polite and gentle manner, ask that person to please stop talking about others. Let them know you would appreciate it if they would not try to engage you in such activity or conversations. We must let others know where we stand in this regard, and eventually, they will get the message and leave us alone.

Judging Others—Casting Stones

Is it okay to judge others? Can we or can we not afford to judge? These are tricky questions.

What does the Bible say about judging others? Does it support or oppose it? The answer is both yes and no. What the Bible says about judging others is often taken out of context.

First, let us look at the Old Testament book of Amos, where we read: "Seek good and not evil, that you may live; So the Lord God of hosts will be with you, As you have spoken. Hate evil, love good; establish justice in the gate. It may be that the Lord God of hosts will be gracious to the remnant of Joseph" (5:14-15). Ask yourself, "Is it possible to hate evil and love good, if we refuse to judge?" It is not.

The concept of judging mentioned in Matthew 7:1 is often lifted out of its original context. On one hand, we cannot be judging all the time, and on the other hand, we cannot *not* judge all the time. There is a time to judge and a time to refrain from judging, but knowing when to judge and when not to judge requires sharp and sensitive discernment.

In the Word of God, the term *judge*, or words closely related to its meaning, is mentioned over seven hundred times. One author points out, "One whole book of the Bible is titled Judges, for it was written at a time when God raised up judges to lead His people" (Melton, 99).

We humans have a bad habit of judging *something* all the time. However, each time we judge, we are not only forming an opinion, we are also coming to some kind of decision. And it does not stop there; what started with one decision often leads to more and more decisions. Jesus' words on the subject are clear: "Judge not, that you be not judged" (Matthew 7:1). The Lord's command does not imply that we should not judge at all, but it does mean, "the Bible is warning us that before we are to sit in judgment of others, we had better make sure that our own motives are pure" (Online Source).

Another Scripture passage dealing with the concept of judging others is found in the New Testament book of 1 Corinthians: "For what have I to do with judging those also who are outside? Do you not judge those who are inside? But those who are outside God judges. Therefore, put away from yourselves the evil person" (5:12-13).

These instructions from the pen of the apostle Paul tell us to do three things:

1. Christians are to judge those who identify themselves as Christians.
2. Believers are encouraged to remove from the church those who are living in open sin.
3. Christians are not to socialize with the sinners in any way or fashion.

This may sound more rude than loving, but remember, we humans love differently than God loves. Man's love, for the most part, is conditional and often subjective or biased, whereas, God's love is always unconditional. The prophet Isaiah explains the difference this way: "'For My thoughts are not your thoughts, nor are your ways My ways,' says the Lord" (Isaiah 55:8). The Lord is always right, and He is always fair.

When we see a brother or sister openly living in sin, we are obligated to warn them. By not doing so, our silence indirectly shows acceptance and even approval of their sin. I would venture to say that almost every church has members who live a compromised life, and we tend to say nothing "not wanting to hurt a brother's or sister's feelings."

We have ignored those compromises and lukewarmness for too long. When someone says not to judge an offending church member, basing his or her argument on Matthew 7:1, it may be because he or she is uncomfortable with the idea of making a judgment call. In all practicality, God expects us to judge, as long as it is a righteous judgment.

Each time we choose not to judge righteously, we may even be committing a sin before God. The psalmist declared: "The mouth of the righteous speaks wisdom, and his tongue talks of justice" (Psalm 37:30). This verse tells us that a righteous person will not hesitate to talk of judgment; therefore, he will not refuse to judge if and when the need arises.

So the question remains: Should we judge others? Absolutely! The apostle Paul rebuked the Corinthians for not judging:

> Do you not know that the saints will judge the world? And if the world will be judged by you, are you unworthy to judge the smallest matters? Do you not know that we shall judge angels? How much more, things that pertain to this life? If then you have judgments concerning things pertaining to this life, do you appoint those who are least esteemed by the church to judge? I say this to your shame. Is it so, that there is not a wise man among you, not even one, who will be able to judge between his brethren? (1 Corinthians 6:1-5).

As one author put it, "If judging is wrong, then Paul needs to confess and repent for misleading these Christians! He clearly told them to judge people" (Melton, 99).

Let us also consider a passage in Malachi that commands us to judge: "Then you shall again discern between the righteous and the wicked, between one who serves God and one who does not serve Him" (3:18).

Author Melton further states, "If the Bible is clear about anything, it is clear about the importance of judging on a regular basis in order to properly serve and honor God. To ignore this fact is to ignore all of the Scripture presented and also the rest of the Bible" (Melton, 99). He has a valid point, and on a personal note, I tend to agree with Reverend Melton.

As we conclude this section, I would like to encourage the readers to maintain a balance when it comes to judging others. Remember, there is a time to judge and a time to withhold judgment. When judging is appropriate, let us make sure we are passing only righteous judgment, based on and backed by the Scriptures. On the same note, let us also not keep ourselves busy judging. In other words, do not be constantly looking for mistakes to judge. More importantly, when others judge us, let us receive the correction in humility and be thankful for it.

The Word of God gives us clear direction and guidance on how to go about judging righteously. I mentioned the word *righteous* several times. In the gospel of John, we read: "Do not judge according to appearance, but judge with righteous judgment" (John 7:24).

Before judging others, make a habit of judging yourself first. Again, consider the words of the apostle Paul to the believers in Corinth: "For if we would judge ourselves, we would not be judged" (1 Corinthians 11:31). If and when we choose to judge others, let us make sure we have all the facts (truth) and not rely on rumors and hearsay (see Jeremiah 5:1).

When we judge, we must make sure we use Scripture to back our conclusion and not do it out of emotions or anger. Again, we turn to the Old Testament book of Isaiah for instruction: "To the law and to the testimony! If they do not speak according to this Word, it is because there is no light in them" (8:20).

I once heard someone say, "When in anger, do not speak." This is sage advice, for we may not use logic or reasoning when we are angry; hence, we should not judge during those times.

Finally, we should be careful (preferably silent) regarding any issue about which the Word of God is either silent or has little to say. An example is food, especially as it relates to eating or abstaining from eating meat. Each one of us must decide for himself whether to judge or remain silent on such issues. Let God be your final judge.

Emotions—Feelings, Reactions, Etc.

Emotions! What are they? *Merriam Webster's Dictionary* defines *emotion* as "strong feeling, a mental reaction marked by strong feeling and usually causing physical effects." Emotions play an important role in our lives; therefore, we should learn how to handle them properly. There seems to be a strong correlation between how one controls his emotions and the level of maturity he displays.

The art of communication includes several components, including timing, mood, right place, content material, and one's emotional state at the time. Many arguments have taken place between two individuals because of the misuse and/or abuse of one's emotions. Our emotions are capable of warning us of imminent danger, and that is why it is important for us to keep them in check and well balanced.

In Genesis 1:27, we read, "God created man in His own image; in the image of God He created him; male and female He created them." Our emotions are part of the image of God we share and experience. God did not create us exactly like Himself, for He has no physical body.

Putting aside the physical aspect, we are to be like God in our character as it relates to faithfulness, compassion, readiness to forgive, kindness, patience, tolerance, understanding, and so on. One's self-worth cannot be measured in terms of material possessions, achievements, physical appearance, career, or status, but being created in God's image gives us plenty of reasons to feel good about ourselves.

I always tell those whom I counsel (and those who are willing to listen) not to make hasty decisions (and choices) when their emotional state is out of balance. Nor is it a good idea to argue or make hasty decisions when they are experiencing anger, hunger, sleepiness, stress, weariness, worry, loneliness, depression, and so on. Few people are capable of making logical and sensible decisions when any of these mental states are present.

On the other hand, it is good to be emotional (sensitive) at times, letting others know how you feel. When we share our feelings and respond in the same way others are emoting in terms of their need, they often feel connected and possibly even accepted and understood. The more a person trusts, the more he or she will open up.

The more transparent you are, the better you will be able to understand a situation or circumstance. We cannot afford to be unemotional like Spock on Star Track, whose response to every situation is to apply pure logic, allowing no room for emotion. That response is not healthy either. Maintaining balance is the key. We have to know when to be emotional and when to respond like Spock. Timing is everything.

Here is the question: What does the Bible say about emotions (or feelings)? Many Scripture passages deal with this issue, helping us face our emotions. These verses also have the power to heal us from the hurt and pain we experience. Jesus cares deeply about our emotional state. One comforting passage that comes to my mind is from the Psalms: "God is our refuge and strength, a very present help in trouble" (46:1).

There is a strong correlation between emotions and one's mental state. A change in one can and will bring a change in the other. How can we control our emotions? We can do that by learning to control our mind (thoughts, etc.).

How do we control our thoughts? The most effective way to bring our thought-life under control is to read God's Word daily, spend quality time in prayer, share with someone we trust, and so on. As an ordained minister, I am often asked to preach (teach), and I always make a point of saying that forgiveness is key to effecting healing to our souls. Unforgiveness leads to anger and bitterness (and more), which in turn gives Satan a foothold in our lives.

The last thing we need is for Satan to have opportunity to put obstacles in our walk with the Lord. God is more powerful than Satan, and He can take care of anything and everything. However, He gives us the tools we need to face and fight the Enemy. God will guide us every step until we learn the right way. Forgiving others is known to bring emotional healing, and I have to admit (and confess) that it has worked for me.

What does the Bible says about emotions? Well, God's Word does not mention the words *emotion* or *emotions* directly; however, it does address many specific feelings, such as anger, joy, grief, mourning, sadness, and so on.

Emotion in and of itself is neither good nor bad. However, the behaviors that result from these reactions can be labeled as either good (positive) or bad (negative).

As we conclude this segment, I would like to encourage you to learn to maintain a balance in how you use and express your emotions and to remember that right timing is the key in many situations and circumstances.

The Bible clearly encourages us to focus more on positive emotions than negative ones: "But now you yourselves are to put off all these: anger, wrath, malice, blasphemy, filthy language out of your mouth" (Colossians 3:8).

We also read the following instructions: "Finally, brethren, whatever things are true, whatever things are noble, whatever things are just, whatever things are pure, whatever things are lovely, whatever things are of good report . . . meditate on these things" (Philippians 4:8).

Those who are optimistic by nature habitually focus on that which is good and positive. So do your best, the best way you know how, as unto the Lord, and put it in His hands. Learn to be patient, learn to wait on the Lord for His direction, and learn to be still. When you put your trust in God, your concerns will become His concerns.

Self-Esteem—Self-Worth, Etc.

The *Oxford Desk Dictionary* defines *self-esteem* as "good opinion of oneself; self-confidence; unduly high regard for oneself; conceit." The following terms are used as synonym for self-esteem: *confidence*, *dignity*, *pride*, *self-pride*, *self-regard*, *self-respect*, *self-worth*, and such like.

The Word of God confirms the importance of how one thinks about (and sees) himself: "For as he [a person] thinks in his heart, so is he" (Proverbs 23:7). A famous French philosopher, Rene Descartes, once said, "I think, therefore I am." We need to realize that God loves us, and He only wants the best for us.

But we have a habit of trying to please others, probably because we fear rejection. Of course, it feels much better to be accepted and loved than to be rejected, but it is wrong to think that way. In the Bible we read: "No one can serve two masters" (Matthew 6:24). We cannot always please both God and the world's system at the same time. In an attempt to do so, we will find ourselves being faithful to one and not to the other.

A Christian's self-identity should be in Christ. Therefore, as His children, we should surrender ourselves to God and choose to serve Him more than anyone or anything else. If and when we refuse to serve the Lord, we must be prepared to answer God when He asks, "Choose for yourselves this day whom you will serve" (Joshua 24:15). Joshua made a bold statement when he responded, "But as for me and my house, we will serve the Lord."

The world's opinion of us is often different than how God sees us. The world, which I call the "secular system," measures us by our physical appearance, education, wealth, career accomplishments, and such like. God makes it clear that how He sees us is in direct contradiction with that of the world's system.

In the Old Testament book of 1 Samuel we read, "For the Lord does not see as man sees, for man looks at the outward appearance, but the Lord looks at the heart" (16:7). The bottom line is simply this: we are not what or who the world says we are; rather, we are who God says we are. Like it or not, God is a better and wiser judge than the world.

In this worldly or secular system, there are those who lose their jobs, are divorced, and get ignored. Some wish they had never been born. This low opinion of one's self is often because of unrealistic expectations. When we do not meet those expectations, we feel we have failed to measure up to some nebulous standard. We open ourselves to ridicule and being labeled.

Whose standards are they anyway? Are they God's? Absolutely not! The Bible declares unequivocally that God loves all mankind and sent His Son to die for everyone. He never discriminates against anyone on the basis of color, race, gender, age, occupation, wealth, and so on. In the gospel of Matthew we read: "Come to Me, all you who labor and are heavy laden, and I will give you rest" (11:28).

An advantage we have with God that we might not always have with others is that we can approach Him without fear of being rejected or judged. He accepts us just as we are. When an individual accepts Jesus Christ as his or her personal Lord and Savior, he or she instantly becomes one of God's own children (spiritually). That is a free gift for which we can be eternally thankful.

The Bible further states that God gave us self-worth when He bought us with His redeeming blood so that we could be His own: "[He] is the guarantee of our inheritance until the redemption of the purchased possession, to the praise of His glory" (Ephesians 1:14). I sincerely believe that only God is known to love unconditionally.

As we wrap up this segment, I would like to bring to your attention a Scripture verse that informs us how we are to treat others. This New Testament passage speaks to every Christian, regardless of how high he or she may have risen with regard to financial success, social status, power, and so on: "Let nothing be done through selfish ambition or conceit, but in lowliness of mind let each esteem others better than himself" (Philippians 2:3).

In the book of Romans we read, "For I say . . . not to think of himself more highly than he ought to think, but to think soberly, as God has dealt to each one a measure of faith" (12:3).

So how does God help us deal with self-esteem issues? Author Wilson states, "Our self-esteem is grounded in the value God places on our life" (Wilson, 2000).

Let us not go from one extreme to the other. Just as we must guard against thinking too highly of ourselves or putting ourselves on a pedestal, we must at the same time resist thinking too little of ourselves. Here again we need to maintain a balance between the two, and the best way to do that is to find our identity in Christ.

It is not always easy to treat others as though they are better than ourselves, especially in a world where we tend to judge others. But the Bible is clear on this topic, and we are to follow what God's Word instructs us to do.

One final encouragement to everyone: Do not take everything others say personally. People can and will say unpleasant words because they are angry, bitter, or resentful. We should only be concerned with truth in what others say about us, whether directly or indirectly.

As stated previously, we must disregard all gossip, especially when it is untrue. We should only be interested in finding and knowing the truth because in John's gospel we read: "And you shall know the truth, and the truth shall make you free" (8:32).

We may not like to hear what others say about us, but we should encourage and entertain any statement that is true. We can be thankful for constructive remarks that can help us make some godly changes.

Since our self-worth is based and depends on Jesus Christ, let us not be too concerned about how this secular system judges us. This does not change the fact that when we are right, we are right, and when we are wrong, we are wrong. The most productive approach we can take is to learn to practice humility daily.

Thoughts—Adaptive or Maladaptive

The *Oxford Desk Dictionary* defines the word *thought* as "the faculty of reason; way of thinking associated with a particular time, people, etc.; reflection; consideration; regard; idea or piece of reasoning produced by thinking; brainstorm; conclusion." Thoughts can be ideas or an opinion or a statement. They can be contemplated either on impulse or as planned.

More than ever before, people seem to struggle with this issue of thoughts. This is especially true because of the highly technological world in which we live. Some grapple with having to choose between human and technological reasoning. Should I use my own logic, or should I depend on and trust in technology?

This kind of situation puts us between the proverbial "rock and a hard place." There is a strong correlation between maladaptive thoughts and emotionalism. I have observed and counseled individuals whose emotions were unbalanced at the time their thoughts were unhealthy.

A pastor friend once told me he believes that the world (secular system) works on our minds, whereas God operates with our hearts. I do not know how much truth lies in that statement; however, I can say with authority that the Word of God has much to say about the heart.

For instance, in the book of Proverbs we read: "Keep your heart with all diligence, for out of it spring the issues of life" (4:23). Also consider 1 Samuel 16:7, which also focuses on the heart from God's point of view. My personal opinion is that the mind and heart are all part of one's being, and born-again believers are to surrender everything to the Lord, including mind, body, spirit, soul, heart, thoughts, and so on.

Not every thought leads to action, but many of them do. Sometimes a thought can survive on its own. But an action cannot survive alone. In other words, there is no such thing as an action without a thought first. For instance, seeing a food commercial on TV often leads me to think of food, prompting me to decide to act on that thought by going to the kitchen and getting something to eat.

For a thought to become an action, we must choose to surrender to it. Only when we choose to yield to our thoughts can they become actions. Hence, there is no such thing as an action without a preceding thought.

Let us never forget that the road to sin begins with thought(s). An impure thought in and of itself is not necessarily sinful. It only becomes sinful only when we choose to act on it.

Now we come to the important question: What does the Bible say about our thoughts? God's Word is replete with advice about thinking (or thoughts). I would like to begin with a Scripture from the book of Proverbs where we read: "The thoughts of the wicked are an abomination to the Lord, but the words of the pure are pleasant" (15:26).

This verse is a gentle warning that thinking beforehand helps us to both speak and act wisely. Wise people carefully plan their words, whereas foolish (unwise) people are reckless with their words because they do not always care about their effects. They tend to do what they want at the moment and may or may not think about it later. Yet, some things in life, such as time, the past, and words spoken, cannot be reversed.

Since spoken words cannot be retrieved, it is important for us to think twice before choosing to release them. There is also the issue of accountability that plays a major role. The Bible makes it clear that someday we will give an account of everything we say and do. On one hand, we can thank God for His mercy, grace, and forgiveness. But on the other hand, there are consequences for sins, especially those we plan and repeat.

God is not only forgiving, but He is also holy, just, and righteous. There are two sides to His nature and character, and we need to heed both. Some people convince themselves that each time they sin they simply need to ask for forgiveness and everything will be forgiven. While that is true, meaning, forgiveness is readily available to us, we must not live a life of repeated sins without expecting to reap their consequences (see Galatians 6:7).

How then can we manage or control our thoughts? I would like to suggest the following methods for taking control of your thoughts, thus freeing yourself to spend quality time serving God and others. Make a habit of writing your thoughts (or recording them, if you can afford to buy a mini recorder). As you write or record, be honest and transcribe your thoughts as they come.

Each night before you go to sleep, spend some time reading or listening to all the thoughts you have written or recorded that day. Consider any thought that is not of God, and ask yourself why you thought those thoughts and what was the motive behind them. I firmly believe nothing happens by accident, chance, or by mistake. Everything happens for a reason and a particular time (see Ecclesiastes 3:1-8).

Just before falling asleep, submit any ungodly thoughts to the Lord in prayer, and ask Him to help you deal with them. If you said or did anything to offend anyone, make it right immediately before it is too late. None of us has a one hundred percent guarantee that when we go to bed each night we will get up the next morning. We will awaken the next morning only when God allows it by His grace and mercy. So let's do it right while we still can.

Second, if you are struggling with unpleasant thoughts, immediately substitute thoughts that are positive, pleasant, healthy, and biblical. Remember the apostle Paul's advice to the Philippians: "Finally, brethren, whatever things are true, whatever things are noble, whatever things are just . . . meditate on these things" (Philippians 4:8).

Last but not least, when you go before the Lord in prayer, ask Him to discipline areas of your thought-life that need to change. Each time you entertain a negative or bad thought, use the "automatic thought stopping" approach, used by cognitive therapist, Dr. Aaron T. Beck. Dr. Beck states that these thoughts can be nagging and repetitive, and one thing that can be applied to take care of this problem is to have an interruption, meaning, not giving in to these thoughts. We can interrupt harmful thoughts by focusing on the Word of God, as mentioned in Philippians 4:8.

Time—Misuse and Wasting

Time is one of those aspects of our lives that is irretrievable. Once it has passed, it will never return. That is why we need to use time wisely and not misuse or waste it. God has given all of us the same amount of time to do what needs to be done. Anyone who is willing and motivated can achieve his or her goals and desires, and yet only a small percentage of people seem to do so. Why? The answer lies with each individual. Time management is not really that difficult to follow. It can be achieved simply, if we have the right level of motivation.

Does the Bible have anything to say about time? Yes, it does. In the book of Ephesians we read: "See then that you walk circumspectly, not as fools but as wise, redeeming the time, because the days are evil" (5:15-16).

One author describes the time issue this way: "Time is short; Life is brief" (Boa, 05). This brief statement is true, and the Bible agrees with it: "The days of our lives are seventy years; and if by reason of strength they are eighty years, yet their boast is only labor and sorrow; for it is soon cut off, and we fly away" (Psalm 90:10). The years of our lives do seem to pass quickly, and they are all numbered and designed by God. He knows each person's life span in great detail, and everything goes according to His will.

In closing, I would like to suggest a simple yet practical and feasible plan for managing time effectively and efficiently. Start by making a list of activities (a to-do list) that need to be attended to. When making the list, remember to prioritize, placing the most important tasks first and then moving to the less urgent. Personally, I prefer to read God's Word and pray first thing in the morning. By doing so, I can ask God to direct and guide me as to how I should spend that day. I start each day with His blessings and end it by thanking Him.

It is also essential to maintain some kind of organizer (or journal). Start by writing the "big picture" first and then break it down into smaller units to understand it even better and eventually fulfill your goals and desires. This can definitely be helpful. I have done it, and it has worked for me.

Whatever we tend to misuse, abuse, or waste (time, money, talents, etc.), God knows how to teach us a lesson. He does so only because He loves and cares for us, and He wants only the best for us. In the book of Jeremiah we read: "'For I know the thoughts that I think toward you,' says the Lord, 'thoughts of peace and not of evil, to give you a future and a hope'" (Jeremiah 29:11).

We all need to do what works for us, as each individual is unique to God. Our plans, goals, and desires may be different, but the common denominator should be the same: motivation, encouragement, and full dedication to do what needs to be done and to do it right, as unto the Lord.

Tongue—Loose and Untamed

The tongue! Is it out of control? Is it well tamed or loose? What does the Bible say about the tongue? Frankly, God's Word has much to say about what James termed "an unruly evil, full of deadly poison" (3:8). The Bible speaks of at least seventeen kinds of tongues, and there are probably more.

Previously, I mentioned that there are certain aspects of life one cannot retrieve. These include our past, time that is spent, words that are spoken, and such like. For whatever reason, we sometimes speak choice words and then, as time passes, we feel compelled to apologize for them. Some choose to let go of these offenses, and some may genuinely (or conveniently) forget about them. In any case, we cannot take back what has been spoken.

"Talk is cheap" is a well-known saying. Talk may be cheap, but it is not free. Secret, unexposed, and unconfessed thoughts may have no consequences, but spoken words and open actions often do. In the book of Galatians we read, "Do not be deceived, God is not mocked; for whatever a man sows, that he will also reap" (6:7).

Someone once said, "You are known by the company you keep." There is some truth in that statement; however, a person's character is better known by the way he uses his tongue. Seneca, a well-known philosopher, once said, "Speech is the index of the mind."

In the gospel of Matthew, Jesus said, "Out of the abundance of the heart the mouth speaks" (12:34). The following two Scripture verses deal directly with the tongue issue: "Death and life are in the power of the tongue, and those who love it will eat its fruit" (Proverbs 18:21). And from the book of James: "The tongue is a fire, a world of iniquity. The tongue is so set among our members that it defiles the whole body, and sets on fire the course of nature; and it is set on fire by hell" (3:6).

Some people have the nasty habit of commenting on practically every subject under the sun. They seldom say, "I don't know," and show no interest in learning something new or unknown. One logical explanation I come up with is simply pride, though there are probably numerous other reasons as well. As long they have a willing listener, these folks feel compelled to talk on and on, sometimes even authoritatively. The book of Proverbs labels these kinds of people as fools: "A fool has no delight in understanding, but in expressing his own heart" (18:2).

It does not take long or much to hurt someone. But the process and time required for a matter to be resolved peacefully may take much longer. Sometimes and in some cases, there is no guarantee that a person or a situation would seek peace. When peace is not an option, the result can be devastating. Anger, bitterness, unforgiveness, and so on, are not worth the offense and are definitely not of God.

The following is a list of seventeen types of tongues recorded in the Bible:

1. Backbiting Tongue (Proverbs 25:23)
2. Cursing Tongue (Psalm 10:7; 109:17-18)
3. Deceitful Tongue (Psalm 120:2)
4. Destructive Tongue (Proverbs 17:4)
5. Flattering Tongue (Psalm 5:9)
6. Healing Tongue (Proverbs 12:18)
7. Lying Tongue (Proverbs 6:17; Psalm 109:2)
8. Mischievous and Wicked Tongue (Psalm 10:7)
9. Overused Tongue (Ecclesiastes 2:3)
10. Perverted Tongue (Proverbs 10:31; 17:20)
11. Piercing Tongue (Proverbs 12:18)
12. Proud Tongue (Psalm 12:3)

13. Silent Tongue (Mark 8:38)
14. Soft Tongue (Proverbs 25:15)
15. Soothing Tongue (Proverbs 15:4)
16. Swift Tongue (Proverbs 18:13; James 1:19)
17. Talebearing Tongue (Proverbs 18:8; Leviticus 19:16)

This impressive list is a courtesy of two authors (Melton, James L., 2001; and Ravenhill, L., 1994).

Conclusion

In closing this section, I would like to encourage every reader (myself included) to be cautious about what you say, and try your best to be gentle, careful, and considerate. Our tongues can deliver blessings as well as curses. In the book of James we read: "With [the tongue] we bless our God and Father, and with it we curse men, who have been made in the similitude of God. Out of the same mouth proceed blessing and cursing. My brethren, these things ought not to be so" (3:9-10).

The good news is that there is always hope, and deliverance is available once we learn to confess, repent, and forsake our sins before God and others.

Chapter Two

Prayer Life

Are Your Prayers Being Answered?

Introduction

What is prayer? Prayer is a means of communicating with God. Each time we dialogue with God (pray), it is intimate, personal, and real. God hears all our prayers; however, His responses may differ. He answers some of our prayers promptly, according to our time schedule. Some He may put on hold, and others He may choose never to answer.

Since God is omniscient, He knows the appropriate response for each of our requests. He knows what we deserve and what we can or cannot handle. Because He loves us, He only wants the best for us and always has a perfect reason for everything He does or does not do. We need to trust Him in every situation.

Most people are familiar with bedtime prayers, saying grace at mealtimes, prayers at funerals, baptisms, and weddings. But prayer is more than these. A well-known Christian author, Thomas Merton, described prayer as "an expression of who people are . . ."

I believe that prayers go up and results come down. We may pray not only for our needs and the needs of others to be met, but prayer is also the means by which we grow closer to God and eventually develop a one-on-one relationship with Him. During our prayer times, we can let God know how much we love Him, giving Him all the praise, glory, honor, and thanks that is due Him all the time.

For a born-again believer, prayer is like breathing. It is easier to pray than not to pray. We pray for a great number of reasons. For instance, we pray as a service and obedience to God. We pray because God commands us to pray: "Be anxious for nothing, but in everything by prayer and supplication, with thanksgiving, let your requests be made known to God" (Philippians 4:6).

Jesus set an example for us by placing a high priority on prayer, and as His disciples, we should do the same. Jesus prayed that He might remain in His Father's will, which is all the more reason for us to communicate with God. As Jesus faced torture and death by crucifixion, He prayed, "Father, if it is Your will, take this cup away from Me; nevertheless not My will, but yours, be done" (Luke 22:42).

So you see, we pray because God commands us to pray, and Jesus set the example of prayer for us to follow. As Christ's disciples, it is nearly impossible for us not to pray, knowing that when we speak to Him, we are actually communicating with God through Jesus Christ, who is interceding before the heavenly Father on our behalf.

As for our motives in our prayers, they ought to be spiritual and not selfish or self-centered. We pray to show our trust and dependence on God. We have a bad habit of complaining and finding lame excuses for troubling situations that arise. Instead of complaining and offering excuses, we should pray. Prayer, after all, is far more productive.

Prayer is known to restore broken relationships between people and with God. In the Old Testament, we read repeatedly how men of God (King David, for example) sinned against God, and through prayer and repentance, their relationship with God was restored. Many more biblical examples could be cited.

Does prayer make a difference today? The answer to that question is an absolute and obvious yes. In fact, prayer can and often does make all the difference.

I admit, there have been times when I have prayed and prayed about a certain issue, and after waiting and waiting for an answer, I found myself disappointed and sincerely doubtful. Then I realized I probably was asking for something that either did not line up with God's Word or it was not part of His will. In those moments, I have been led to read a particular Scripture as encouragement: "Trust in the Lord with all your heart, and lean not on your own understanding; in all your ways acknowledge Him, and He shall direct your paths" (Proverbs 3:5-6).

Sometimes a person engaged in prayer can experience a degree of loneliness. On the surface, the communication may seem to be one-sided, as if the pray-er is talking to himself, without any assurance or promise from the Lord. But when those feelings arise, take heart, knowing that is not the case at all. The Bible assures us that God hears all our prayers; however, He may not answer all of them. Sometimes we petition God for things that may not be right for us, which is why He puts some of our prayers on hold until the time is right for us to receive without any reservations.

Prayer is absolutely essential for all who believe in God. When we do not pray, we are revealing not only a lack of faith but also our lack of trust. The importance of prayer is so critical that one author describes it as "our primary means of seeing God work in others' lives" (Houdmann, 2009). The Bible clearly states, "The effective, fervent prayer of a righteous man avails much" (James 5:16).

Are there any benefits in praying? Absolutely. The values include but are not limited to the following:

1. Prayer is direct communication with God, meaning, it is speaking with God.

2. Prayer is an awesome privilege and honor. Through prayer we can have an audience with our heavenly Father. Incidentally, when we go before God in prayer, we do not need to be ashamed or afraid. We can approach Him just as we are, with assurance that He loves us.
3. Prayer gives us an opportunity to line up our plans and desires with His will. When we are willing and obedient to obey Him, He will reveal His will for us. Being in God's will is the key to answered prayer.
4. Prayer gives us the opportunity to put our trust in Him who is not known to fail. Jesus said, "I will never leave you nor forsake you" (Hebrews 13:5).

How should we pray? Here are some specific attitudes and approaches to prayer:

1. Be honest.
2. Show respect and awe for God.
3. Express your love for God.
4. Ask for His direction and guidance.
5. Pray with humility.
6. Pray for others. Praying for others comes under the category of intercessory prayer.

Do we learn how to pray, or is prayer something that comes naturally? The answer may be yes to both of these questions. Prayer does not always come naturally for some, and not everyone has a spiritual mentor willing and ready to teach him or her how to pray. As a matter of fact, we do not always know what to ask and what not to ask, because we do not always know God's will; therefore, it is not easy for us to pray naturally. Some people use "common sense" when they petition God for something, either for themselves or for others. And yet the Bible tells us to "pray without ceasing" (1 Thessalonians 5:17).

Is there a right or wrong way to pray? Not really. We are not given a specific format or structure on how to pray. Our primary concern when we approach the heavenly Father should be that our petitions line up with His Word.

Some individuals pray according to some sort of guidelines. One example would be to open their prayers with praise. They move from there into giving God thanks for all He is and does. The next step would be to confess one's sins and asking God for His forgiveness. Finally, they present their case (needs and wants) before God and ask Him to meet their needs. When I pray, I always say toward the end, "Let thy will be done." We can always depend and rely on the Holy Spirit to help us know what to say and how to pray.

Different Types of Prayers

As for the different types of prayer, I offer no definite recommendations because different people use and follow a format that is suitable for them. As a general rule, most prayers seem to follow a regular prayer format, such as giving praise, being thankful, asking God to bless someone, making a petition for one's self and others, using the Word of God, listening and not talking, singing a song, and, most importantly, saying the Lord's Prayer, which is recorded in Matthew 5:9-15.

Common Reasons for Unanswered Prayers

Are there occasions when God does not answer some of our prayers? Yes! I would like to direct your attention to two important Scripture verses that directly relate to prayer and its consequences.

In Matthew's gospel, we read a promise Jesus made to His disciples: "Whatever things you ask in prayer, believing, you will receive" (21:22). On the other hand, we also read, "You ask and do not receive, because you ask amiss, that you may spend it on your pleasures" (James 4:3). The word *amiss* means, "wrong motive."

Do these verses contradict each other? Of course not! God's Word is never contradictory. God always has a perfect explanation for everything

He says and does. We do not always understand His ways. He Himself said, "'For My thoughts are not your thoughts, nor are your ways My ways,' says the Lord" (Isaiah 55:8).

Allow me to list some common reasons why God may choose not to answer our prayers or may put them on hold:

1. Discouragement (Colossians 4:2; Romans 12:12; 1 John 3:4; Ephesians 4:14; 1 Peter 3:7)
3. Selfishness and Self-centeredness (Psalm 10:4; Philippians 2:3; 2 Timothy 4:3; James 3:16-17; James 4:3)
3. Dishonoring One's Companion (Spouse) (Ephesians 5:22-24)
4. Disobedience (as in Rebellion) (1 Samuel 15:23; 2 Timothy 3:5; 1 John 4:1)
5. Double-mindedness and Unstable (2 Timothy 3:5; James 1:8; James 4:8; 2 Peter 3:16)
6. Encouraging and Entertaining Wrong Motives (James 4:3)
7. Failure to Apply Spiritual Authority (Mark 11:23; Acts 16:18; Ephesians 6:12; James 4:7)
8. Forsaking God (Joshua 24:20; 1 Samuel 8:8; Jeremiah 22:9)
9. Hard-heartedness (Ezekiel 3:7; Hebrews 3:8, 13, 15)
10. Hypocrisy (Matthew 7:5; 22:18; 23:28; Galatians 6:3; 1 Peter 2:1)
11. Lack of Charity (Proverbs 21:13; Mark 10:21)
12. Lack of Faith (Mark 11:24; Romans 10:17; Ephesians 2:8; Hebrews 11:6)
13. Lack of Fear of God (Psalm 19:9; 34:9; 36:1; 111:10; Ecclesiastes 12:13)
14. Lack of Fellowship with God (John 15:7)
15. Lack of Perseverance (Galatians 6:9)
16. Living According to the Flesh (Romans 8:5, 13; 2 Corinthians 10:3)
17. Not Asking in His Will (1 John 5:14)
18. Not Knowing How to Pray (Luke 11:1)
19. Not Seeking to Please the Lord (Mark 12:30-31; Galatians 5:6; Hebrews 4:16; James 2:20; 1 John 3:22)

20. Provoking God (Psalm 78:56; Jeremiah 7:19)
21. Refusing to Confess (and Repent) (Isaiah 59:2; 1 Peter 3:12)
22. Refusing to Hear the Truth (2 Timothy 3:8; 2 Timothy 4:4)
23. Refusing to Humble One's Self (Exodus 10:3; James 4:6)
24. Refusing to Tithe (Leviticus 27:30; Deuteronomy 8:18; 14:23; 16:17; Psalm 116:12; Malachi 3:8-19; Matthew 6:19-20; 23:23; 2 Corinthians 9:7)
25. Regarding Inequity (Psalm 66:18; Isaiah 59:2)
26. Unbelief and Doubt (Deuteronomy 32:20; Mark 4:40; 9:24; 2 Thessalonians 3:2; Hebrews 3:12; 11:6; James 1:6-7)
27. Unforgiveness (Bitterness, Etc.) (Matthew 6:14-15; 18:21-22; Mark 11:25; Luke 6:37; Ephesians 4:32)
28. Vain Repetitions (Parading Prayer Life) (Ecclesiastes 5:2; Matthew 6:7)

What should we do when God withholds an answer to our prayers? It is not always easy to just sit around and wait, not knowing if the answer to a particular prayer will ever come to pass. Waiting patiently does not come easy for many people. By nature, human beings prefer to reason and use their own logic as a substitute for waiting on the Lord. This is especially true when the prayer involves matters of importance or of great need. If and when an answer does not come promptly, or as soon as we had hoped, we begin to doubt God, wondering if He even heard the prayer.

When it comes to waiting for God to answer prayer, a well-known saying, "An idle mind is the Devil's workshop," seems to describe many people. The truth is, when we pray, we should leave the matter in God's hands, knowing we have nothing to be concerned about. This is surely what the apostle Paul meant when he wrote: "Be anxious for nothing, but in everything by prayer and supplication, with thanksgiving, let your requests be made known to God" (Philippians 4:6).

If a prayer does not get answered, we must not blame God because it is not His fault; He is always right. Instead, let us examine our own thoughts, motives, desires, goals, expectations, and so on. We also need to learn how to resist every temptation to doubt God, realizing it is not from Him. Temptations come either through Satan or from ourselves, and God gives us the strength to "resist the devil" (James 4:7). As for the issues with ourselves, we are to exercise self-control, which happens to be one of the nine fruits of the Spirit mentioned in the book of Galatians (5:22-23).

Does God Answer Prayer?

Absolutely. God is known to be a prayer-answering God, but He does not fulfill every petition; and He has a good reason for not answering. Those who are convinced that God does not answer prayer should read Daniel 9, where the prophet pleaded with God for the release of his people from captivity.

Verses 24 and 25 helps us understand that God answers prayer on His terms, meaning, in His will, by His timetable, and according to His divine purpose.

A key factor in getting a prayer answered is praying in His will. But how is this possible? The answer is simple: know God and His Word. To know God and understand His nature and characteristics, we must read the Bible, His Word.

Once the Bible becomes an integral part of our daily lives, prayer will slowly and surely become a priority in our daily routine. First, we begin to know God. Second, we may ask of Him whatever we need. The Lord Himself has commanded and encouraged us to ask: "So I say to you, ask, and it will be given to you; seek, and you will find; knock, and it will be opened to you. For everyone who asks receives, and he who seeks finds, and to him who knocks it will be opened" (Luke 11:9-10).

Do not be concerned about the "right" or "wrong" ways of prayer. The important thing is to pray according to God's will. Regardless of our need, thoughts, logic, or reasoning, God knows what is best for us not only as it relates to timing but also to our ability to receive and handle it. When God chooses to withhold an answer to our prayer, it may not be because we failed to ask in His will. It may be because God sees that we are unable to handle an answer. Writing to the Christians in Corinth, the apostle Paul said: "No temptation has overtaken you except such as is common to man; but God is faithful, who will not allow you to be tempted beyond what you are able, but with the temptation will also make the way of escape, that you may be able to bear it" (1 Corinthians 10:13).

As we wrap up this segment, let me once again encourage you to follow these guidelines when praying for anything:

1. Pray according to the Scriptures.
2. Pray according to His will.
3. Pray for things that honor and glorify God.
4. Ask for wisdom as you pray. In the book of James, we read, "If any of you lacks wisdom, let him ask of God, who gives to all liberally and without reproach, and it will be given to him" (1:5). A good place to begin learning how to pray is found in 1 Thessalonians 5:12-24.
5. Above all and most importantly, rely on the Holy Spirit.
6. Pray the Lord's Prayer, as recorded in Matthew 6:9-13, for comfort and encouragement.
7. Read the Psalms for healing and the Proverbs for wisdom. This is a personal practice of mine.

Intercessory Prayer

What is intercessory prayer? It is the act of praying on behalf of others. In other words, we intercede for others' needs according to their prayer requests and known needs. Because we are taking others' needs and requests before God, we are acting as a mediator. Several Old Testament characters took on the role of mediator: Abraham, Daniel, David, Elijah, Elisha, Ezekiel, Hezekiah, Jeremiah, Moses, Noah, Samuel, and so on.

In the New Testament, Jesus Christ is pictured and presented as the ultimate intercessor, which is why we conclude all our prayers to God the Father in Jesus' name: "For there is one God and one Mediator between God and men, the Man Christ Jesus" (1 Timothy 2:5). Therefore, Jesus Christ is the intercessor and mediator between God and man.

Praying for others is not always easy because the list and task can be rather long. For instance, if we mention the names of every person we know and care for, the list would be very long, as each person on that list may have numerous needs. If we were to pray for each need of every person on that list, it could take hours each day, and that is not possible.

Of course, we also have our own list of needs and concerns, including those of our immediate households, over which we must pray. This being true, how do we decide what and for whom to pray? In a situation like this, we have no better choice than to go before the Lord and ask Him to bring to our attention those who most need prayer each day.

God knows everyone and everything, and because He is faithful and loving and cares for each one of us, we can trust Him to take care of our needs as well as those of others. God honors that we are willing and care enough to pray for others. He will no doubt bring to our attention those needs and individuals about whom we must pray. We can be rest assured of that.

It is also a good idea to make a list of prayer needs, and have that list handy each time we go to the Lord in prayer. We may work on the list, but He will remind us what to do. It can be a beautiful teamwork, working together, hand in hand.

Another Scripture verse that needs our consideration reads as follows: "Who is he who condemns? It is Christ who died, and furthermore is also risen, who is even at the right hand of God, who also makes intercession for us" (Romans 8:34).

True intercessory prayer contains certain elements, and a perfect model of such intercessory prayer is found in Daniel 9. One author gives a verse-by-verse description of the prophet's prayer: "It is in response to the Word (v. 2); characterized by fervency (v. 3); and self-denial (v. 4); identified unselfishly with God's people (v. 5); strengthened by confession (vv. 5-15); dependent on God's character (vv. 4, 7, 9, 15); and has as its goal God's glory (vv. 16-19)" (Houdman, 2009).

We believers can take the prophet Daniel as a good example (role model) and go before the Lord on behalf of others with a broken and contrite spirit and also with a repentant attitude. True intercessory prayer seeks only God's glory and does not and should not focus on our own needs and wants.

For whom do we intercede? Since I cannot and will not speak for others, my own list looks something like this: I begin by praying for my spouse, my children, my extended family (parents, siblings, etc.), brothers and sisters in the Lord, friends, etc.

The Bible does give us a list for whom we should pray:

- those in authority (1 Timothy 2:2)
- ministers (Philippians 1:19)
- the Church (Psalm 122:6)
- fellow countrymen (Romans 10:11)
- the sick (James 5:14)
- enemies (Jeremiah 29:7; Matthew 5:44)
- those who persecute us (Matthew 5:44)
- those who forsake us (2 Timothy 4:16)
- all men (1 Timothy 2:1)

In closing, allow me to encourage all believers to be intercessors because God calls all Christians to this ministry. We are encouraged to "bear one another's burden" (Galatians 6:2), and we are also commanded to "pray for one another" (James 5:16).

There seems to be a misconception that those who offer intercessory prayers are "super-Christians." But that is not the case. All believers are called to be intercessors, and every believer has the same Holy Spirit; therefore, God allows no exceptions and no favoritism of any kind.

Fasting

What does the Bible say about fasting? The Bible does not command Christians to fast. God neither requires nor demands it. However, fasting is mentioned in the Bible and presented as "something that is good, profitable, and beneficial" (Houdman, 09).

Fasting is mentioned several times in the Bible. Three good examples are found in Zechariah 7:5, Acts 13:3, and Acts 14:23. There is a false notion (misconception) among many that fasting relates nearly always to food, either because of a lack of provision or for dietary purposes. But that is not true at all. The primary purpose for fasting is to draw one's attention away from food and the things of this world and shift the focus completely onto God and His will.

Fasting is another way (besides prayer, Bible study, etc.) to build a serious and intimate relationship with God. For the most part, the fasting mentioned in the Bible focuses on food. However, there are other ways to fast than just food alone.

Houdman describes fasting as "anything given up temporarily in order to focus all our attention on God" (Houdman, 09; see 1 Corinthians 7:1-5). Those who choose to fast should limit it to a set time (short duration) especially when fasting from food, mostly due to medical conditions, such as diabetes and other disorders.

Doctors may not encourage or even recommend that a person fast from food for extended periods of time because it can be harmful to the body. Believers who fast should not consider it as a means for losing weight because that is not considered to be a biblical fast. The purpose of a biblical fast is to build a deeper, intimate relationship with God.

Finally, when we fast, there is no need to put on a show as did some hypocrites mentioned in the Matthew 6. There is no need to prove anything to anyone; we are to keep it only between God and ourselves.

Like prayer, fasting does have its benefits. It helps us discipline not only our thoughts and time but also our walk with the Lord as we are committed to Him.

Prayer and Fasting

Prayer by itself is effective and powerful. The same holds true for fasting. So combining the two is all the more effective, meaning, it has twice the effect. In the Bible, we can see that fasting and praying are often linked. Evidence of such can be found in Luke 2:37 and Luke 5:33.

I would like to close this section with a Scripture that deals with the issue of prayer and fasting head-on. In Matthew 17, we read about a certain boy who was possessed by a demonic spirit. The boy's father brought his son to Jesus' disciples for prayer. The disciples prayed and nothing happened, meaning, the boy was not delivered.

When Jesus learned about the situation, He told His disciples to bring the boy to Him. When they did so, He "rebuked the demon, and it came out of him; and the child was cured from that very hour" (Matthew 17:18). The disciples then asked Jesus why they could not cast out the demon. Jesus told them, "This kind does not go out except by prayer and fasting" (v. 21). Such is the effect and power when people pray and fast.

Conclusion

In this chapter, I presented many truths about prayer and fasting. I urge and encourage all believers to diligently seek the Lord, pouring out your heart's desire before Him and asking Him to direct and guide all your paths and ways. If and when all else fails, pray and wait on the Lord.

Chapter Three

Self-Deception

Being a False Witness

Introduction

Right or wrong, I have always assumed that the best counseling is self-counseling. Likewise, the worst deception is self-deception. My reasoning lies in that no one besides God knows us better or worse than ourselves.

For instance, when I am hungry, thirsty or tired, only my own body and mind knows how much to eat or how much to drink or how much rest I need. The great Greek philosopher Socrates once said, "Know thyself." The more we know ourselves, the better it will be for us and even better for others.

Socrates also is credited with another quote that is worth reading and remembering: "An unexamined life is not worth living." There is some truth in this statement. Some might misinterpret Socrates' meaning and go so far as to consider ending their lives, but I hope that will never be the case. I don't know exactly which direction the philosopher was going with this remark, but we do know that each of us is precious to God and that God formed us in His image (Genesis 2:7).

So how can one deceive him- or herself? Several attitudes and actions can lead to self-deception:

1. Believing lies
2. Telling lies
3. Misleading others
4. Controlling, manipulating, and conning others, and so on

This chapter focuses on some important life issues, such as being a false witness, giving empty promises, breaking promises, cheap talk, and so on. Being a false witness involves such corresponding actions and character traits as lying, gossiping, dishonesty, misrepresentation, and so on.

Self-deception reaps some serious penalties, but the consequences are more severe when we deceive others. When we deceive ourselves, we hurt only ourselves. But when we deceive others, we hurt both others and ourselves. Remember: God loves His children, even those we choose to deceive and hurt. In either case, we may be grieving the Holy Spirit, and in the book of Ephesians we read, "Therefore, putting away lying, let each one of you speak truth with his neighbor; and do not grieve the Holy Spirit of God, by whom you were sealed for the day of redemption" (4:25, 30). I can say from firsthand knowledge, you do not want to grieve the Holy Spirit.

There was a time in my life when I experienced spiritual separation for awhile, and that was difficult to bear. I admit I was scared. However, as soon as I confessed, repented, and turned around, God extended to me His forgiveness, grace, and mercy. What joy and peace I felt as I returned to His fold.

The spiritual separation happened because I chose voluntarily to deceive others as well as myself. Regardless of how I look at it, it was not worth the pain involved. Consequently, I learned a valuable lesson.

Let us examine a few Scripture verses that deal directly with the issue of self-deception. In the book of Proverbs we read: "He who speaks truth declares righteousness, but a false witness, deceit; deceit is in the heart of those who devise evil. But counselors of peace have joy" (12:17, 20).

The prophet Jeremiah penned the following warning: "Everyone will deceive his neighbor, and will not speak the truth; they have taught their tongue to speak lies; they weary themselves to commit iniquity. Your dwelling place is in the midst of deceit; through deceit they refuse to know Me, says the Lord" (9:5-6).

And finally, the Bible passage I am personally guilty of abusing and misusing is found in the apostle Paul's letter to believers in Galatia: "Do not be deceived, God is not mocked; for whatever a man sows, that he will also reap" (Galatians 6:7).

(Personal note: I am quoting an abundance of Scripture verses for two reasons. First, God's Word can encourage, edify, and bring wisdom to those who are willing to turn around and make changes. My second and most important reason for including the Bible passages is that I feel spiritually led to share every verse, and I want to be obedient and do what is right.)

Is self-deception tied or closely related to pride and ego? Of course it is. Many people tend to elevate themselves above others. In other words, putting self on a pedestal comes as second nature to those who think more highly of themselves than they ought. We all may know someone who displays a "holier-than-thou" attitude. But John the Baptist gave us the perfect answer for this way of thinking when he said, "He [Jesus Christ] must increase, but I must decrease" (John 3:30).

Though we may try, we cannot hide our sins from God. In fact, no one can. Jesus taught in parables, and in one of His illustrations, He said, "Nothing is secret that will not be revealed, nor anything hidden that will not be known and come to light" (Luke 8:17). From God's perspective, all our thoughts, motives, desires, evil schemes, etc., are all visible. He is omnipotent (all-powerful), omniscient (all-knowing), omnipresent (everywhere present), infinite (immeasurable), eternal, and so on.

It is difficult to overcome any sin we do not or cannot identify. How then can we detect self-deception in ourselves? We do so by digging into God's Word, which happens to be the ultimate standard for all areas of our lives.

The author of the book of James clarified this point when he said, "Be doers of the word, and not hearers only, deceiving yourselves; if anyone among you thinks he is religious, and does not bridle his tongue but deceives his own heart, this one's religion is useless" (1:22, 26). Therefore, let us keep ourselves busy, taking planks out of our own eyes before trying to remove specks from other people's eyes (see Matthew 7:8).

Fear of Rejection

I mentioned earlier that I believe two of mankind's most common fears are that of rejection and of the unknown. I have yet to meet anyone who is comfortable with the idea of being rejected. There may be an exception to the rule (there usually is), but nearly every human being longs to love and be loved. We not only want to be accepted and loved by others, we also like to reciprocate that love. It is a mutual give-and-take kind of thing.

It is amazing what some people are willing to do and the distance to which they are willing to go to avoid rejection. We try so hard to be accepted by others that in the process we learn to say and do "the right things" at the expense of compromising our own conscience and convictions.

Knowing we are loved and accepted is always a great feeling. What we do not realize is that in order to achieve that conditional and possibly temporary acceptance, we may be hurting only ourselves in the long run and possibly grieving the Holy Spirit. Let us come to an understanding that only God's love is permanent and unconditional.

Rejection can come from any number of sources, including supervisors, coworkers, friends, neighbors, relatives, family, spouses, and so on. We can become overwhelmed by this fear. Perhaps this is what prompted

King Solomon to say, "The fear of man brings a snare, but whoever trusts in the Lord shall be safe" (Proverbs 29:25).

Jesus recognized that trait in the Pharisees, the religious leaders of His day: "They loved the praise of men more than the praise of God" (John 12:43). Why do we want to be accepted by others? Because acceptance sends a message that we are worth something. On the flip side, disapproval conveys the idea that we have little worth.

Since we innately resist feelings of worthlessness, we tend to spend inordinate amounts of time and energy (and sometimes money) trying to please others. In doing this, we take our eyes and attention away from God and His love and purpose for us. When dealing with humans, we must realize we are engaged in a battle we may never win.

The reason for this is simple: We cannot please everyone all the time. There will always be those who disapprove of what we say and do. After awhile, this kind of struggle (a losing battle) will become tiring, pushing us into a place where we experience loneliness and emotional isolation.

Two Scripture passages speak directly to this topic. The first is from the writings of the apostle Paul: "There is therefore now no condemnation to those who are in Christ Jesus, who do not walk according to the flesh, but according to the Spirit" (Romans 8:1). The second verse is a word of edification from the writer of Hebrews: "So we may boldly say; The Lord is my helper; I will not fear, what can man do to me?" (Hebrews 13:6). Allow these two Bible verses to give you the assurance and confidence you need to battle against any rejection you may face from others and from Satan as well.

From a counseling standpoint, let me say that just because you are rejected occasionally does not always mean something is wrong with you. It could be a problem with those rejecting you. They may be facing issues they do not know how to handle or resolve. Be careful not to allow their problems to be your problems. I have observed that those who judge wrongly are often guilty of the same things about which they find fault.

In closing, I would like to suggest that you follow a simple protocol with regard to criticism. Find out who is saying what about you (directly or behind your back). If what they are saying is untrue, ignore it without any ill feelings. On the other hand, if what they are saying is true (based on God's Word), be thankful for the criticism, even if it hurts. Take that truth to the Lord and ask Him to help you deal with it. Be sure you are open, ready, and willing to not only accept the truth but also to make positive and productive changes.

Misrepresentation

This section focuses on two issues: (1) being a false witness, and (2) living a lie. Bible has quite a lot to say about both topics, but it speaks early on about being a false witness. You may be familiar with the Ten Commandments. The ninth commandment reads as follows: "You shall not bear false witness against your neighbor" (Exodus 20:16).

God takes seriously certain aspects of our lives and culture, including abortion, adultery, homosexuality, lying, and so on. Though sin is sin, I believe some transgressions are more egregious than others. Because of the severity of these sins, their ramifications and consequences can be far-reaching.

The Bible clearly states that God despises lying. In the book of Proverbs, we read:

> These six things the Lord hates, Yes, seven are an abomination to Him: a proud look, *a lying tongue*, hands that shed innocent blood, a heart that devices wicked plans, feet that are swift in running to evil, *a false witness who speaks lies*, and one who sows discord among brethren (6:16-19, emphasis added).

Why do we lie? Why do we misrepresent ourselves? Why do we bear a false witness? We may have several reasons, one of which surely refers back to the fear of rejection discussed above. When we choose to lie, it may be for two reasons: to improve our image in the eyes of other people or to make others appear less acceptable or worthy.

I have searched the Word of God as it relates to lying and being a false witness and was dumbfounded to discover how seriously and personally God takes these actions. The Bible makes it clear that lying reaps severe consequences, leading even to hell if it is not confessed, repented of, and abandoned altogether.

Once again, in the book of Proverbs, we read, "Lying lips are an abomination to the Lord, but those who deal truthfully are His delight" (12:22). In what ways can we lie or be dishonest? People seem to find numerous ways to deal deceitfully. The list includes but is not limited to:

1. Cheating on exams
2. Cheating on income tax returns
3. Cheating on God's tithes
4. Giving compliments that we don't really mean
5. Exaggerating
6. Speaking evil against another person
7. Asking household members to say you are not home when you are
8. Speaking slander
9. Telling bill collectors the check is in the mail when it has not been sent
10. Spreading gossip or rumors
11. Practicing false teaching
12. Using flattery
13. Telling "little white lies"

Lying is a plague that has crept into the church. Even many of God's ministers engage in speaking falsehoods and think little of it. But lying is an "abomination" (abhorrence) to God. In the book of Revelation we read: "But the cowardly, unbelieving, abominable . . . and all liars shall have their part in the lake which burns with fire and brimstone, which is the second death" (21:8).

How did lying begin? The first Bible record of lying is found in the book of Genesis where the serpent (Satan) spoke deceitfully to Eve in the garden of Eden. Jesus called Satan—also known as the Devil, Lucifer, and other appellations—the "father of lies": "When he [Satan] speaks a lie, he speaks from his own resources, for he is a liar and the father of it" (John 8:44).

How does the Bible define a lie? As anything that is not the truth. As we read the entire Bible, we discover the definition of a lie's antithesis, truth. In fact, we believers must look to the Scriptures as the standard or measuring tool in determining what truth is and how we can accept it and be set free (see John 8:32).

The next time we accuse others of dishonesty (lying), let us also examine carefully our own minds (thoughts), hearts, actions, and so on, as we may be guilty of the same offenses. If that is not hypocrisy, I don't know what is.

An online article states that the "two main reasons people lie are usually rooted either in fear or pride" (www.bible.com/bible answers). Another author gives additional reasons people lie: "To protect oneself, to gain an advantage, or simply to impress others" (Fowler, 2007).

What can be some aftereffects or results of lying? In other words, what can we expect from it? Lying is known to dissolve any existing trust between individuals. It hurts others by destroying friendships as well as relationships (marriages, etc.). It can and will ruin a good name (one's reputation).

From a spiritual standpoint, untruthfulness can sever a person's fellowship with God. It definitely incites God's judgment because, as the Bible clearly states, God hates lying, and it is an abomination to Him: "A false witness will not go unpunished, and he who speaks lies shall perish" (Proverbs 19:9).

The very idea that liars are barred from entering heaven is scary even to read, much less imagine. But such punishment does not have to apply to anyone, for there is always a way to prevent it. The only way for liars to escape certain banishment from God's presence is explained clearly in the New Testament book of 1 John: "If we confess our sins, He is faithful and just to forgive us our sins and to cleanse us from all unrighteousness" (1:9).

We are told not only to confess our sins to God, we must also confess them to others: "Confess your trespasses to one another, and pray for one another, that you may be healed" (James 5:16). So the formula for healing is to confess, repent, change (turn around), and apply godly principles on a daily basis.

In his letter to the church at Ephesus, the apostle Paul encouraged the Christians there to "speak the truth in love." He continued by explaining why this type of speech is necessary: That they [we] "may grow up in all things into Him who is the head—Christ" (Ephesians 4:15).

I would like to conclude this section with the following suggestions, which I personally am trying to apply:

1. Talk less
2. Listen more
3. Think twice before speaking
4. Stay neutral when you have nothing good to say about a person or situation
5. Wait for every opportunity to confess and make it right before God and man
6. Avoid passing judgment
7. Offer an opinion or advice only when asked

8. Most importantly, if you feel you must confront, be sure you are being led by the Holy Spirit and then share your concerns in love.

Besides obeying the Holy Spirit, take into account a couple of other important aspects of helpful communication: (1) wait for the right mood, and (2) make sure the timing is right. Following these guidelines could keep you out of trouble.

Making Empty Promises and Breaking Promises

By our very nature, we humans find it fairly easy to make promises, but few of us are faithful to always keep our word. Since the latter requires more diligence (often more than we imagined), fulfilling our promises may prove to be difficult indeed.

What does the Bible say about making vows? You may be surprised to learn that Jesus opposed making vows of any kind: "'You shall not swear falsely, but shall perform your oaths to the Lord.' But I [Jesus] say to you, do not swear at all . . . Nor shall you swear by your head, because you cannot make one hair white or black. But let your 'Yes' be 'Yes,' and your 'No,' 'No.' For whatever is more than these is from the evil one.'" (Matthew 5:33-37).

The Bible makes it abundantly clear: We are not to make any vows either to the Lord or to one another. I see this more of a commandment than a personal choice. God is the only One who is known to keep His word flawlessly. I remember giving my word to many people in the past and not being able to keep all of them, even though my intentions were good.

At times, I have given my word under pressure or under obligation or I was persuaded to give it. The problem with giving vows is that we can never be sure if we will be able to keep our promises, for nothing is guaranteed. As humans, we are prone and susceptible to error.

A second concern associated with making promises is the uncertainty of the future. None of us knows what the future holds for us, much less for others. In the book of James, we read: "Whereas you do not know what will happen tomorrow. For what is your life? It is even a vapor that appears for a little time and then vanishes away" (James 4:14).

God is in control, and He is the only One who knows everyone's past, present, and future. We have to learn to trust Him because "All things work together for good to those who love God, to those who are the called according to *His* purpose" (Romans 8:28, emphasis added).

Remember Jesus' strong warning for His followers to choose to respond simply with either yes or no? We all know people who try to operate in a gray zone. That is not only not of God, it is also risky, for living in the gray area indicates spiritual "lukewarmness," which God strongly rebukes: "I know your works, that you are neither cold nor hot. I could wish you were cold or hot. So then, because you are lukewarm, and neither cold nor hot, I will vomit you out of My mouth" (Revelation 3:15-16).

When a person tries to live in the gray area (uncommitted fringes), he may slowly but surely begin to take matters into his own hands and away from God's will. Knowing God's will is a key issue of being a Christian, and when that is not possible, life can become tough as we operate in our own strength.

With God out of the picture, life becomes empty and lonely. From personal experience, I can attest that spiritual loneliness is a difficult place, as I have been there one too many times. It is not worth the pain of being isolated from God. Not everyone who goes the distance away from God is able to return. Though God is always willing to receive the wayward ones, some may not want to come back for whatever reason(s).

Therefore, we must be careful not to make any empty promises. In the event we do make a vow, let us use every effort to keep it. If for some reason we cannot keep it, it is important that we find someone who can fulfill the promise on our behalf. By doing so, we are letting the other person know that we care enough to keep our word either on our own or through someone we trust. Let us not "bite off more than what we can chew," as the saying goes.

Talk Is Cheap (But Not Free)

Most of us have heard this phrase many times. Though the statement is true, it has a serious side that relates to the issue of accountability. Some talk may be cheap, but according to the Word of God, it is never free: "So then each of us shall give account of himself to God" (Romans 14:12).

It is one thing to possess knowledge, but if we do not apply that knowledge, we miss the point of having gained it in the first place, especially as it relates to developing an intimate relationship with our heavenly Father. Herbert Armstrong taught, "Knowledge is of no value unless applied." He was right about that.

Knowledge is good as long as we know how to use it properly and do not abuse or misuse it. The more one has or knows, the more he or she is expected to perform (or prove): "For everyone to whom much is given, from him much will be required; and to whom much has been committed, of him they will ask the more" (Luke 12:48).

King Solomon, who has been called the wisest man who ever lived, wrote about the consequences of having more knowledge: "For in much wisdom is much grief, and he who increases knowledge increases sorrow" (Ecclesiastes 1:18). There is nothing wrong with possessing a great amount of knowledge as long as we know how to use and apply it properly and wisely as unto the Lord.

We may possess two types of knowledge: head knowledge and heart knowledge. Head knowledge is nothing more than accumulated information, facts, statistics, and so on. One can attain head knowledge in various ways, such as by reading, listening, observation, instincts, and through education, experience, and so on. Heart knowledge is the result of applying or activating the head knowledge. Simply put, head knowledge deals with "what," and heart knowledge deals with "how." Wisdom, on the other hand, comes from God.

The Bottom Line

"One too many lies, told to one too many people, for too long a time." This seems to be the sad but true story of a great number of people. On a more personal note, I have been guilty of this bottom-line statement for most of my Christian life, a fact I am ashamed to admit.

We all have our reasons why we exaggerate and fabricate, but one of my reasons has been the fear of rejection, especially as it relates to living as a foreigner in a predominantly Caucasian nation. I continue to experience more than my share of racial and gender discrimination, which I resent.

Because of my fear of rejection, I have tried in the past to take matters into my own hands. As a result, I found myself engaging in "smooth talk"—saying whatever others wanted to hear. My biggest mistake was failing to trust the Lord and not placing every situation into His hands. I am improving now, and I am always ready and willing to receive complete deliverance.

Conclusion

In closing this chapter, I wish to remind you that it does not matter what people think or say about you behind your back. Do not pay attention to everything everyone says. Focus only on the truth because, as we read in John 8:32, the truth has the power to set you free.

There is no need to fear other people; neither is there a need for you to always be accepted and loved by others, especially if it is for the wrong reasons. In the gospel of Matthew, we read: "Do not fear those who kill the body but cannot kill the soul. But rather fear Him who is able to destroy both soul and body in hell" (10:28).

If given the choice between having a relationship with the Lord and enjoying friendships with other humans, I would choose God without a doubt or reservation. When God is for me, and as long as I am willing to obey Him and walk with Him in love and integrity, I have nothing to fear. God is always faithful and always keeps His word; therefore, those who trust Him and depend on Him for everything will never be disappointed.

One author encourages us to "ask ourselves these questions before saying anything questionable about or to some else: Is it true? Is it necessary? and, Is it kind? Unless we can answer 'yes' to all these, we are probably better off leaving it unsaid" (Fowler, 2011).

Chapter Four

Establishing a Comfort Zone

Creating Our Own Safety Zone

Introduction

This will be a short chapter. Whatever needs to be said will be said simply and to the point. This chapter focuses on those individuals who insist on living strictly within the confines of their comfort zones. As the saying goes, "Birds of a feather flock together."

Based on my observations, as well as stories and incidents I have heard, this type of behavior is characteristic of many, many individuals. They tend to pick and choose who they talk to and with whom they mingle or socialize.

Choosing Our Inner Circle

I have been a born-again Christian since January of 1986. Since that time, I have lived in about nine different cities and five states. During those years, I have visited and been a member of many churches affiliated with various denominations.

On numerous occasions, I have gone to lunch or dinner with several pastors, other church leaders, and Christian friends from within the church. At each of these meetings, I realized that the group included almost the same people. I do not remember nor can I recall a single time when a new person was invited or volunteered to join us in fellowship, which struck me as odd. Should it be that way? Even if someone did join us, he or she almost always was a member of the same church and denomination.

Many individuals seem uncomfortable around others who have a different ideology or opinion. For instance, I have yet to see Charismatic/Pentecostal and non-Charismatic and non-Pentecostal people come together.

Not Open and Willing to Invite Others; Not Open and Willing to Join Others

Some Christians (one too many, in my opinion) refuse to invite others to join or associate with them. On the other hand, some believers (one too many, again) hesitate or avoid joining or associating with other believers. I am sure each one probably has his or her personal reason(s). But I have my doubts if any of their excuses line up with the Word of God. Despite all excuses and reasons, the Bible does say there is "one Lord, one faith, one baptism" (Ephesians 4:5).

What might be the reasons believers offer for their exclusiveness, for avoiding and ignoring one another. Beyond what I have heard in counseling session, I can only make an educated guess. After all, most of us live by the saying, "To each his own."

The reasons and excuses for social exclusiveness include but are not limited to the following:

1. Educational differences
2. Emotional inequity
3. Financial incompatibility
4. Inferior intelligence
5. Cognitively distant
6. Spiritual disagreement

Open and Willing to Learn; Open and Willing to Teach

The Bible declares that we are "fearfully and wonderfully made" (Psalm 139:14). Each one of us is special and unique to God. He loves us so much He died for our sins and rose again. It is God's desire and will that we not only love each other but also serve one another whenever a need or opportunity arises.

We should put aside all differences and work diligently toward cooperating with one another. Why do so many people refuse to learn from others? I can think of at least one reason: pride, which of course is "false pride," along the lines of self-righteousness.

Along with many other traits, pride seems to be a universal issue and is prevalent around the world. Much of my life growing up in India, I noticed two things about many Indians in general: (1) Older individuals rarely ask younger people for their advice, feedback, or suggestion, and (2) Those same elderly people seldom apologize to anyone younger than they.

In the Bible we read, "All have sinned and fall short of the glory of God" (Romans 3:23). That being true, it is up to each person to either choose to accept others on an equal footing or practice a form of religion that is of no help to them.

On the contrary, apostle Paul encourages believers to treat others as though they are *better* than themselves: "Let nothing be done through selfish ambition or conceit, but in lowliness of mind let each esteem others better than himself" (Philippians 2:3).

I sincerely believe that no one knows everything. Only God is omniscient. Therefore, it is important that we look for opportunities to learn everything we can from everyone with whom we come in contact, whether through a face-to-face encounter or via e-mail, texting, or telephone conversations.

We never know who we may need and for what reason we may need them. Avoiding and ignoring others for the sake of our own personal comfort zone is unwise. Once again, the apostle Paul gives us a perfect explanation of how we need each other:

> The body is not one member but many. If the foot should say, "Because I am not a hand, I am not of the body," is it therefore not of the body? And if the ear should say, "Because I am not an eye, I am not of the body," is it therefore not of the body? If the whole body were an eye, where would be the hearing? If the whole were hearing, where would be the smelling? But now God has set the members, each one of them, in the body just as He pleased . . . . And the eye cannot say to the hand, "I have no need of you"; nor again the head to the feet, "I have no need of you." No, much rather, those members of the body which seem to be weaker are necessary (1 Corinthians 12:14-22).

We must be careful not to allow pride to block opportunities to learn as well as to teach if and when the need arises. More importantly, we should thank God for creating avenues by which we may benefit from others' knowledge and expertise as well as occasions to share our own gifts. In the New Testament, we read, "In everything, give thanks" (1 Thessalonians 5:18).

Learning to Be Humble

What does it mean to be humble? The word *humble* has many meanings, some of which include: not being prideful or arrogant, to be modest, to be subservient, not viewing self in high regard, not putting self on a pedestal, and so on.

Just to cite one example for easy understanding: Imagine several well-known and popular individuals (let's say authors, to make it more personal) are assembled in a room. I can honestly say that in the presence of such an elite group, I would feel humble.

It is one thing to know little and remain humble, but it is another thing to be well educated and well-informed and still choose to remain humble. Humility is an absolute essential for those who call themselves true believers. The Bible is emphatic in that regard.

Before I go further with this topic, I would like to provide at least one Scripture from both the Old and the New Testaments. In the book of Proverbs we read: "Surely He [God] scorns the scornful, but gives grace to the humble" (3:34). And two New Testament writers address the issue almost verbatim: "Humble yourselves in the sight of the Lord, and He will lift you up" (James 4:10); and "Humble yourselves under the mighty hand of God, that He may exalt you in due time" (1 Peter 5:6).

The flip side of humility is arrogance, and the Word of God is straightforward when dealing with those who are filled with pride. In the book of Proverbs, we read, "Pride goes before destruction, and a haughty spirit before a fall" (16:18).

I know many individuals (including myself) who act prideful at times. One of many problems associated with proud people is that to them everything seems to be fine as it is; therefore, they see no need for change or correction. It is difficult to deal with an extremely prideful individual.

One cannot always reason with such people because they tend to reject and disdain the logical approach, especially when the logic deals with their faults or weaknesses. I know, because I used to be prideful, and I remember many occasions when others tried to convince me there might be another way (other than mine) of viewing things. I would grow impatient, annoyed, and judgmental in these conversations.

Over the years, however, I have worked diligently to correct my prideful attitude, and by God's grace, mercy, and kindness, I have come a long way. Yet I also realize I have not arrived, but at least I am making some progress and moving (slowly) in the right direction. As indicated by

God's Word, I am taking one day at a time: "Sufficient for the day is its own trouble" (Matthew 6:34).

The Bible encourages believers to live their lives as Christ lived His. Jesus was born in a stable, probably surrounded by smelly farm animals. Being born of the Virgin Mary (a human) does not change the fact that Jesus is part of the Trinity. Even so, he began His earthly life in absolute humility, in a stable.

Jesus loves and cares for us so much that He gave us His word (promise): "Take My yoke upon you and learn from Me, for I am gentle and lowly in heart, and you will find rest for your souls" (Matthew 11:29). Jesus lived in complete humility and obedience to His Father's will.

In the book of Philippians we read, "He humbled Himself and became obedient to the point of death, even the death of the cross" (2:8). In a nutshell, Jesus Christ is the ultimate example of a humble person. On many occasions, He simply walked away as opposed to defending Himself as He had every right to.

Going back to the issue of pride, when do we show our pride? We tend to show our pride (the most) when we see other Christians fall and fail. But that is very wrong. When we see a believer fall and fail (go astray), we are to make it our job and duty to help that brother or sister, as we read, "If a man is overtaken in any trespass, you who are spiritual restore such a one in a spirit of gentleness, considering yourself lest you also be tempted" (Galatians 6:1).

In what ways can we humble ourselves? I would like to suggest the following guidelines:

1. Set aside some time every day, giving it to the Lord. Read the Word of God and pray during this time.
2. Learn to maintain a "servant" attitude. Make the question, "How may I be of service?" your life motto.

3. Never try to prove yourself to anyone, especially as it relates to education, intelligence, career, social status, or financial standing.
4. Refrain from making sarcastic or judgmental comments. Instead, choose to remain calm, quiet, and learn to be a good listener. "An intelligent person knows how to put others in their place. A wise person knows how to put himself in his place" (Vemuri, 2011). If I had to choose, I would rather be wise than intelligent.

Learning to Practice Humility

What exactly is humility? The dictionary defines the concept as "the quality or condition of being humble; modest opinion or estimate of one's own importance, rank, etc." Even though the terms *humble* and *humility* are presented separately, they can be perceived as the same.

Prideful and pride are the antitheses for *humble* and *humility*, respectively. The Bible describes humility as "meekness, lowliness, and absence of self" (*The Ultimate A to Z Resource*, 2001).

The Greek term we translate as *humility* literally means "lowliness of mind." What a powerful meaning! Who would choose lowliness of mind? Probably very few, yet for a true believer, lowliness of mind should be his or her ultimate goal, desire, motive, and intention. The apostle Paul underscored this thought when he said, "Let nothing be done through selfish ambition or conceit, but in *lowliness of mind* let each esteem others better than himself" (Philippians 2:3, emphasis added).

Notice that the apostle Paul used the terms *lowliness* and *mind* in the same sentence. In a worldly system, these two words would be viewed as contradictory and even as an oxymoron. Contradictory because the word *lowly* usually applies to those with minimal or no intelligence. In Paul's days, as in modern times, nearly everyone honored and respected those whose thinking was at a high level. But the Word of God does not endorse or support the logic of the secular or worldly system.

Biblical humility means one is not to think highly of himself: "For I say, through the grace given to me, to everyone who is among you, not to think of himself more highly than he ought to think, but to think soberly, as God has dealt to each one a measure of faith" (Romans 12:3).

Instead, we are to acknowledge who and what we are in Christ and find our identity in Him. True humility does not mean we must always try to remain neutral and live in the gray areas. An individual should not feel guilty when talking about his or her own strengths and weaknesses, successes and failures. In other words, there is no beating around the bush: "What you see is what you get."

How can we develop true humility? The most effective way is by establishing a consistent and persistent relationship with God. The secular world may not always accept or appreciate when we practice humility. They can take it the wrong way and even perceive it as immaturity or childishness at times.

But what unbelievers think or say about us should be of little concern to us because God's view of humility is the opposite of the world's perspective. In Matthew's gospel we read, "Blessed are the poor in spirit, for theirs is the kingdom of heaven" (5:3). Jesus appreciates and actually praises those who are humble and poor in spirit.

I see humility more as a commandment than an option, much like the concept of tithing. Paying a tithe of your income into the "storehouse" is a commandment, whereas giving a "love offering" is a choice. Where commandments are concerned, we have no choice but to obey and surrender or be willing to face the consequences.

In the worldly system, we often hear the phrase, "I am just looking out for number one," which is self-centeredness. From a biblical viewpoint, it is the opposite of the biblical teaching on humility. Speaking of Jesus, John the Baptist said, "He must increase, but I must decrease" (John 3:30). We are told to have that same attitude toward others. We see the term *one another* mentioned repeatedly in the Bible. For instance, we are encouraged to pray for one another, encourage or edify one another, confess your faults one to another, and so on.

Why is humility an important part of our spiritual life? One Christian author answers this question by offering three wise suggestions. He says, "Humility is the proper attitude before God, humility keeps us from depending on our own strengths, and humility makes our prayers direct and honest" (Wilson, 2000).

Yet humility is not only about "lowliness of mind." I believe it also means maintaining a servant attitude. As mentioned above, believers must always be ready and willing to ask others: "How may I be of service to you?" Having this mind-set is important to our spiritual growth and maturity.

Jesus set the example for us as One who maintained a perfect servant's attitude. As God the Son, Jesus is part of the Holy Trinity, yet being the Messiah and Savior, He humbled Himself and washed His disciples' feet: "After that, He poured water into a basin and began to wash the disciples' feet, and to wipe them with the towel with which He was girded" (John 13:5).

Serving others is a way of serving God. Someone once asked me, "What is a Christian?" to which I answered, "Being Christlike." As authentic Christians, we are to always do our best (the best way we know how) to imitate Christ wherever and whenever possible.

As we imitate Christ, we demonstrate His characteristics through love, forgiveness, patience, empathy, sympathy, and prayer. Maintaining a servant attitude is a big one for me, as it is through serving that we become more like Christ, who is our perfect role model and example.

Conclusion

My father once told me, "You cannot give what you do not have." In other words, we can only give what we have and who we are. As Christians, it is essential that we first understand our true identity before trying to understand who others are.

As I conclude this chapter, I would like to share a few words of wisdom that have come to me from different sources, including the Bible, my parents, my wife, my siblings, and my friends inside and outside the church family. I am still following these helpful guidelines:

1. First, *learn about yourself*, your true identity as it relates to your strengths, weaknesses, plusses, minuses, and so on. A good way to do that is to acquaint yourself with the book of Proverbs, which contrasts wisdom and foolishness. In other words, there is a right way (wisdom) and a wrong way (foolishness) to conduct your life.

   The book of Proverbs has thirty-one chapters. By reading one chapter a day, you will be able to complete the entire book in a month. As you read daily, God will speak to you through your conscience, which will gently remind and caution you about where you stand in terms of your thoughts, actions, deeds, desires, goals, intentions, and motives.

   I have been a fool long enough, for most of my adult life. I would like to be wise instead. What must I do to be wise? To begin with, I need to fear God: "The fear of the Lord is the beginning of wisdom" (Psalm 111:10; Proverbs 9:10). Then, I must desire and seek motivation to grow.

   In order to learn, I need to be a good listener. But most importantly, I need to trust God, knowing that He loves me and wants only the best for me. The Lord has given me His word that He will be with me forever: "Lo, I am with you always, even to the end of the age" (Matthew 28:20).

2. *Shift your focus from yourself to others*; learn from them.

    I believe we meet three types of people as we go through life. Some are at a higher level academically. They have more education, knowledge, experience, wisdom, etc. Others are at a lower level because they happen to know less (for reasons already mentioned). And then there are those who are at the same level as us, give or take a few variables.

    But I have never met anyone who either knows everything or who knows nothing at all. My advice is to learn from those who are at a higher level. Teach those who are at a lower level, assuming they are open, willing, and ready to be taught. And enjoy and share what you can with those who are your peers.

    In a nutshell, from the time we arise in the morning until we go to bed at night, we should be either learning something from someone or teaching something to someone. Doing neither of these is nothing short of a waste of precious time that will never be regained.

3. *Seek counsel.* We need to follow certain godly principles in order to remain humble and to maintain a teachable spirit. One of those principles is to seek godly counsel. As an assistant professor of psychology, having taught at several colleges, I have always encouraged my students to ask when in doubt.

    Asking is always better and probably wiser than assuming. Let us examine a couple of Scripture passages from the book of Proverbs that directly deal with the issue of seeking wise counsel or advice: "The way of a fool is right in his own eyes, but he who heeds counsel is wise" (12:15). And: "Without counsel, plans go awry, but in the multitude of counselors they are established" (15:22). We can now see the importance and significance of seeking counseling.

Encourage and receive constructive criticism. At first, you may feel uncomfortable listening to someone telling you that your ideas and/or actions do not measure up to their standards or to the Word of God. But let us turn once again to the book of Proverbs where we read: "The ear that hears the rebuke of life will abide among the wise. He who disdains instruction despises his own soul. But he who heeds rebuke gets understanding" (15:31-32).

4. Finally, the best way to understand humility is to *see yourself through God's eyes*. For example, assume that a certain individual considers himself to be a righteous man. Even if this assumption is true, we must remember that God sees things differently: "But we are all like an unclean *thing,* And all our righteousness is like filthy rags" (Isaiah 64:6, emphasis added).

We can follow several steps toward humbling ourselves and practicing humility, thereby enjoying our walk with the Lord and learning to serve Him and others:

1. The first step on the path is to confess your sins to God and to others. In the book of Psalms, we read that King David not only confessed his sins before God, he also asked God to examine and search his thoughts and heart. But we are also encouraged to confess our sins to others: "Confess your trespasses to one another" (James 5:16).

2. The next step on the path to humility is to learn to be thankful. Someone once said, "The more one has, the more one wants." This is true of many people, including many pastors, evangelists, and other church leaders. Greed is not of God, and it will put a stumbling block in our walk with God.

We are to be thankful in what we have and content with what we do not have (see 1 Thessalonians 5:18).

3. Step three is to crucify pride and self-righteousness and develop a habit of dying daily to self. Bearing our cross is part of the title of this book and a portion of Jesus' invitation to become one of His disciples: "If anyone desires to come after Me, let him deny himself, and take up his cross daily, and follow Me" (Luke 9:23).

4. The fourth step along the way of humility involves our need to learn patience, especially with regard to the wrongdoings of others. I recall many instances where I lost my patience when I saw others breaking God's laws. I would become emotional and judgmental, not realizing that I too was guilty, if not for that sin then certainly for others.

    Patience is a virtue, as the saying goes, and it happens to be one of the nine fruits of the Spirit described in Galatians 5:22-23. One too many friendships and relationships have ended or been lost because of someone's impatience.

5. And finally, take the important step of learning the godly characteristic of forgiveness. I once taught a four-hour class on "How to Give and Receive Forgiveness." I am convinced that God takes the issue of unforgiveness very seriously. It is like a poison that will take its toll on every aspect of your life if not dealt with swiftly.

    In the gospel of Luke, we read, "Judge not, and you shall not be judged. Condemn not, and you shall not be condemned. Forgive, and you will be forgiven" (6:37).

Following these five critical steps can and will bring a positive and productive change in your life. Once others see these virtues manifested in you, they too might want to experience these same changes in their lives.

Once again, I encourage you to learn what you can, teach what you should, remain humble and practice humility, and, above all, maintain a servant mentality. By doing so, not only will you develop a closer relationship with God, but you will also help others do the same. Whatever you do for others (as unto the Lord) will not go unnoticed, and God will reward you when the time is right.

Chapter Five

Tithing

Robbing God or Ourselves?

Introduction

Money can be like fire; "a good servant but a bad master," as the saying goes. Most of us know what happens when we play with fire: It can destroy and even kill.

In a sense, money works in a similar fashion. I have read and heard many stories about individuals who won or were bequeathed a fortune (lottery, inheritance, etc.) and soon lost most or all of it. When a person does not use resources wisely, he or she can expect to lose them shortly.

Someone once said, "Money cannot buy happiness, but it surely can make misery more tolerable." There seems to be a great amount of truth in that statement. Money is definitely one aspect of life that gets nearly everyone's attention.

I mentioned earlier that I have done (and still do) Christian counseling, an approach that uses the Word of God to deal with human nature as it relates to sin and so on. I do individual, marriage, and family counseling, using the Bible as the primary tool, when possible. In all my years of counseling, I have yet to see even one case where money was not an issue. Problems related to finances have been involved in every one of my counseling cases. That gives us an idea of the important role money plays in our lives. However, other issues of life are actually far more important than money. These overarching aspects include but are not limited to the following: compassion, forgiveness, healing, love, patience, prayer, salvation, understanding, and such like.

When I counsel people, one of the many things I tell the counselees about life is simply this: If you do not have money, you can earn or borrow it if someone is willing to lend. If you need employment, you can apply for and get a job; if you need food, you can buy it, and so on. But, if you do not have love, patience, understanding, and such like, where can you turn?

The point is this: Some things in life can be earned, borrowed, or received as gifts. Other things, such as those mentioned above, cannot be bought with money because they are not for sale. One either has or does not have them. Each one of us must work hard to learn, earn, and develop these qualities.

What does God's Word say about money or managing resources? There are literally hundreds of Scripture verses that deal with money and its stewardship. The Bible covers different aspects of finances as they relate to financial independence. These topics include borrowing, co-signing, accumulating debt, giving, lending, saving, stewardship, and so on. The Word of God clearly states, "Money does not solve problems."

Allow me to begin with the most important biblical aspect of finances—tithing. Tithing is an Old Testament concept that is not mentioned in the New Testament. In the Old Testament, tithing was a requirement of the law whereby all Israelites were commanded to give ten percent of everything they earned. The concept of the tithe operates on *gross* earnings and not on the *net*.

Scripture passages that deal directly with the concept of tithing are Leviticus 27:30; Numbers 18:26; Deuteronomy 14:22; and 2

Chronicles 31:5. One verse pastors of every denomination tend to use, misuse, and even abuse is Malachi 3:8-10:

> Will a man rob God? Yet you have robbed Me! But you say, in what way have we robbed You? In tithes and offerings. You are cursed with a curse, for you have robbed Me, even this whole nation. Bring all the tithes into the storehouse, that there may be food in My house, and try Me now in this, says the Lord of hosts.

Why should we tithe? I can think of at least two reasons:

1. We tithe because God commands us to do so. The Bible talks about the tithe and also about giving "love offerings." Some Scripture verses are to be considered commandments; others give believers an option, meaning we are not obligated to do anything. So tithing is one of those commandments. We have no choice but to obey and give as the Lord has commanded.

   On the other hand, giving a love offering is a choice that is entirely up to the discretion of each believer. What is considered a love offering? A good example would be a special financial gift received to bless the church's senior pastor on his birthday, wedding anniversary, during pastor appreciation month, or even to send him and his spouse on a short vacation or retreat.

2. The second reason we tithe is to support the church—the spiritual storehouse. The church's elders, deacons, or administrative board prepare monthly and annual budgets to cover overhead costs, such as salaries for the pastoral staff and other employees, pay the utility bills, replace and repair damaged equipment/furnishings, pay the mortgage, and handle other expenses as they arise.

Most churches also have additional disbursements of funds including benevolent (or charity) work that involves helping the needy within the church and in the community. Benevolent giving usually provides food, clothing, shelter, and even some medical supplies/expenses for the poor.

And last, but not least, many churches support itinerating evangelists and missionaries, who labor diligently doing God's work in their own countries and in other nations around the world.

The total of all these expenditures can amount to a great sum of money. The tithes and love offerings are designed by God to cover every legitimate expense as it appears on a regular and consistent basis each month.

These are the two primary reasons why we should and must tithe. (Of course, there may be more.) It is sad and unfortunate that not every believer understands his obligation and opportunity to tithe. A recent survey reported that only twenty percent of professing Christians tithe, covering the expenses for the other eighty percent.

I am sure those who choose not to tithe have convinced themselves that it is okay and that God will understand. God does understand, but do *they* understand the consequences for disobeying His command to tithe? We have no idea, nor can we imagine the financial and spiritual risk we are taking when we choose to ignore this solemn command.

I mentioned earlier that tithing is only an Old Testament concept. What does the New Testament say on the subject? Nowhere in the New Testament do we find the terms *tithe* or *tithing*, nor is there any mention of a specific percentage. How then do we decide what or how much to give?

Please keep in mind that the New Testament does affirm the importance and benefits of giving. In the apostle Paul's first epistle to the Corinthians, we read: "On the first day of the week, let each one of you lay something aside, storing up as he may prosper, that there be no collections when I come" (16:2).

We are to give as we are able with no specific percentage prescribed. Some can give much more than ten percent, and some are able to give far less than the expected ten percent. If we do not know what to give or how much to give, we can pray and seek God's wisdom: "If any of you lacks wisdom, let him ask of God, who gives to all liberally and without reproach, and it will be given to him" (James 1:5).

It is important to maintain a pure motive when giving. We give because God commands us to and also because we want to give from the heart. The truth of the matter is, God owns everything, and no man or woman on earth comes close to God's vast wealth.

No one can out-perform God when it comes to giving, as well as in many other ways. In the Psalms, we read, "For every beast of the forest is Mine, and the cattle on a thousand hills" (50:10). Therefore, let us not act as if we have it made. God knows how to teach all of us a lesson or two because He loves and cares for us.

Giving Conveniently

I find no Scripture verse that deals directly with this type of giving; therefore, I will have to explain as best I can, based on what I have read and heard. This is the type of giving where individuals do not follow or abide by God's standards with regard to the tithe. Instead, they choose to give *conveniently*, following the "play-it-by-ear" technique. In other words, they let their circumstances dictate their giving. And as we all know, circumstances can change without a moment's notice. Convenient givers have no standard guiding their decisions.

It is one thing not to have much to give, but it is another thing to have it and choose to withhold it. I know many individuals personally who strongly believe that giving ten percent is strictly an Old Testament concept that does not apply in the New Testament era. I am not here to judge anyone, nor will I try to put anyone on a guilt trip because that is not biblical either. Certain issues or aspects of life tend to be rather delicate and sensitive, and how to deal with them is up to each individual and God. From their perspective, they may be exercising their free will, but from God's view, He does and will expect an answer from every person for all they say and do: "So then each of us shall give account of himself to God" (Romans 14:12).

We know God is forgiving; however, He has another side that is holy and just. We need to understand and revere both sides of His character. When much of our giving depends on our mood, emotions, and circumstances, we might consider that to be *convenient giving*.

Some people tend to give *conditionally*. For instance, they present their terms to God and then withhold their monies to see if and when God will bring their prayer conditions to pass. A conditional giver might say, "Lord, if you do this or that, I will put this amount of money in the offering plate." But it does not and should not work that way. God's love toward us is unconditional, and we do not have to do anything extra or special to earn it.

When we go before the Lord in prayer, we must approach Him on His terms. We cannot afford to act and react any way we want and still expect Him to answer and bless. God is always ready and willing to forgive speedily, but He will not always answer or bless us with what we want unless we are asking according to His divine will.

Giving Grudgingly

Much of what was said above about convenient giving also applies to this type of giving. The attitude behind convenient giving is usually based on one's emotions or moods. The attitude behind giving grudgingly usually is based on the emotions of anger, disappointment, or dissatisfaction.

Once again, I know individuals who fall under this category of giving. When I ask them their reasons for giving, they admit they really don't want to give the full ten percent, or even most of it, but they do it anyway. They may say they are afraid God will "do a number" on them if they don't give. That sounds to me like a spirit of condemnation, which is not of God, for He does not condemn. He only convicts, and even then He moves gently and in love. Satan is the one who condemns. Even if we choose not to give, God does not love us any less.

God does not discriminate or show partiality toward anyone: "Then Peter opened his mouth and said: 'In truth I perceive that God shows no partiality. But in every nation whoever fears Him and works righteousness is accepted by Him'" (Acts 10:34-35).

The Bible tells us it is wrong to give grudgingly. In Paul's second letter to the Corinthians we read, "So let each one give as he purposes in his heart, not grudgingly or of necessity; for God loves a cheerful giver" (9:7). Let us make sure not to give selfishly, always expecting something in return just because we are giving.

There is no need to expect anything in return for our generosity; God has already promised that He will reciprocate our giving: "Give, and it will be given to you: good measure, pressed down, shaken together, and running over will be put into your bosom. For with the same measure that you use, it will be measured back to you" (Luke 6:38). Giving grudgingly will only hurt yourself.

Giving Sacrificially

Of all the types of giving, this is my favorite. Sacrificial giving is an honor and privilege, and there are few who practice it.

I have heard and read that more and more pastors are looking for second or part-time jobs. Why? Some of my pastor friends tell me there has been a noticeable decrease in tithes, which has forced many of them to take a second job in order to feed their families. None of my pastor friends gave any names; therefore, all our conversations in this regard were general in nature.

I would like to offer some biblical examples of sacrificial giving. This type of giving does not always follow a formula as in the required ten percent. In other words, sacrificial giving does not always find itself as part of one's planned expenditures.

The tithe should be part of a person's budget. Since sacrificial giving is not part of that planned weekly or monthly outlay, once we give it, we must find ways to recover financially from it, which means we may have to make a sacrifice somewhere else, preferably in the area of *wants* as opposed to *needs*.

The Bible is replete with examples of sacrificial giving:

1. At the top of the list is God, our heavenly Father, who sacrificed Jesus, His Son. Here we are—all of us sinners and very good at it. We do not deserve the love God lavishes upon us.

    Yet He loved us so much that He gave His only begotten Son, as we read in the verse that has been called the "Golden Text of the Bible": "For God so loved the world that He gave His only begotten Son, that whoever believes in Him should not perish but have everlasting life" (John 3:16).

    God's gift is so beautiful and precious that the apostle Paul expressed his thankfulness for it: "Thanks be to God for His indescribable gift" (2 Corinthians 9:15). How much more could God give us than His own begotten Son? He simply sacrificed His best on our behalf.

2. Our second example is Jesus Christ, who lived a perfect and sinless life when He was on Earth. Jesus is the Lord and Savior of all who believe in Him and call Him on His name. He loves every person and shows no partiality toward anyone.

Despite our sinfulness, Jesus gives us the equal opportunity to belong to God, to become His children: "But as many as received Him, to them He gave the right to become children of God, to those who believe in His name" (John 1:12).

If I look at Jesus' life in terms of what He said, what He did (for us), and how He lived, there is so much to be thankful for, and I should have no blaming, complaining, or excuses to offer. Above everything, Jesus made the ultimate sacrifice when He gave His life on the cross. Could He have given a greater gift than His own life?

3. The next example is found in Mark's gospel (12:41-44). Mark presents an interesting picture of a widow who gave all she had. This woman's story has a valuable lesson to teach us.

One day, Jesus was sitting near the treasury in the temple. The treasury was not a building, but more than likely a trumpet-shaped chest. The Bible refers to the treasury as "the offering box." Offerings placed in this treasury were used for sacrifices as well as for the upkeep of the temple. The Bible tells us that this occasion was Jesus' last public appearance in Jerusalem as a free man; He was killed just a few days later.

As He sat near the treasury, Jesus observed the people's giving habits, how they were putting money into the treasury. Some rich people probably dropped in large sums of money (pocket change for them). But Jesus was unimpressed with their seeming generosity because He knew their motives and intentions.

However, one person, a widow, caught Jesus' attention. We are told that she was poor. What did she put in the treasury? Two small copper coins. Her contribution was not worth much monetarily. In fact, it was next to nothing when compared with the contributions made by the rich people. And yet, of all the gifts placed into the treasury that day, only this widow's gift earned not only Jesus' attention but also His blessing. Jesus was pleased with her offering, given sacrificially and without expectation.

Jesus called His disciples to Him and said, "Assuredly, I say to you that this poor widow has put in more than all those who have given to the treasury; for they all put in out of their abundance, but she out of her poverty put in all that she had, her whole livelihood" (Mark 12:43-44).

The preceding examples of sacrificial giving are from the Bible. Now I would like to pose two contemporary scenarios:

1. Suppose you own four television sets and come across someone who is in need of a television but cannot afford to buy one. No one but you and God know that you own four televisions. You could donate one of your sets to this individual and pretend you have made a huge sacrifice.

    On the other hand, suppose you have only one television, to which you have become attached, spending many hours every day watching your favorite shows. Then someone brings to your attention the need of the individual who cannot afford to buy one. If you choose to give away your set, but do not let him or anyone else know you have given away the only set you own (and need), that would be considered *sacrificial giving*.

    I hear several of my friends confessing that they cannot always tithe because they live from paycheck to paycheck. They say they plan to give when they can afford it. Yet these same individuals own and maintain several gadgets—smart phones, electronic tablets, expensive cameras, camcorders, pricey watches, and cable TV. They also seem to be able to afford going to the movie theatre regularly and eating out at nice restaurants. In addition, many of them indulge in buying upscale gifts for birthdays and anniversaries, taking short trips, and so on.

My questions is this: how can someone not afford to tithe and yet have enough money to take care of unnecessary and sometimes unwanted expenses? I am not sure everyone understands the difference between *needs* and *wants*. Learn to buy because you need something, not because you want it.

Jesus made it clear that seeking His kingdom is to be our first priority: "But seek first the kingdom of God and His righteousness, and all these things shall be added to you" (Matthew 6:33). God has and always will take care of believers who put their trust in Him.

Giving Cheerfully and Joyfully

Under the section, "Giving Grudgingly," we read the apostle Paul's words to the Corinthians on the subject. Now let us look at that same passage from the perspective of giving cheerfully: "So let each one give as he purposes in his heart, not grudgingly or of necessity; *for God loves a cheerful giver*" (2 Corinthians 9:7, emphasis added).

Though the New Testament contains numerous Scriptures about giving, its teachings differ from the Old Testament in that it does not prescribe a specific percentage one is to give. Churches and some individuals focus heavily on giving cheerfully, joyfully, and liberally. These teachings include the words of Jesus and the apostle Paul.

Paul "walked the walk and talked the talk" when it comes to giving, and he did it by living his life as an example for others to follow. The churches he cited for giving include Antioch, Jerusalem, Macedonia, and others. Individuals who gave generously include Barnabas, Dorcas, and so on.

Examples of generosity can be found in Deuteronomy 15:13-14; 24:19; and James 1:27. These Scripture verses address the importance of showing benevolence toward certain individuals—foreigners, orphans, slaves, widows, etc.—and being blessed as a result. Today, the individuals on this list might include a family member, a single parent, a friend, or sibling who has lost his or her job, and children in need of food, medical attention, shelter, etc.

It seems that almost anyone is able to receive without hesitation or reservation. However, few people actually like to give. Yet the Bible says: "It is more blessed to give than to receive" (Acts 20:35). I can honestly say there is great joy in giving. I know this to be true because by God's grace and mercy, my wife and I have been able to be giving people. I say this not to boast but rather to encourage others to do the same when opportunities arise.

Of course, we should always give "as unto the Lord" and not for any selfish motive or reason. Each time I give, I try to follow two important rules:

1. Expect nothing in return
2. Give unselfishly

Since God loves a cheerful giver, we can be sure He will provide so all our needs are met. In other words, if we sow generously, we will reap generously in return. Yet, we should have pure motives in our giving; we give because we love God and love to meet a need, not because we might receive something in return. God knows who to bless, when to bless, and how much to bless, and we cannot manipulate His giving with our giving.

Before I end this chapter, I would like to address briefly other aspects of financial stewardship besides tithing and love offerings. My advice includes the following:

1. Avoid borrowing money for any reason (see Proverbs 22:7).
2. Avoid debt at all costs (see Psalm 37:21).
3. Give generously to help the needy and poor (Proverbs 19:17).

4. Leave an inheritance for your descendants (Proverbs 13:22).
5. Invest for the future (Proverbs 6:6-8)
6. Lend money like you give: expecting nothing in return (Luke 6:35).
7. Do not charge interest (Luke 19:23).
8. Manage money wisely (Proverbs 21:5).
9. Save (Proverbs 6:8; 21:20).

Conclusion

In his article, "Five Bible Verses About Money Every Christian Should Know," Bob Lotich strongly recommends that all believers acquaint themselves with the following five Scripture verses: Philippians 4:19; Malachi 3:10; 1 Timothy 6:10; Acts 20:35; and Proverbs 22:7 (Lotich, 08).

I would like to close this chapter with a simple-to-follow plan that will help you overcome any financial challenges that may come your way. I am not a financial expert and do not pretend to be one; however, I can recommend what has worked for my wife and me.

First, before anything else, we set aside the ten percent of our gross income as the tithe recommended in the Old Testament. Of course, there have been times (once or twice) when we held onto it. But as soon as we could, we gave the full tithe.

Please understand that there is neither guilt nor any type of judging from neither my perspective nor from the Lord's heart. Regardless of what we say and do (for personal reasons, etc.), God understands, and His love for us will never change.

As you prepare a workable plan, write down a realistic budget (like a balance sheet), where you can see at a glance all your expenses as well as your income. You may not have much say when it comes to certain expenses, such as rent, mortgage, utilities, food, etc. But a budget will help you see areas of discretionary spending that may need to be altered.

Where giving is concerned, let us work diligently, do our best, seek counsel (or advice) when and where necessary, and put it in God's hands before and after we do what needs to be done.

Chapter Six

God, Our Heavenly Father

Who He Is and How We See Him

Introduction

This is my favorite chapter in this book because it focuses on God, my heavenly Father. Please remember that Jesus and God are the same: "I and My Father are one" (John 10:30).

The concept of the Trinity is not mentioned in the Old Testament; however, in Genesis 1 we read: "Then God said, 'Let Us make man in Our image, according to Our likeness'" (v. 26). Notice this verse uses the term *us*, which indicates plurality. That does not mean, however, that there is more than one God.

The word *us* refers to the Trinity. The prefix, *tri*, means three, therefore, the word *Trinity* means three persons in one. These three persons of the Godhead are God the Father, God the Son, and God the Holy Spirit. The Holy Spirit is also referred to as the Holy Ghost and the Comforter.

Christianity is one of three religions, along with Islam and Judaism, that is monotheistic (*mono* being "one"; *theistic* being "belief in God"), which means its adherents believe in only one God. "Hear, O Israel: The Lord our God, the Lord is one" (Deuteronomy 6:4).

So who is God, and what is He like? What does the Bible say about God? Its pages include more information about Him than we can fathom. In order to comprehend (to the extent our finite minds can grasp), it is important to understand God as it relates to His attributes (character), names, nature, and so forth.

Before we begin to explore the vast subject of who God is, let us keep in mind that we can only know Him in terms of what He has chosen to reveal of Himself. The Bible tells us not only what God is like but also what He is not like. It is crucial that we understand who God is because any false or incorrect perceptions of Him would be considered idolatry.

One Christian author defines God as "the supreme Being; the Creator and Ruler of all that is; the self-existent One who is perfect in power, goodness, and wisdom" (Houdmann, 2009). Let's start by considering the attributes or character of God, which includes but is not limited to the following:

- compassionate (Psalm 86:15)
- fair (Psalm 119:137)
- faithful (Deuteronomy 7:9; Psalm 89:1-8)
- forgiving (Psalm 130:4; 1 John 1:9)
- genuine (1 Samuel 15:29)
- good (Psalm 25:8; Mark 10:18)
- gracious (Psalm 103:8; Romans 5:17; 1 Peter 5:10)
- light (Isaiah 60:19; James 1:17)
- love (John 3:16; Romans 5:8)
- merciful (Psalm 103:8-17; Daniel 9:9; Romans 9:15)
- righteous and just (Deuteronomy 32:4; Psalm 11:7; 119:137)
- true and truth (Psalm 31:5; John 14:6; Titus 1:1-2)
- unchanging or immutable (Psalm 102:25-27; Malachi 3:6; Hebrews 13:8)
- wise (Proverbs 3:19; 1 Timothy 1:17)

Now we can talk about His nature, which includes but is not limited to the following characteristics:

- eternal (Psalm 90:2; Jeremiah 10:10)
- holy (Leviticus 19:2; 1 Peter 1:15)
- immaterial (Luke 24:39)
- immortal (1 Timothy 6:16)
- incomparable (2 Samuel 7:22; Isaiah 40:18-26; Micah 7:8-20)
- incomprehensible (Psalm 145:3; Isaiah 55:8-9)
- infinite (Job 26:14; Jeremiah 23:24; Revelation 22:13)
- intangible (John 4:24)
- invisible (John 1:18; 1 Timothy 1:17)
- light (James 1:17; 1 John 1:5)
- omnipotent, meaning all powerful (Genesis 18:14; Revelation 19:6)
- omnipresent, meaning present everywhere (Psalm 139:7-12)
- omniscient, meaning all-knowing (Psalm 139:2-6; Isaiah 40:13-14)
- one (Deuteronomy 6:4; Isaiah 45:5; 1 Corinthians 8:4; Galatians 3:20)
- self-existent and self-sufficient (Psalm 50:10-12; Colossians 1:16)
- source of all life (Psalm 36:9; Acts 17:25)
- sovereign (2 Samuel 7:22; Isaiah 46:9-11)
- spirit (John 4:24)
- trinity or triune (Matthew 28:19; 2 Corinthians 13:14)

Before explaining more about God as it relates to His names and His work, I wish to comment on a couple of issues. First, some individuals (atheists, for example) do not believe in God and His existence. My comment to these individuals is simply this: God's existence is conspicuously evident not only in His creation but also through our conscience. The Bible calls an atheist a fool: "The fool has said in his heart, there is no God" (Psalm 14:1).

Second, in Hinduism (and possibly in other religions) some men are treated as gods. I know for a fact that once or twice a year (if not more often), certain Hindus belonging to a particular caste affix eyes, nose, mouth, and even earrings onto a coconut, creating a "goddess" for worship. But the Word of God contradicts and disagrees with this type of belief: "They have mouths, but they do not speak; eyes they have, but they do not see; they have ears, but they do not hear; noses they have, but they do not smell; . . . those who make them are like them; so is everyone who trusts in them" (Psalm 115:5-6, 8; 135:16-18).

In addition, Hinduism also teaches reincarnation. In other words, once a human dies, he or she returns to Earth as a human or perhaps as an animal, a plant, or a tree, and so on. But the Bible strongly opposes the concept of reincarnation.

Having read the Bible from cover to cover, I have concluded that the Bible does not *prove* the existence of God. Instead, it supports His existence from the opening verse, "In the beginning, God created the heavens and the earth" (Genesis 1:1), to the closing "Amen."

As a born-again Christian, I believe in creationism and not in evolution. There is much in the Bible that we do not understand with our finite minds and intellect. From time to time, I have tried to grasp certain issues about life but all in vain.

The Names of God

Thus far, we have focused on God's characteristics and nature. Now let us look at His different names and the meaning behind each. We will also examine His work, or what He does. First, we will study the Hebrew names of God in the Old Testament with their English meanings.

Besides the Hebrew names of God, I also would like to present other names of God, as it is important for us to understand who God is and what He means to us.

One might ask the questions, What is in a name, and why should a name be so important? One article explains, "In the Old Testament times, a name was not only identification, but an identity as well. Many times a special meaning was attached to the name. Names had, among other purposes, an explanatory purpose" (http://www.blueletterbible.org).

The Hebrew names of God in the Old Testament are as follows:

- Adonai (Lord)
- El (The Strong One)
- El Elohe Yisrael (The God of Israel)
- El Elyon (Most High)
- Elohim (Strong One)
- El Olam (Everlasting God)
- El Roi (The God Who Sees Me)
- El Shaddai (Almighty God)
- Immanuel (God With Us)
- Jehovah (I AM)
- Jehovah-Jireh (The Lord Will Provide)
- Jehovah-Mekaddishkem (The Lord Who Sanctifies)
- Jehovah-Nissi (The Lord Is My Banner)
- Jehovah-Rapha (The Lord Who Heals)
- Jehovah-Rohi (The Lord Is My Shepherd)
- Jehovah-Sabaoth (The Lord of Hosts)
- Jehovah-Shalom (The Lord Is Peace)
- Jehovah-Shammah (The Lord My Companion)
- Jehovah-Tsidkenu (The Lord Our Righteousness)
- Qanna (Jealous)
- Yah or Jah (I AM); Yahweh (I AM).

This impressive list is from Rose Publishing (www.rose-publishing.com).

The next list presents the biblical names of God (and Jesus). This list was compiled by Ms. Mary Fairchild on a website titled: http://www.christianity.about.com/namesofgod. Ms. Fairchild states, "Studying the names of God is one of the most uplifting Bible adventures a Christian can explore." I hope and pray you will enjoy and get to know God up close and personal, just as I have. It has been a blessing for me to realize that God is all I need and there is no satisfaction elsewhere. I pray it will be the same for you as well. Here are the names in alphabetical order:

A. Advocate, Almighty, Alpha, Amen, Angel of the Lord, Anointed One, Apostle, Author and Perfecter of our Faith
B. Beginning, Bishop of Souls, Branch, Bread of Life, Bridegroom
C. Carpenter, Chief Shepherd, Christ, Comforter, Consolation of Israel, Cornerstone
D. Dayspring, Day Star, Deliverer, Desire of Nations
E. Emmanuel, End, Everlasting Father
F. Faithful and True Witness, First Fruits, Foundation, Fountain, Friend of Sinners
G. Gate for the Sheep, Gift of God, God, Glory of God, Good Shepherd, Governor, Great Shepherd, Guide
H. Head of the Church, High Priest, Holy One of Israel, Horn of Salvation i AM
I. Jehovah, Jesus
J. King of Israel, King of Kings
K. Lamb of God, Last Adam, Life, Light of the World, Lion of the Tribe of Judah, Lord of Lords
L. Master, Mediator, Messiah, Mighty God, Morning Star
M. Nazarene
N. Omega, Offspring of David
O. Passover Lamb, Physician, Potentate, Priest, Prince of Peace, Prophet, Propitiation, Purifier
R. Rabbi, Ransom, Redeemer, Refiner, Refuge, Resurrection, Righteousness, Rock, Root of David, Rose of Sharon, Ruler of God's Creation
S. Sacrifice, Savior, Second Adam, Seed of Abraham, Seed of David, Seed of the Woman, Servant, Shepherd, Shiloh, Son

of David, Son of God, Son of Man, Son of Mary, Son of the Most High, Stone, Sun of Righteousness
- T. Teacher, Truth
- V. Vine
- W. Way, Wonderful Counselor, Word

I need to mention that there are biblical references for all the names mentioned here, both the Hebrew ones as well as the others.

Who is God as it relates to His work? One author explains God's work this way: "We cannot understand God apart from His works, because what God does flows from who He is. Here is an abbreviated list of God's works—past, present, and future:

> God created the world; He actively sustains the world; He is executing His eternal plan, which involves the redemption of man from the curse of sin and death; He draws people to Christ; He disciplines His children; and He will judge the world (Houdmann, 2009).

Over the years, I have known many Christians who perceive God in whatever way fits and suits their lifestyle. Some make Him a God of convenience. Others only see God as One who forgives. Still others recognize Him as holy, just, and righteous.

Let's examine each one of these perceptions only to acknowledge and realize how wrong we are to have and maintain a narrow-minded perception. God is, has always been, and will always be the same as He proclaimed Himself to be: "For I am the Lord, I do not change" (Malachi 3:6).

God of Convenience

Modern technology has provided us with numerous conveniences. Take for instance cell phones, faxes, the Internet, microwave ovens, drive-in banking, credit cards, online shopping, and so on. Those of us who live in the Western world (the United States in particular) should thank God for the types of conveniences available to us.

The downside is that living a life of convenience has turned many people (including some churchgoers) into technology addicts, for lack of a better description. We depend so much on technology that if and when one of our gadgets doesn't work properly, we lose our cool—become restless, uncomfortable, and uneasy. For example, if a rainstorm or heavy winds knock out the power, nothing in the house works until the power is restored. This means no television, no microwave, no computer, etc. This sort of inconvenience makes many people irritable and hard to live with.

Why is that the case? Because many of us have not learned to cope effectively and efficiently in situations or circumstances that require patience and self-control. The truth is, this great nation called United States is a land of comfort and convenience.

Comfort and convenience are good, except when these blessings are not used properly. Then they can (and will) offer great temptation to anyone who chooses to fall for it. We can begin to feel entitled to the comforts and conveniences we enjoy instead of seeing them as gifts from God. In the Bible, we read, "For everyone to whom much is given, from him much will be required" (Luke 12:48). Having become accustomed to so much comfort and convenience, we must be careful not to turn Jehovah-Jireh (God Will Provide) into a God of convenience.

In the secular (or worldly) system, one's success or failure is measured by career, money, power, status, and popularity. However, for a genuine believer, both his success and failure are based on whether he is living in God's will, trusting God, maintaining a consistent prayer and devotional life, being faithful with regard to giving, and so on.

One of the key issues for Christians is to know and operate in God's will, which is where we find our safety and security. If we are not living in God's will, who is to blame? I can assure you from experience that the only one at fault is "self."

A pastor once said, "An easy way to fall out of the will of God is [to] make God a matter of convenience in our lives" (Perryman, 2005). This is so true. We have a habit of projecting our own idiosyncrasies not only onto others but also onto the Lord Himself.

God will not, nor has He ever, put up with this sort of game-playing. It is true that "convenience affects the pace of life and how our society functions. We need to open our eyes and see how we have been sucked in and how it's playing a role in our own lives, even in how we relate to God" (Kraft, 2005). Mr. Kraft makes a valid point. Let us remind ourselves daily that each time we approach God, it is on His terms and not our own. We may put demands on other human beings and occasionally get away with it, but it never works with God.

On the contrary, when we try to place demands and conditions on God, it backfires every time, and we may not like or be ready for the consequences that result from such presumption. I say from experience that God knows how, when, and where to teach us a lesson, and He is good at it. Yet His motives are always based on His great love and care for us because He only want the best for us.

Many people tend to associate convenience and life. In other words, the more the convenience, the better life can be. You can see the strong correlation between the two: life and convenience. It is quite the opposite in the Word of God. For instance, in most cases where you see the term *life*, you also see such words as *persecution*, *trials*, *tribulation*, and *trouble*. To confirm this statement, let us look at what Jesus said on the subject: "Whoever desires to come after Me, let him deny himself, and take up his cross, and follow Me" (Mark 8:34).

We now have a comparison between how we like our lives to be as opposed to God's viewpoint. No wonder He said, "For My thoughts are not your thoughts, Nor are your ways My ways; For as the heavens are higher than the earth, so are My ways higher than your ways, and My thoughts than your thoughts" (Isaiah 55:8-9).

Before I close this section, I would like to give another example that seems to be close to home for too many people, especially those in the church. It seems like we do not show much interest in spending quality and quantity time with God when things are going well. However, whenever something goes wrong—a broken relationship, divorce, loss of a job, separation—we find ourselves spending time before God, asking (even begging) Him for a blessing, favor, and immediate solutions.

This is a classic example of perceiving Him as a God of convenience. If I were in God's shoes (hypothetically speaking, of course), I would have a few questions:

- First, give Me one good reason why I should bail you out now, when you showed no regard for Me all along?
- Am I not the same every day, month, and year? Didn't I explain that "I am the Lord, I do not change" (Malachi 3:6)?
- When life was good, you ignored Me, but now you want an immediate bailout. Is this your request or more of a demand?

If God bailed out everyone in similar situations, what would be the meaning and purpose behind persecution, tests, trials, tribulations, and troubles?

God is always quick and ready to forgive and forget, which means our transgressions are gone for good, but God sometimes purposefully allows certain things to happen to teach us important life lessons. May we not consider these times as punishment but rather as correction: "For whom the Lord loves, He corrects, just as a father the son in whom he delights" (Proverbs 3:12).

We also read, "As many as I love, I rebuke and chasten. Therefore be zealous and repent" (Revelation 3:19). The lesson to be learned here is to stop treating God like a vending machine. Instead, we need to humble ourselves before Him in prayer, confessing and repenting and asking Him to forgive us and give us direction and strength to accept and see Him for who He is, all the time.

God Who Forgives

We serve a God whose very nature is to forgive, and He takes pleasure in doing so. He is known to forgive the moment we ask. Not only does He forgive, but He also forgets: "For I will forgive their iniquity, and their sin I will remember no more" (Jeremiah 31:34).

Throughout the New Testament, we find numerous references on forgiveness. I am thankful and consider it a privilege to know I am being forgiven each time I ask. On the other hand, I am concerned about the consequences that surely will come my way as a result of repetitive sins.

For example, imagine I am a state trooper who has a son with a "lead foot." The boy loves to speed and thinks nothing of it, especially on the highway. He has convinced himself that he will never get a ticket because of his "inside connections."

One day, the young man is zipping down the highway at about twenty-five miles per hour over the speed limit. Just to help him understand life and its realities, I pull him over and give him a hefty ticket. "As your father, I forgive you for speeding," I say, after issuing the citation, "but as an officer of the law, I have to give you a ticket in order to do what is right before God."

In this scenario, my son has experienced not only his father's forgiveness but also the consequences (a ticket) for breaking the law. Some may expect me to give him a break, since he is my child. But if I do that, how can I give an account for my actions before God?

In the New Testament, we read that God shows no partiality, meaning, He does not discriminate for or against anyone: "God shows no partiality" (Acts 10:34). As a child of God, we are to do what is right. If the above scenario were true, I would be compelled by conscience to give my son a ticket, because I also do not believe in partiality or discrimination.

Too many Christians choose to see God only as a forgiving God and nothing more. I can recall on many occasions approaching a brother or sister in the Lord in love to gently remind him or her of wrongdoing. I thought surely they would thank me for the concern and care I was showing. Instead, almost all of them became angry and tried to justify their wrongdoing by quoting a few well-known Scripture verses. Most Christians tend to use the following three passages to get out of any personal discomfort:

1. "Judge not, that you be not judged" (Matthew 7:1).
2. "First remove the plank from your own eye, and then you will see clearly to remove the speck from your brother's eye" (Matthew 7:5).
3. "He who is without sin among you, let him throw a stone . . . first" (John 8:7).

We try to validate our wrongdoing by misquoting these verses.

Many Christian friends, including some leaders such as pastors, have told me that God is forgiving by nature, and when He forgives (with no questions asked), who am I to challenge or question? I was told in essence to "get lost."

I have even tried to share the example of the state trooper to make a point but to no avail. I also have been told not to lecture, especially when the correction/counsel is not requested. I was under the impression that I was obeying the injunction presented in Galatians: "If a man is overtaken in any trespass, you who are spiritual restore such a one in a spirit of gentleness" (6:1).

In closing this section, I would like to encourage you to change your view of God. See Him for who He is and not as whatever you want Him to be. Remember His words spoken through the Old Testament prophet Malachi: "I am the Lord, I do not change" (3:6).

The God we serve is a loving and forgiving God. Someone once said, "God is known to forgive even before we ask." That is because He knows our intentions: "Man looks at the outward appearance, but the Lord looks at the heart" (1 Samuel 16:7).

God Who is Just

Just as some people only wish to see God as forgiving, others, probably fewer, recognize Him as holy, just, and righteous. Personally, I prefer to see Him as more than forgiving for reasons only I can explain and justify. But as the saying goes, "To each his own." As employees, we tend to behave and do what is right if we know the employer is watching. When unsupervised, we tend to loosen up.

We know God is just because the Bible tells us He is. But what exactly does that mean? Being just means God insists on and supports what is right—how things ought to be as they relate to the truth.

How can we understand God's justice? The answer is simple: just look at our sins, especially those we repeatedly and frequently commit. There seems to be a close connection between our sin nature and God's justice.

I already explained that God is always ready and willing to forgive. But the buck does not stop there. Putting aside His forgiveness, let's ask ourselves this question: Does God treat us fairly? Absolutely, and there is no room to argue here. How do we know that?

First, God shows no partiality, nor does He discriminate against anyone. Second, God does not punish. Some people assume (even believe) that God is waiting with a big stick to punish us for our sins, but that is not true. He corrects (or chastens) us for our own good because He loves and cares for us.

So how do we know He is fair in His dealings with us? The prophet Jeremiah answered this concern: "I, the Lord, search the heart, I test the mind, even to give every man according to his ways, according to the fruit of his doings" (17:10). Remind yourself often that God is always right even though you may not always feel that way. It is His nature to be holy and right; therefore, He cannot be bribed, conned, duped, or manipulated. Those tactics will never work.

God knows everyone's past, present, and future. He knows what we need and what we don't need. Each time we decide to take matters into our own hands, He will step aside because of the free will He has given us. He will not remove or recall that freedom, but He does give us the tools necessary to fight the Enemy and his evil schemes.

God does not force us to say or do anything. Whatever we say or do, He prefers that we do it from our heart rather than doing it under some kind of guilt, fear, or obligation. God sees the big picture, and He judges us accordingly: "God will bring every work into judgment, including every secret thing, whether good or evil" (Ecclesiastes 12:14).

To conclude this section, I wish to offer the following encouragement and suggestion: On one hand, be thankful for God's forgiveness, grace, and mercy. On the other hand, resist living in fear or guilt, assuming He is ready to punish you each time you fail and fall.

We all have struggles, as no one is perfect except God, but we can ask God to help us in those troublesome areas. God wants to work with us as a team: "'Come now and let us reason together,' says the Lord" (Isaiah 1:18). Let's do it by accepting and taking His invitation seriously.

In addition to going before the Lord in prayer, we can also confess our shortcomings and weaknesses to those with whom we feel comfortable and at ease. These individuals may include one's spouse, pastor, parent, grandparent, sibling, friend, neighbor, an employer, or a colleague.

Accept and receive God's forgiveness when it is needed and also accept and receive His correction each time it is given. Some individuals blame Satan for everything, but remember this: Satan can do nothing on his own. For him to work, either God must give His permission, as in the case of Job, or we allow him to attack and tempt us.

Two related Scriptures come to my mind: "God will not give us more than what we can handle" (1 Corinthians 10:13), and "Rebuke the devil and he will flee from you" (James 4:7). So focus more on responsibility and less on blaming.

Heavenly Father—God Who Forgives and Judges

Either out of curiosity or confusion, the topic we will be examining in this section seems to be of interest to many Christians, including myself. To be honest, I have struggled with this issue for quite some time: the God of the Old Testament versus the God of the New Testament. Some compare the two as the God of hate (or wrath) versus the God of love (or mercy). The truth is far from these assumptions or perceptions. God is always who He says He is.

I will try to remove any confusion you may have about this fascinating and interesting topic as it relates to God. I believe it is more of a misunderstanding than anything else, for God was, is, and will always be the same (read Malachi 3:6).

I will provide sufficient information identifying the God of the Old and New Testaments as not only the same God but also revealing two sides of His nature—anger, just, wrath versus grace, love, mercy—in both divisions of the Bible.

God in the Old Testament

Scripture passages supporting or defending God's anger, judgment, wrath, and so on, include Genesis 15:13-16 and Romans 12:19.

Passages supporting or defending God's compassion, grace, love, and mercy are Exodus 34:6; Numbers 14:18; Deuteronomy 4:31; Nehemiah 9:17; Psalm 108:4; Psalm 145:8; and Ezekiel 18:23.

Last but not least, let us examine two important Scripture verses in which Jesus Himself reveals information and affirms the God of the Old Testament: "You shall love the Lord your God with all your heart, with all your soul, and with all your mind" (Matthew 22:37).

Jesus also made it clear that God in the Old Testament always desired love and mercy rather than sacrifice (see Matthew 9:13; 12:7).

God in the New Testament

Some Scripture verses supporting (or defending) God's anger, judgment, and wrath include Matthew 10:34-35; Matthew 23; Romans 1:18; Romans 9:14-18.

A couple of New Testament passages that support (or defend) God's compassion, grace, love, and mercy include John 3:16; 1 John 4:10.

Conclusion

There are more passages in the Word of God that support or defend both sides of God's nature. I mentioned only a few just to make a point. Based on the information as well as the facts provided, we can safely conclude the following:

1. God is the same throughout both the Old and New Testaments. God does not change; He is immutable.

2. God in the Old Testament has shown anger, judgment, and wrath, but He also has shown compassion, grace, love, and mercy.
3. God in the New Testament has also shown anger, judgment, and wrath, and He also has acted with compassion, grace, love, and mercy.
4. God does not contradict Himself.

Like others, I struggle from time to time with certain life issues. For instance, I would like to know why God allows hurricanes, floods, tornadoes, etc. Where was God on September 11, 2001? Why do so many children die of hunger, disease, and abuse?

I am sure there are many more questions we would like answered, but we have to believe that God knows what He is doing, and we can trust Him without doubt and reservation. I have chosen to believe that:

1. God is always right.
2. God is always on time.
3. God shows no partiality.
4. God does not lie.

Let us therefore take comfort in knowing we are in good hands, and as we learn to put our faith and trust in Him, He will in turn direct and guide our life and its many paths. Let me close this chapter with one of my favorite verses from the book of Romans: "And we know that all things work together for good to those who love God, to those who are the called according to His purpose" (8:28).

One author states, "God's nature and character includes both mercy and love together with anger and judgment against sin. God displays all sides of His personality consistently across both the Old and New Testaments. Furthermore, God is just when He displays His wrath against sin, but in mercy He chooses to show grace to some when He desires. This is the inherent right of a sovereign God" (Church, 2007).

Chapter Seven

Equal Opportunity Destroyers

Areas That Can Bring Us Down

Introduction

This chapter focuses on some of the most crucial aspects of a person's life. I have chosen ten areas I feel need our immediate and sincere attention. Please keep in mind, however, that there are probably other matters that are also important.

I am addressing these specific concerns from a counseling perspective. In all my years of biblical counseling, I can recall discussing these issues again and again with clients. In my personal and professional opinion, of the ten areas of concern we will be discussing, the two that are of utmost consequence are anger and impatience. I believe these issues together account for at least sixty percent of counseling and stress-related problems.

So let us begin our journey, talking about areas of our lives that cause us a great amount of discomfort, dissatisfaction, uneasiness, and unhappiness. When I say these issues "cause" discomfort, I realize that nothing ever does anything on its own unless we choose to give it power. It is one thing to entertain thoughts, and it is another thing to yield to those thoughts and take action.

Anger—Explosive and Impulsive

Once upon a time, a young couple climbed a high mountain. There they saw a wise, old man, who motioned for them to sit. He told them they could ask him any question.

The couple responded by inquiring about the meaning of life. He told them. They asked him the recipe for happiness. He wrote it down. They asked him about all the secrets of the universe. No problem.

Then they posed a hard question for the old man: "Oh, Great Master, we are angry so often. We hurt each other when we get angry. What can we do?"

Suddenly, the master glared at them, snapped his pencil in two, cursed loudly, and stomped back into his cave. "Alas," he muttered over his shoulder, "if I could figure that out I wouldn't be sitting here all alone on this mountain" (Efron and Efron, 1995).

What do we learn from this short story? Even some wise and knowledgeable people can feel helpless when it comes to issues like anger and so on.

What is anger? The dictionary defines it as "a strong feeling of displeasure and belligerence aroused by a wrong; wrath; ire." Simply put, anger is an emotion. The subhead to this section mentions two kinds of anger: explosive and impulsive.

Explosive anger is an uncontrollable and even unstable emotional outburst. Impulsive anger is spontaneous or sudden. In either case, one tends to say and do things that can be damaging at the time and may be regretted later. However, feelings of regret or remorse may not always apply to those individuals with a seared conscience.

What comes to mind when you think of anger? I made a short list of synonyms that are closely related to anger:

- aggravated
- annoyed
- bitter
- blowing-off steam
- boiling point
- emotional outburst
- explode (as in thoughts)
- fed-up
- flying off the handle
- fretting
- frustration
- fury
- hostility
- hot
- irritable
- mad
- on edge
- rage
- temper
- upset
- vengeance
- violence
- wrath

Many people have problems dealing with anger. It does not take much to set them off; in other words, for them getting angry is easy. It is not uncommon for some people to become angry or mad several times a week over one thing or another.

One author states, "Anger is not in itself sinful" (Kruis, 2000). So is it always bad or wrong to get mad? Not necessarily. God's Word allows Christians to be angry but with a catch. In the New Testament we read: "Be angry, and do not sin" (Ephesians 4:26). Anger is not always a sin, especially when it is focused toward standing up for what is right.

The Bible refers to "righteous anger," or righteous indignation. From a biblical standpoint, this is the only type of anger that is not considered sinful. As recorded in the gospel of Matthew, Jesus demonstrated righteous indignation when He saw merchants misusing the temple: "Then Jesus went into the temple of God and drove out all those who bought and sold in the temple, and overturned the tables of the money changers and the seats of those who sold doves" (21:12; the incident is also described in Mark 11:1 and John 2:15).

Why do we struggle so much with sin? Because we live in an imperfect world, and the reason this world is so imperfect is because we humans are imperfect. For selfish reasons, we are turning this world into a difficult and unsafe place to live. It seems that for every one person who wants to do what is just and right before God, at least one hundred individuals are intent on doing the opposite. We read, "For many are called, but few are chosen" (Matthew 22:14).

So why are we filled with rage? What drives an individual to become irate? Answering this question is not easy because different people express outrage for different reasons. I sincerely believe many people get angry because of one or more of the following issues: impatience, pride, and selfishness.

Impatience

Why impatience? We humans are impetuous by nature. We feel obligated to be either saying or doing something constantly. When we are not saying or doing, we become uncomfortable and even restless.

Impatient people are not always easy to deal with. (The same is true for those who are prideful and self-centered.) I have watched many impatient people lose their tempers at a moment's notice. They generally prefer immediate answers and seldom ask for or welcome any suggestions from others.

But what about pride? I have some friends who think they know everything about any subject; so much so that they are unwilling to entertain any thought that contradicts or differs from their own. In essence, what they are saying is, "I am such a well-informed and well-read person, I don't need you to tell me anything unless I solicit your input."

Why selfishness? We humans are creatures of habit, and habits are difficult to break. Most of us resist change because it disrupts the routines we have established for our lives. When someone tries to offer advice, feedback, or suggestions, we become agitated and try to brush aside that person and his or her advice.

Another element—insecurity—plays a key role in helping us understand what triggers anger. What makes a person insecure? Again, the reasons may vary from person to person. Insecurity usually has to do with some unresolved issue(s) in one's past and/or present circumstances.

Because of unresolved issues, the person may feel restless and stressed out. Those who wish not to deal with these situations tend to use anger, control, domination, manipulation, and such like to deal with or escape from the circumstance at the time.

It is often difficult to reason with those who are insecure. The more you try, the quicker they lose their cool and put up an argument. Eventually, you find yourself dealing with an irrational person.

Those who feel insecure tend to see things their way and do not always accept a second opinion. Worse yet, they may not be open to admitting or confessing their wrongdoing. The best ways to help an insecure individual is to show patience and empathy and by being a good listener.

If used improperly, anger can wreak havoc, including but not limited to the following: loss of friendship, unemployment, divorce, separation, violence, destroyed property, and even death. Most importantly, it can break communication, ruin one's health, and eventually steal a person's joy and peace.

Hurting others in what we say and do does not compare to how much we are hurting ourselves in the long run. Most anything in life (good or bad/positive or negative) has a way of accumulating if done consistently and repeatedly for a long period of time.

How then can anger be dealt with? Let's examine the Word of God where we can find many references dealing with anger:

1. Priority one: confess your sins to God (1 John 1:9).
2. Next, realize that you chose to sin on your own terms; therefore, you have no one else to blame.
3. Develop the habit of confessing to others as well to God: "Confess your trespasses to one another, and pray for one another, that you may be healed" (James 5:16).
4. Understand that the trials and tribulations you are facing could be opportunities God has given to make you stronger and more mature in your faith.
5. Deal with the problem; do not attack the messenger. Communication is the best thing to solve the problem. In the book of Ephesians, the apostle Paul encourages us to follow four rules of communication (4:15; 25-32).

One piece of advice I give counselees and anyone else who is willing to listen is this: You cannot change or control others in terms of how they act, respond, or speak; however, you can always change and control yourself. Do your part, and you can always count on God to do His. He always keeps His word.

Selfishness/Self-centeredness

On one end of the continuum lies anger and impatience, doing enough damage when the opportunity arises. On the other end of the continuum is selfishness and pride. By selfishness, I mean self-centeredness, and by pride, I mean self-righteousness.

Self-centered individuals are totally absorbed in themselves. Their motto (figuratively speaking) is, "Looking Out for Number One." Another term used for selfishness is *narcissism*. The dictionary defines self-centeredness as "limited to or caring only about oneself and one's own needs."

Selfish people by nature are not capable of thinking of anyone other than themselves. Even if they are capable of thinking of others, they choose not to and shift the focus to themselves instead. It is difficult to reason with self-centered people because they see every issue from their own perspective.

Of all the individuals with whom I have dealt, the ones who cause me the most angst are those who are selfish and self-centered to the core. Selfish people use every kind of tactic to get what they want, including: slander, exaggeration, gossip, lying, stealing, telling stories, and so on.

Selfish people are self-sufficient, meaning, they rely on themselves and not on God. "The Buck Stops Here," might also be their mantra. They are obsessed (preoccupied) with thoughts about themselves and allow no room for God and others in their minds and hearts.

They not only elevate themselves, they also put their own needs and wants on a pedestal, meaning, what they think and want comes first before anything or anyone. Here are some examples of selfishness in its purest form. I offer only a few incidences because of their daily occurrence:

> Smokers standing next to the main entrance of a public building. Except on one or two occasions, I have observed as these smokers refuse to move away from the door. When I have requested them to move away from the door, they get

angry, are ready to argue, and even pick a fight. Some young people have actually given me the finger when I asked them nicely to move away from the door.

These smokers show no concern about the effects of secondhand smoke. Why should a nonsmoker be forced into a situation where he or she has to accept such nonsense? Nonsmokers have rights too.

1. Each time I watch a movie in a theatre, I observe at least two incidents taking place while the movie is being played. First, some people talk loudly on their cell phones, and second, many people put their feet up onto the chairs in front of them.

    This is inconsiderate. I paid full price to watch and enjoy a movie in peace and quiet. But some selfish people highjack that peace, not to mention my rights and privileges. It seems to me that victims have few rights while criminals and wrongdoers are given every advantage. But God sees everything.

    Some drivers enjoy cranking their music to a fever pitch (louder than the legal limit). Then, just to agitate other motorists and pedestrians, they roll down their windows, forcing their "music" onto others. It doesn't matter that those nearby may not care for that type of music, not to mention the decibels at which it is being played.

    Sadly and unfortunately, these drivers get by with such violations only because some police officers are neglecting their duty. If the officers were to ticket these drivers, the offenders might consider reducing the volume a bit.

I am sure you and I would be able to cite many more examples. However, I chose to mention these three because they seem to happen on a daily basis. I am sure you get the idea and understand my point of view.

What does the Bible say about selfish or self-centered behavior? Let's examine some key Scripture verses that directly deal with this issue:

In the book of Psalms we read, "The wicked in his proud countenance does not seek God; God is in none of his thoughts" (Psalm 10:4). And in Jeremiah's prophecies we read: "Thus says the Lord: 'Let not the wise man glory in his wisdom, let not the mighty man glory in his might, nor let the rich man glory in his riches'" (9:23).

Like heads and tails on the same coin, love and self-centeredness are complete opposites. True love seeks and wishes the best for others, whereas self-centered people seek and wish the best only for themselves. In Paul's first letter to the Corinthians, we read: "Love does not seek its own" (1 Corinthians 13:4).

A self-centered person trusts his or her own wisdom as opposed to trusting in God. God made it clear that we are to trust Him: "Trust in the Lord with all your heart, and lean not on your own understanding" (Proverbs 3:5). When we choose to go our own way, we are taking (spiritual) matters in our own hands. When we do that, we cannot expect God to defend and support our actions and decisions. He is ready and willing to help us only when we are ready and willing to walk in His will, instead of doing things our way. The key to understanding God and His purposes is to be in His will.

Self-centeredness is a very old concept, beginning with Lucifer (Satan). In the book of Isaiah we read words attributed to him: "I will ascend above the heights of the clouds, I will be like the Most High" (14:14). Instead of trying to elevate ourselves to a lofty position, God wants His children to be a blessing, and one way of serving Him is to dethrone self and serve others.

Self-centered people sometimes covet what belongs to others and do not rest until they get their way. This is not only wrong, it is a character flaw that God takes very seriously. We are not to covet (lust for) anything that belongs to others: "You shall not covet . . . anything that is your neighbor's" (Exodus 20:17). Notice this statement is one of the Ten Commandments God gave His people.

To help us understand better, let's compare the ultimate struggle between good and evil—being sacrificial versus selfishness. On one hand, Lucifer wanted to be like the Most High (Isaiah 14:14). On the other hand, Jesus, God's Son, took the form of a bond servant (Philippians 2:6-7). The Savior gave us a perfect example of serving others when He knelt and washed His disciples' feet (see John 3:3-17).

To wrap up this section, I would like to encourage you to abandon all selfish thoughts and behaviors. Regardless of how you look at it, the consequences are not worth the risks. Even if you are able to obtain what belongs to someone else, God can and will restore to that person what he or she needs and deserves. Being selfish can and will only hurt you, and the consequences can be more than you expected.

Die to self. That may be something you are unable to do on your own, so allow God to work in you by bringing positive and productive changes. You may choose to work with someone you trust, and with his or her help, you can conquer this issue and look to a bright future.

Ingratitude and Lack of Appreciation

This section focuses on those individuals who do not always show appreciation for who they are and what they have. In other words, they are not always thankful and do not take time to count their blessings. They tend to take life and everything in it for granted. Some even take God for granted.

There are those who seem to do what is convenient and right only a few times a year:

1. They attend a church service only a few times a year for a baby dedication, Christmas Eve, Easter, funerals, weddings,

etc. Other than at these few special services or events, you may not see them in church.
2. During Thanksgiving each year, many families travel long distances just to be with their loved ones. But instead of enjoying each other's company and fellowship and sharing some joyous moments, they argue and fight with each other all year long, right up to the Thanksgiving holiday and continue right after it is over.

Not appreciating what one has and not being thankful seems to be common among humans. Instead of appreciating what God has given us, we maintain an attitude where we are convinced that we have a right to receive more. Frankly, we do not have any rights. Even the air we breathe is a gift from almighty God.

Is the glass half empty or half full? One half of that glass represents those who have less than we have, and the other half represents those who have more. We can either look at those who have more and be ungrateful (complain), or we can look at those who have less than we do and be thankful (content). Which half are you focusing on?

What does the Bible say about being thankful? Enough to open our eyes. To begin, let's examine two key verses:

- "In everything give thanks, for this is the will of God in Christ Jesus for you" (1 Thessalonians 5:18).
- "You ask and you do not receive, because you ask amiss [with wrong motives]" (James 4:3).

God does not owe us anything, nor is He obligated to give. Yet He gave us life and many blessings to go with it. The only thing we can and should say is "thank you." I mentioned once before that God can take away anything He wants, and no one can stop Him from fulfilling His will. I am not saying that He will remove anything, but I am saying that He can.

We are living in the last days, and there are many signs pointing in that direction. Ungratefulness is one of those signs. In his second letter to Timothy, the apostle Paul talked about the condition of being unthankful in the last days: "For men will be lovers of themselves, lovers of money, boasters, proud, blasphemers, disobedient to parents, *unthankful*, unholy" (2 Timothy 3:2, emphasis added).

As the apostle Paul explained in the book of Romans, ingratitude accompanies unbelief: "Although they knew God, they did not glorify Him as God, nor were thankful, but became futile in their thoughts, and their foolish hearts were darkened" (1:21). Being thankful is an attitude that comes from the heart and not an issue of the mind. This means, when someone is not thankful, his or her heart is not right before God.

The Bible talks about many people being called but only a few are chosen (see Matthew 22:14). Likewise, God has shown His grace and mercy to all, and yet only a few have chosen to receive it. In the gospel of Luke, we read a story about how God healed ten men with leprosy, but only one of them returned to give God thanks (Luke 17:11-19).

Those who live in the United States of America should not only consider it a privilege and honor to call this nation their home. They also should be thankful for the many blessings God has bestowed upon America, freedom being the most precious one. Of all the blessings God has given us, the two for which I am most grateful are freedom of speech and freedom of religion. To be able to speak one's opinion and to be able to attend church and worship God without fear and guilt deserves our thankfulness.

And yet we not only take God for granted, we also lose our focus on what He stands for as well as what He expects from us. Slowly and surely, we are distancing ourselves from the strong foundation upon which this nation was established. Evidence of this can be seen in rules that remove the Ten Commandments from government buildings, school properties, and so on. It is a shame and an insult to God.

Not only are we to be thankful to God, we also need to be thankful to others (see Colossians 3:15). Jesus was a perfect role model of gratefulness. The Gospels describe Him as a praying man who gave thanks continually.

God has given us what we need and allows only as much diversity and pain as we can bear (or handle). Therefore, let us focus on the goodness of God and not on what He has withheld from us.

Make a list of all God has given you, which will help you learn to be thankful, enjoy His blessings, and never take God or others for granted. And remember, God is not subject to human reasoning; instead, we are subject to His reasoning. Each time you approach God, remember to approach Him on His terms, not your own.

Expectations—Awards and Rewards

This section focuses on those individuals who expect to be awarded and rewarded because of what they have given, either a gift or help to someone in time of need. It is a natural tendency to expect something in return for kind deeds, but it does not have to be that way.

I always practice and advise others to follow these four principles when it comes to giving:

1. Give secretly. Do not make it a public display.
2. Give unconditionally. Do not put any conditions when giving, especially in your favor.
3. Give unexpectedly, without expecting anything in return.
4. Give unselfishly, with no personal ambition or motive.

In the gospel of Matthew we read: "But when you do a charitable deed, do not let your left hand know what your right hand is doing, that your charitable deed may be in secret; and your Father who sees in secret will Himself reward you openly" (6:3-4). In this passage, Jesus commands that we do nothing publicly like the Pharisees and Sadducees. Their motive for open displays of generosity was to make themselves look good. Anyone who blows his or her own trumpet is tagged a hypocrite (see Matthew 6:2).

God knows and sees every act, and He knows who to bless, when to bless, how to bless, and through whom to bless. We must trust Him, knowing that He will do what is right for each one of us, especially when we are ready and willing to obey and walk in His will. There is no need for us to expect anything in return because God will take care of us.

The following Scripture verses deal with God's provision without our even having to ask or expect some type of recompense: In the book of 2 Corinthians we read, "He who sows sparingly will also reap sparingly, and he who sows bountifully will also reap bountifully" (9:6). Then, in the book of Galatians we read, "Whatever a man sows, that he will also reap" (Galatians 6:7).

Finally, look at what Jesus had to say on the topic: "Give, and it will be given to you: good measure, pressed down, shaken together, and running over will be put into your bosom. For with the same measure that you use it, it will be measured back to you" (Luke 6:38). These verses confirm that when we give (sow) bountifully, God will see to it that we reap bountifully. No need to expect anything in return.

I have quoted these Bible verses to remind you that God knows what and how to give. He looks at your heart—your desires, goals, intentions, and motives. When you are in right standing with Him, God will reciprocate that blessing, and you can "take it to the bank," as the saying goes.

Once again, I would encourage you to help others often, and in doing so, expect nothing in return. Of all the people you help, even if one person chooses to return the favor, simply accept it and be grateful. The advantage of not expecting anything in return is that you will not be disappointed or discouraged.

People who are selfish by nature may not return the favor. But do not let that stop you from blessing. On the flip side, try not to be *too* generous. There will always be those who are ready to take advantage of your generosity.

Help when and where you can as the Lord directs, and not out of emotions or when you feel "checked" in your spirit. The key in giving is to feel good about it, meaning, your giving, along with your actions, will make the other person feel good as opposed to dwelling and focusing on receiving something in return.

Another advantage to helping and giving to others is that it can motivate those individuals to help others in need. In other words, they will consider returning the favor. We give because someone has given to us when we were in need. Jesus said, "Freely you have received, freely give" (Matthew 10:8). Let us follow our Lord's advice.

Food—Overeating and Wasting; Gluttony

Mahatma Gandhi, a famous Indian freedom fighter, lawyer, philosopher, and politician, "Eat to live, but do not live to eat." We should remember and heed that down-to-earth advice because it came from a man who is considered to be practical and wise.

I try to follow some simple principles with regard to food:

1. *Eat only when you are hungry.* I understand the temptation to eat a lot and frequently. This enticement is an ongoing struggle I am trying my best to win.
2. *Eat (or snack) only to fulfill a medical need or obligation*, such as diabetes, hypoglycemia, and other diseases.
3. *Never overeat just because the food is available.* In other words, eat no more than is necessary or needed.
4. *Try not to waste food.* Only God knows the millions of people, especially children, who go without food for days at a time.

5. *Begin with small portions.* When I eat at home, at a restaurant, or at someone's house, I begin by taking small amounts. I can always return for second and third helpings, if necessary.

Some people are annoyed when I advise them to neither overeat nor waste food. "It is my body and my money and my right, and I will do what I want and wish with it," they sometimes respond. I know they are right in their own way; however, I give the counsel only because I care and wish the best for them. Plus, I try to offer advice I am willing to follow. Otherwise, I would be a hypocrite, and I sure do not want to be known as a fraud.

Because something belongs to a person does not give him or her the right to abuse or misuse it. It is only his or hers in the first place because God has allowed and permitted it to be under his or her stewardship. I say from experience that God not only *can* but is also known to reclaim what He has given.

The following two Scripture verses will help us understand this topic. In the gospel of Luke we read: "For everyone to whom much is given, from him much will be required; and to whom much has been committed, of him they will as the more" (12:48).

Next, look at Jesus' parable of the talents, explained in the gospel of Matthew (25:14-30). The lesson to be learned from this parable is simply this: when God gives us ability, gifts, money, strengths, etc., He expects us to use them wisely. When we do, God increases our blessings because He knows we can be trusted with what He has given us. This parable also teaches that if and when we do not use our God-given talent(s) wisely, it can be taken away and given to those who can be trusted.

The parable of the talents may not refer directly to the use of food, as it deals with the issue of financial stewardship, but the principle behind it applies to *everything* God entrusts to us. God expects us to be wise overseers of whatever He places in our care, and when we abuse or misuse those things, God can remove them, just as the master took the one talent from the unwise servant.

Overeating is considered an abuse of one's body, and we have no right to do that. When a person accepts Jesus Christ as his Lord and Savior, that individual belongs to God, meaning, his body, mind, soul, spirit, thoughts, etc. are God's, and he cannot do whatever he want or wishes with it.

This applies to everything in our lives, whether it is food, money, talents, and even life itself. The apostle Paul made this point clear in his first letter to the Corinthian believers:

> Do you not know that your body is the temple of the Holy Spirit who is in you, whom you have from God, and you are not your own? For you were bought at a price, therefore glorify God in your body, and in your spirit, which are God's (1 Corinthians 6:19-20).

Gluttony is another term used for overeating. It is sad that hypocrisy seems to be on the rise among many Christians today. Take for instance our inconsistency with regard to sin. On one hand, we are quick to label drinking alcoholic beverages and smoking as sins, and we constantly judge those who smoke and drink. On the other hand, out of selfishness or for whatever reasons, we tend to accept, excuse, and even tolerate gluttony. Does this not qualify as hypocrisy? I understand there may be different kinds of sins and different degrees and variations of committing them; however, in one sense, sin is a sin, and there is only one way to deal with it: confess and repent.

Any argument or logic we may use in opposition to drinking and smoking, i.e. it is an addiction; it ruin's one's health, etc., can be applied to gluttony as well. It is no different. Yet if we look at the eagerness with which we approach the lunch or dinner table, our actions speak louder than words.

On the flip side, wasting food is also an abuse of resources. I could not afford to waste food, even if I had the money to do so. That would be an insult to God the provider, as well as to those who may need that portion of food to survive.

The principle of abusing and misusing applies not only to food but also to everything in our lives. Three specific Scripture verses from the book of Proverbs speak directly to the issue of gluttony. Read Proverbs 23:2; 23:20-21; and 28:7.

We can enjoy God's bountiful blessings, which include various kinds and types of foods (fruits, meats, vegetables, grains, etc.) that are delicious, nutritious, and pleasurable. But we must learn to control our appetites and not allow the appetite to control us. With hard work and diligence, we can do it.

Greed—Materialism

The dictionary defines *greed* as "excessive desire to acquire or possess more (especially material wealth) than one needs or deserves." *Materialism* is defined as a "preoccupation with or emphasis on material objects, comforts, and considerations, with a disinterest in or rejection of spiritual, intellectual, or cultural values." In this section, I will be using the terms *greed* and *materialism* interchangeably, treating each as a synonym to the other.

Two additional words, *needs* and *wants*, play a major role in our lives. How do these terms differ? The difference is quite simple: Everyone has three basic necessities and a few other minor needs. We learned in elementary school that the three basic needs are *food* (which also includes water), *clothing*, and *shelter*. Other minor needs include *medical* and *school supplies, transportation*, etc. These do not necessarily apply to everyone.

Anything other than these basic essentials falls under the designation of wants. These desires taken to extreme may also be categorized as greed or materialism. A question I routinely ask myself is, should I buy this item because of a need or simply because I want it?

Thinking in practical and realistic terms, the basic needs are the only acquisitions essential to our very existence. The truth is, however, each basic necessity can become a want. For instance, am I satisfied with affordable clothing that is within my means, or do I crave expensive garments purchased at an upscale shop, even when I know I cannot afford them? Where and how do we draw a line between needs and wants?

How does the Bible approach the subject of greed? Since avarice for the most part is associated with money or wealth, there are literally hundreds of Scripture verses that address the topic of finances, money, and wealth. Not only do we find several warnings about yielding to greed, but the Bible also cautions us against yearning for riches.

Several key passages will help us understand the seriousness of the issue, open our eyes of understanding, and direct us toward the narrow and right path. First, let us look at Jesus' comprehensive warning: "Take heed and beware of covetousness [greed], for one's life does not consist in the abundance of the things he possesses" (Luke 12:15).

The Bible tells us that Jesus was perfect in all He said and did while on Earth as the Son of Man. If He had wanted to be rich, I am sure He could have achieved great wealth. Nothing could have stood in His way, but He never pursued status of any kind. On the contrary, the Bible says Jesus became poor for our benefit: "Though He was rich, yet for your sakes He became poor, that you through His poverty might become rich" (2 Corinthians 8:9). In addition, we have Jesus' own words: "Foxes have holes and birds of the air have nests, but the Son of Man has nowhere to lay His head" (Matthew 8:20).

Jesus chose twelve disciples who not only walked with Him but also followed Him wherever He went. One disciple, Judas, became greedy and chose to betray Jesus for thirty pieces of silver. Those who fall into the sin of greed may end up selling their consciences for materialistic gain and pleasures.

When an individual becomes greedy, he or she is inviting destruction. A well-known saying is also a Scripture verse with which most of us are familiar: "The love of money is a root of all kinds of evil" (1 Timothy 6:10). Also in his first epistle to Timothy, the apostle Paul warned his readers "not to trust in uncertain riches but in the living God" (6:17). We are to put our trust in the Lord and definitely not in wealth. Some people constantly covet things that belong to others. And then there are those who wish to have more. Both of these types of greed fall under the category of idolatry.

Idolatry means worshipping anything other than Jehovah God. This includes money, vehicles, expensive homes, pleasure, and even our own bodies. Idolatry is a serious spiritual sin. Consider what the Bible says about those who worship at the altar of materialism: "For you know, that no fornicator, unclean person, nor *covetous man, who is an idolater*, has any inheritance in the kingdom of Christ and God" (Ephesians 5:5, emphasis added).

Money itself is not a problem, but the love of it is deadly. The closer we get to the love of money, the farther we move away from God. As stated above, the love of money is idolatry, and there is no doubt about it. Jesus clarified this issue when He said, "Assuredly, I say to you that it is hard for a rich man to enter the kingdom of heaven" (Matthew 19:23).

Jesus told the story about a certain young, rich ruler who came to Him, inquiring about how to enter heaven. The Lord told the man to sell all his possessions and donate the proceeds to the poor. But this advice was not what this young ruler wanted to hear. So instead of following the Lord's advice, he went away sad because he was very wealthy (see Matthew 19:16-22; Luke 18:18-23).

What was this young man's basic problem? Obviously, it was greed. The reason he could not follow Jesus was because he loved his riches more than anything else. That seems to be true with many people today (especially those who are wealthy). In the gospel of Matthew, we read, "No one can serve two masters" (Matthew 6:24).

In closing this section, I wish to point out some overarching truths:

1. The Bible is not anti-money; however, it does condemn the love of money.
2. The focus of our lives should be more on being humble, able to bless (give) and serve others, and so on, rather than on amassing riches.
3. We are to "seek first the kingdom of God" (Matthew 6:33).
4. We are admonished to be content with what we have (Hebrews 13:5).
5. And finally, we are to be thankful in every circumstance (1 Thessalonians 5:18).

Jealousy—Envy

The dictionary defines the word *jealous* as "feeling resentment against someone because of that person's success or advantages." Examples would be "He was jealous of his rich brother," or "She envied her friend's great wealth." Envy is defined as "a feeling of discontent or covetousness with regard to another's advantages, success, possessions, etc."

The Bible seems to agree with this definition. For example, consider Solomon's words on the topic: "I saw that for all toil and every skillful work a man is envied by his neighbor" (Ecclesiastes 4:4). The terms *jealousy* and *envy* are actually synonyms. When we are jealous, it means we envy someone who happens to possess something we wish to have.

Socrates, a well-known Greek philosopher, once said, "Envy is the daughter of pride, the author of murders and revenge, the begetter of secret sedition, the perpetual tormenter of virtue. Envy is the filthy slime of the soul; a venom, a poison, a quicksilver, which consumeth the flesh and drieth up the bones."

What makes a person jealous? I may not have all the answers, but I can suggest few common reasons:

1. Lack of confidence
2. Failure to trust God to take care of basic needs
3. Selfishness
4. Insufficient provision for needs and/or wants
5. Lack of gratitude for blessings
6. Greed
7. An assumption that either God or others are unfair

One specific issue that I think accounts for most envy is insecurity. Other factors are involved, of course, such as deception, fear, etc., but why does insecurity play such a huge role in the envy issue? Because we tend to rely heavily on what other people think of us. Insecurity takes root when we feel rejected or unloved.

It is human nature to compare ourselves to those who appear to be doing better than we, and we perceive their strengths as potential threats to our own well-being. But this is erroneous thinking. Most importantly, we should care what God thinks of us. He made it clear that He loves us unconditionally, just as we are. We should take comfort in knowing that and not worry about what others have or what they think.

Jealous and envious people are what the Bible calls covetous, which means they yearn to obtain or possess something that belongs to another person. "You shall not covet your neighbor's house; you shall not covet your neighbor's wife . . . (Exodus 20:17).

The source of envy is within ourselves:

> From within, out of the heart of men, proceed evil thoughts, adulteries, fornications, murders, thefts, covetousness, wickedness, deceit, lewdness, an evil eye, blasphemy, pride, foolishness. All these evil things come from within and defile a man (Mark 7:21-23).

If an individual learns how to be satisfied with what God has given him or her, the issue of jealousy or envy does not even arise. We need to be content and thankful for at least two reasons:

1. God knows what and the amount we need, when we need it, and how much of it we can handle. In the book of 1 Corinthians we read: "But God is faithful, who will not allow you to be tempted beyond what you are able, but with the temptation will also make the way of escape, that you may be able to bear it" (10:13).
2. Whatever God gives, He can also take away, and no one can stop Him from doing whatever He wills: "For who has resisted His will?" (Romans 9:19). God owes no explanations, because He is sovereign. He works independently, and we can be assured that He will always do what is right.

I can understand worldly people craving riches and always wanting more, but Christians "are not of this world." The apostle Paul gave us wise counsel when he said, "Do not be conformed to this world, but be transformed by the renewing of your mind, that you may prove what is that good and acceptable and perfect will of God." (Romans 12:2).

How do we overcome jealousy? Allow me to make the following suggestions:

1. Learn to control and discipline your thoughts. Instead, renew your mind so that it aligns with God's Word.

2. Deal with insecurity by forming an intimate relationship with God.
3. Do not seek approval, fame, or a name for yourself.
4. Learn to be content with what you have.
5. Substitute the lies with the truth, which is God's Word.
6. Never compare yourself to others, especially those of the world.
7. Avoid and/or cancel greedy and envious thoughts, knowing that God provides your needs.
8. Do not grow angry or frustrated about the riches of others. Instead, celebrate their prosperity, knowing that God will provide whatever He feels we need and deserve, and no man can take it away.

Lust—Actions, Deeds, Desires, Motives, Etc.

The dictionary defines the word *lust* as "A strong sexual desire; self-indulgent sexual desire (personified as one of the deadly sins); to have a craving, appetite, or great desire for."

Most of us have heard the phrase, "The Seven Deadly Sins." Are these transgressions listed in the Bible? We cannot find a specific listing of these sins in the Bible; however, it has been said that they can be found in chapters 5 through 7 of Matthew's gospel. Along with vanity (pride), gluttony, avarice (greed), sloth (laziness), wrath (anger), and envy, lust is considered as one of those seven deadly vices.

I wish to make two things clear about lust:

1. Lust is not always a male issue. It is possible and likely that men experience this temptation more than females; however, lust is a human problem. One Scripture verse that explains this concept is found in the book of Romans: "All have sinned and fall short of the glory of God" (3:23).
2. Lust does not always have a sexual connotation, though that may be its most prevalent context. Putting aside anything that

is sexual, an individual can lust for other things, such as a particular type of car, a better home, expensive jewelry, and so forth. Job viewed lust as a moral sin (failure): "For that would be wickedness; Yes, it would be iniquity deserving of judgment" (Job 31:11).

The following "facts and stats" are from an online article by Paul S. Taylor. Please keep in mind that this information was reported in 2001. We can only imagine to what proportions these numbers and percentages have risen or increased by now.

1. Nearly a one-third of children ages 10-17 from households with computers say they have seen a pornographic website (National Public Radio, 2000).
2. Forty-four percent (44%) of teenagers have visited a sexually-explicit website (*Time* magazine, 2000).
3. There are more than 200,000 pornographic websites on the Internet today, with 3,000 new ones being added every day.
4. *Playboy* magazine's website, which offers free glimpses of its playmates, now averages about 5 million hits a day.
5. One in four regular Internet users visits a sex site at least once a month (*New York Times*, 2000).
6. At least twenty percent (20%) of American adults (Christian and non-Christian) have looked at a sex site online. The ratio is the same for Christians: one in five people in the pews has looked at web porn. The same study shows that one in every three men has looked at a sex site; close to half for men under the age of 35 (*Focus on the Family*, 2001).
7. Visits to porn sites comprise a third of all Internet usage (*Newsweek* Magazine, 2000).
8. Thirty percent (30%) of all unsolicited emails are pornographic (ChooseYourMail.com, 1999).
9. There are now more outlets for hardcore pornography in the United States than there are McDonald's restaurants.
10. The porn industry takes in more than 8 billion dollars in one year—more than all revenues generated by rock and country

music, more than America spends on Broadway productions, theater, ballet, jazz, and classical music combined (*U.S. News and World Report*, 2000).

These stats are mindboggling. The sad truth is that these figures and percentages have probably doubled (maybe even tripled) in the last ten years. We do not have money to tithe or help someone in need, but we seem to be always able to fulfill the lusts of the flesh. God must grieve over it!

What does the Bible say about lust? It speaks of lust as "sexual impurity," for the most part. However, it presents lust in several other ways: adultery, covetousness, lawlessness, seduction, and so on. The Old Testament character, Job, said, "I have made a covenant with my eyes; why then should I look upon a young woman?" (31:1).

I mentioned once before that everything starts with a thought. A thought, which is an idea, is not a sin. However, when we act on those thoughts, it becomes a sin as we read, "Therefore, to him who knows to do good and does not do it, to him it is sin" (James 4:17).

Jesus considered lust such a serious issue that He said, "Whoever looks at a woman to lust for her has already committed adultery with her in his heart" (Matthew 5:28). Lust is known to ruin friendships and has led numerous couples to separate and even file for divorce.

Many commercials, especially those on television, magazines, billboards, etc., are very provocative and seductive and present females as sex objects. In addition, many young women (high school and college-age girls) tend to dress in such a way to attract men in the wrong manner. Modesty for these women is out the window.

Those who yield to lust are not always concerned about the consequences of promiscuity and have what I call "roving eyes." They spend much of their time scanning the road and television, but even more on the

Internet. It is sad but true. Do they wonder why their prayers are not being answered?

God promises forgiveness the second we ask for it. However, I do not recall reading anywhere in the Bible where He also promises an immediate answer or solution for those who live a life of continual and repeated sin without conviction.

When a person lives according to the sinful nature, he or she tends to set their mind on what that sin nature desires. Eventually, he or she will yield to fulfilling the lust of the flesh, which usually leads to some kind of action, whether it is spending money or committing adultery or fornication.

In his first letter to the Corinthians, the apostle Paul shared a list of sins and warned that those who are guilty of committing any of them will not inherit the kingdom of God (see 1 Corinthians 6:9-10). Lust is a serious sin and should be dealt with immediately.

I would like to share a word or two for both men and women, speaking to men first. Men who lust tend to focus on a woman's outward appearance. That is how it starts. When thoughts are not controlled, one thing can lead to another. Next thing you know, you find yourself in a big mess that is not always easy to escape. King Solomon gave good advice in this regard: "Do not lust after her beauty in your heart, Nor let her allure you with her eyelids. For by means of a harlot a man is reduced to a crust of bread; and an adulteress will prey upon his precious life" (Proverbs 6:25-26).

Any single man, woman, widow, or widower who cannot control themselves either in thoughts or (more so) in actions, should marry, assuming you have a desire to get married (1 Corinthians 7:8-9). However, some men and women feel led to remain single and serve God and others. But let me make clear that lust can destroy any individual, whether that person is single or married.

My advice for women is to be careful how you dress. Displaying provocative parts of the body is wrong and is not of God (see 1 Timothy 2:9-10).

So what can we do to overcome lust? Here are some steps we can take that will help us overcome lust:

1. Spend quality time in prayer and reading the Word.
2. Meet with a pastor, and share your concerns and thoughts with him.
3. If you are married, sit down with your spouse and be honest with one another and also with the pastor.
4. Admit and confess you have a problem, and do not live in denial.
5. Understand the concept of accountability.
6. If you can financially afford it, speak to a licensed counselor.
7. If you belong to men's or women's prayer or study group, share your concerns if you feel comfortable and safe doing so.

I pray that we do what is right before God for others as well as ourselves. A simple maxim comes to my mind: "Prevention is better than cure." It is a good idea to follow this rule. We do not always know or can guarantee a cure, but if we can learn self-control (the prevention part), we don't have to be concerned about the cure.

Pride—Self-Righteousness

The dictionary defines *pride* as "a high or inordinate opinion of one's own dignity, importance, merit, or superiority, whether as cherished in the mind or as displayed in bearing, conduct, etc." *Self-righteous* is defined as "confident of one's own righteousness, especially when smugly moralistic and intolerant of the opinions and behavior of others."

Some synonyms used for pride are *arrogance, conceit, egotism, vainglory, vanity,* and such like. Pride can be perceived in two different ways. There is a pride that God hates, as we read, "The fear of the Lord is to hate evil; Pride and arrogance and the evil way and the perverse mouth I hate" (Proverbs 8:13).

Then, there is the kind of pride we feel when we do something unexpected or met a challenge to achieve or attain something. For instance, I dropped out of high school three different times. Now I have earned doctoral degrees. If my parents were alive, they definitely would say, "We are proud of you."

The kind of pride God deplores is self-righteousness, which is a sin. The reason God hates this sin is because it hinders people from seeking Him. Those who are full of pride are so preoccupied with themselves their thoughts and actions are far from God (see Psalm 10:4).

Just as heads and tails are opposite sides of the same coin, pride, or self-righteousness, and humility are opposites. Being humble is what the Bible describes as being "poor in spirit." Jesus explained that those who are "poor in the spirit" are blessed "for theirs is the kingdom of heaven" (Matthew 5:3).

What does it mean to be "poor in spirit"? It means one is ready and willing to acknowledge that he or she is spiritually bankrupt and not worthy to approach God, except through His divine grace and mercy. The proud, on the other hand, are so full of themselves, they think they do not need God. Someone has said that no one is so empty as a person who is full of himself. I would categorize those who are proud or self-righteous as either "new agers" or "secular humanists."

A pastor once said, "Pride has kept many people from accepting Jesus Christ as Lord and Savior." That is an absolutely true statement, and I personally have many friends who would fit into that category in that they denied and rejected all witnessing I have offered and shared. In fact, they told me to leave them alone.

One of the hardest things for prideful people to do is to admit and confess their sins, not to mention the ability to acknowledge their need of the Savior. Not only can proud people be too optimistic, but they can also be perfectionists. Trying to get the words *I am sorry* from them is no less than a miracle.

When you confront a prideful person about his or her wrongdoing, you can expect one of three reactions: They will get angry and not hesitate to show it, they will immediately defend themselves, or they may give you the silent treatment for awhile. I have experienced all these responses and more.

What does the Bible say about pride and self-righteousness? Actually, the Bible has much to say about it. The following Scripture verses are key to helping us understand God's stance on this topic:

1. *God hates pride*: "These six things the Lord hates, Yes, seven are an abomination to Him: a proud look . . ." (Proverbs 6:16-17). Further into the book we read, "Everyone proud in heart is an abomination to the Lord; though they join forces, none will go unpunished" (Proverbs 16:5).
2. *Pride is an outright sin* that should be dealt with immediately. In the book of 1 John we read, "For all that is in the world—the lust of the flesh, the lust of the eyes, and the pride of life—is not of the Father but is of the world" (2:16).
3. *Pride diverts attention and focus away from God* and puts it on ourselves. Instead of accepting the accolades of the crowds, John the Baptist declared, "He [Christ] must increase, but I must decrease" (John 3:30). God will distance Himself from the prideful (James 4:6), and we are told, "we cannot serve two masters" (Matthew 6:24; Luke 16:23).

We are not to sound our own trumpets; instead, we should let others speak their opinions of us. Yet, despite what others say about us, we should only be concerned with the truth and nothing else. As for the prideful, they not only think they are wise, they also give the impression that they actually do "know it all."

The Bible cautions us clearly "not to be wise in your own eyes; Fear the Lord and depart from evil" (Proverbs 3:7). The apostle Paul, in his first letter to the Corinthians, made a bold statement about such folks: "And if anyone thinks that he knows anything, he knows nothing yet as he ought to know" (1 Corinthians 8:2).

Pride will not only cause our downfall (Proverbs 11:2), it can even bring death: "There is a way that seems right to a man, but its end is the way of death" (Proverbs 14:12). Eventually, pride can (and will) bring anyone to his knees (Proverbs 29:23).

What causes an individual to be prideful? The answer to that question would vary from person to person. However, some common causes may include academic achievement, outward beauty, intelligence or intellect, material possessions, power, status, wealth, and so on.

At one time, Satan was the highest angel, and God put him over other angels. He was also in charge of music, meaning, praise and worship. He became filled with pride. Thinking he could do better than God, He plotted to take over the throne of God. Satan's downfall from heaven is the direct result of pride (see Isaiah 14:12-15; Ezekiel 28:17).

Self-righteous people mistakenly think they are better than others. The following two verses confirm this erroneous thinking. First, we read, "He who is without sin among you, let him throw a stone first" (John 8:7). Second, "For all have sinned and fall short of the glory of God" (Romans 3:23).

We are commanded and encouraged to put others above ourselves: "Let nothing be done through selfish ambition or conceit, but in lowliness of mind let each esteem others better than himself" (Philippians 2:3). This does not and will not come easy for a prideful person.

God knows how to bring prideful people to their knees. He has done it many times, and He will do it again and again, whenever and wherever He sees the need.

In closing, I would like to encourage you to take to heart every Scripture verse quoted in this section. Take time to examine your thoughts and hearts and follow King David's prayer request before God: "Create in me a clean heart, O God, and renew a steadfast spirit within me" (Psalm 51:10).

We need to realize that we are what we are only because of God's grace (see 1 Corinthians 15:10). Only as God permits (and not of ourselves) are we capable of being of benefit and value to others and the kingdom of God (see 2 Corinthians 3:5).

One does not want to rebel against a holy and righteous God. In doing so, he or she is fighting a losing battle. The Lord gave a strong warning through the prophet Isaiah about those puffed up with pride: "For the day of the Lord of hosts shall come upon everything proud and lofty, upon everything lifted up—and it shall be brought low" (Isaiah 2:12; see also Isaiah 13:11 for additional confirmation).

Conclusion

This chapter has included much support material relating to many debilitating issues most of us face daily. Regardless of how large one's problem appears, remind yourself often that God is bigger and can handle anything. He has everything and everyone under control.

So what can we do to draw closer to God? King David gave us the answer to that question: "The Lord is near to those who have a broken heart, and saves such as have a contrite spirit" (Psalm 34:18). The key is to practice humility because God helps the meek (see Psalm 9:12).

It is time we shifted our attention and focus from self to God and then move toward serving others. It is okay to confess our faults to one another. In fact, we are commanded to do just that (see James 5:16).

Chapter Eight

Personality

Self-Identity: Who Am I?

Introduction—What Is Personality?

When we describe or talk about someone's personality, we are usually pointing out his or her attitudes and behavior. Seldom do we bring one's physical appearance into the discussion, at least not as much as their character. But there is more to personality than just attitude and behavior.

The dictionary defines *personality* as "the visible aspect of one's character as it impresses others; the sum total of the physical, mental, emotional, and social characteristics of an individual; the organized pattern of behavioral characteristics of the individual."

One psychologist defined *personality* as "the dynamic and organized set of characteristics possessed by a person that uniquely influences his or her cognitions, motivations, and behaviors in various situations" (Rychman, 2000). Some synonyms used for personality are *charm, disposition, emotions, identity, individuality, nature, self, temperament,* and so on.

To put it in simple terms, personality actually reflects how a person thinks, feels, and behaves in all situations. In other words, it has to do with an individual's consistent behavioral traits. A trait is a behavioral characteristic that determines a person's character. Examples include being friendly, impulsive, moody, prideful, stubborn, and so on.

In one sense, personality is difficult to define because it means different things to different people. However, there are certain components (or fundamental characteristics) within one's personality that seem to be common to almost all human beings. These fundamental characteristics are consistency, physiological and psychological factors, actions and impact behaviors, and multiple or various expressions.

The consistency component states, "people act in the same ways or similar ways in a variety of situations" (Cherry, 2011). We humans are creatures of habit, and habits are hard to break. We tend to show consistency in our behavior toward others whether the situation is positive or negative.

A second fundamental characteristic is that our personality is influenced by both physiological and psychological factors. The physiological (also referred to as biological) aspect focuses on body language, or nonverbal communication. The psychological factor emphasizes our behavior, feelings, and thoughts.

The third fundamental characteristic concerns our actions and impact behaviors, meaning, how we respond (or act) toward others in various situations. We tend to act one way in one situation and totally different in a similar situation.

And the fourth fundamental characteristic takes into account multiple or various expressions. Our personality does not just focus on behavior alone; it also takes into consideration our emotions, feelings, and thoughts as they relate to close relationships and social interactions with other people.

Personality is a topic that really fits more in the field of psychology and sociology than the Bible. Psychologists have written hundreds of books on this topic. The Bible does not directly mention the word *personality* in either the Old or New Testament. The Bible focuses more on one's sin nature as opposed to the technical terminology associated with one's personality.

If I started explaining personality from a psychology standpoint, it would take too long and require more space than allowed in these pages. My goal, however, is to define personality in general terms rather than to write from an academic or textbook viewpoint.

There are well over twenty different personality theories, and I cannot cover all of them. But I would like to draw your attention to two common statements we either have said or heard others say: (1) He or she has a magnetic (or pleasing) personality; and (2) His or her personality stinks.

People who make these types of remarks do not always know the other individual on a personal basis, so why do they say such things? What makes one say authoritatively that a person's personality is either pleasing or displeasing?

Before I answer these questions, let me present another interesting statement people make (and some even believe) that may shed some light on this intriguing topic. Nearly every day, we see individuals and form impressions about them that make us want to either avoid them or approach them and engage them in conversation. What makes the difference?

I do not know all the answers to these questions, but I will relate a reason with which am I personally familiar. Growing up in India, I often heard people say that the "face is the index of mind." I believe this statement has some truth in it.

Body language, especially facial expressions, speaks volumes. Some people seem quite adept at using nonverbal signals to convey strong messages. What makes people show the emotions or expressions they do? I sincerely believe that one's cognitions (or thoughts) have much to do with it.

Our expressions have a strong correlation with how we feel inside, both emotionally and mentally. A person who is optimistic and easygoing by nature will display relaxed facial expressions that match his or her inner tranquility. The same holds true for those who are having a disturbing or rotten day.

We are familiar with statements like, "You are what you eat," "You are what you talk," and so on. I tend to disagree with these kinds of statements in general because I do not find sufficient truth in them. For instance, because I choose to snack on junk food does not mean I am worthless junk. On the contrary, the Bible says we are created in God's image: "So God created man in His own image; in the image of God He created him; male and female He created them" (Genesis 1:27). I consider it a privilege and honor to be identified as a child of God.

A similar statement with which I strongly agree goes like this: "You are what you think." Descartes, a well-known French philosopher, once said, "I think, therefore I am," Even the Bible agrees and confirms this premise: "For as he thinks in his heart, so is he" (Proverbs 23:7).

We humans make a habit of comparing ourselves with others. We do so because we love to figure things out by using our own reasoning powers. Despite all the logic we may use, though, we are not always correct because we see only bits and pieces and not the big picture, which only God can see.

Being able to define personality is not good enough. There is more to know and learn about an individual as it relates to the "why." We just learned the "what" portion; now let us explore the "why," meaning asking ourselves, "Why study personality?"

Why Study Personality?

Knowing and learning about personality can be beneficial not only in understanding oneself but also others with whom we interact on a daily or regular basis. Studying personality is important because we not only tend to influence each other (either directly or indirectly), but we also can be role models to those who have expectations of us.

Personality is what makes a person in terms of who he is and why he acts in a particular way. Therefore, it is important and beneficial to know, learn, and study those factors that make and shape one's personality. The more we know, the better it is.

Studying personality helps us understand the many facets of an individual's character as well as his or her lifestyle as it relates to emotions, feelings, goals, mental illness, nature, nurture, productivity, success, and the like. The same holds true regarding the discovery of negative qualities.

Among all the aspects that make studying personality so interesting is the attention-getting "nature versus nurture" controversy. Some argue that nature plays the key role; that is, a major portion of our personality is predetermined, or inherited through our genes (DNA).

On the other hand, some people strongly support the thought that nurture determines the development of one's personality. They say nurture, which consists of life experiences and environment, is responsible in shaping who a person is and how he or she approaches life. I am convinced that neither nature nor nurture contributes one hundred percent of the determining factors, as both play key roles.

Studying personality can also help us assist others before a situation or disorder moves to the point of no return. For instance, an individual who suffers from a mental illness, such as depression, generally show symptoms as being withdrawn, wanting to be alone, quiet, and so on.

Understanding this individual's personality will help us detect and possibly prevent similar symptoms in others.

Finally, studying personality also can help us in other significant areas of our lives, such as careers, friendships, jobs, relationships, and so on. For instance, if I am an employer, I would like to know ahead of time if I am hiring the right person for the job.

DSM-IV-TR

The initials DSM stand for *The Diagnostic & Statistical Manual of Mental Disorders*, a text edited and published by the American Psychiatric Association. The DSM, currently in its fourth edition, is used primarily by clinicians and psychiatrists to diagnose psychiatric illnesses. The volume covers and deals with all categories and types of mental health disorders for children, adolescents, and adults. The DSM-IV version, originally published in 1994, lists about 250 mental disorders.

An updated version, the DSM-IV-TR, was published in 2000, and lists at least four hundred mental disorders. The initials TR stand for "text revision" due to minor amendments to the descriptions of some disorders. The DSM-IV-TR is not intended for use by therapists, as it focuses mostly on medical-related disorders, such as anxiety, mood, psychotic disorders, and so on.

The DSM-IV-TR describes in great detail conditions or symptoms that must be present in order for an individual to be diagnosed with specific mental health conditions. The DSM-IV-TR consists of five different "axes," or dimensions. The details of these five axes are as follows:

- Axis-I: Clinical Disorders. This level comprises at least 95 percent of all the 400 disorders (possibly more) of the entire DSM-IV-TR. To give a general idea, axis-I covers the following disorders, to name a few: adjustment, anxiety, developmental, mood, pervasive, schizophrenic, somatoform, and so forth.

- Axis-II: Mental Retardation (Developmental Disorders) and Personality Disorders. Personality disorders affect how an individual behaves, feels, and thinks. Mental retardation is defined as intellectual impairment associated with deficits or drawbacks in other areas (besides intellectual) as in interpersonal skills and self-care.
- Axis-III: General Medical (Physical) Conditions as in Health-Related Issues
- Axis-IV: Psychosocial and Environmental Problems (Severity of Psychosocial Stressors)
- Axis-V: Global Assessment of Functioning (Level of Functioning)—The GAF Score

The DSM-IV-TR identifies ten personality disorders, which are categorized under three main "clusters":

Cluster A: Eccentric, Odd, and Suspicious

1. Paranoid Personality Disorder
2. Schizoid Personality Disorder
3. Schizotypal Personality Disorder

Cluster B: Emotional, Erratic, and Impulsive

1. Antisocial Personality Disorder
2. Borderline Personality Disorder
3. Histrionic Personality Disorder
4. Narcissistic Personality Disorder

Cluster C: Anxious and Fearful

1. Avoidant Personality Disorder
2. Dependent Personality Disorder
3. Obsessive-Compulsive Disorder

It has been said that people with personality disorders often find it difficult to "control their feelings and behavior, get on with friends and family, get on with people at work, keep out of trouble, and make or keep relationships" (Online Article, 2011).

For several reasons, it is not always easy to diagnose personality disorders:

1. Not everyone acknowledges he or she has issues that need to be addressed. Most probably also deal with pride.
2. Some resist seeing a counselor or a therapist because they would like to "keep it in the family" and will try to handle it "internally." This approach does not always work.
3. Some do not object to seeking counseling, but they cannot always afford it financially. This becomes even more difficult when an individual works a part-time job and is not eligible to receive medical insurance.
4. Some prefer to see a pastor, priest, or another religious or spiritual leader. These men and women of God may be knowledgeable in God's Word, but many of them are uneducated, inexperienced, and unskilled in the field of human behavior.
5. Some refuse to see a counselor or a therapist because they are shy and do not feel confident opening up and sharing. They may be embarrassed, uncomfortable, and uneasy discussing sensitive areas of their lives with a total stranger.

Axis-IV deals with environmental and psychosocial events or problems in a person's life, such as college, death of a loved one, economics, education, healthcare, housing, legal issues, marriage, new job, unemployment, and the like.

Axis-V allows the practitioner or clinician to rate an individual's overall level of functioning at the present time. Each patient is scored on a scale of 0 to 100, and the closer the score is to 100, the healthier a person is thought to be. It is my understanding that almost all serial killers would score under 30.

The DSM is primarily used by psychiatrists who have a medical degree (MD) and by psychiatric nurse practitioners. Psychologists have doctorate degrees, such as EdD, PhD, or PsyD. The psychologists who do consult, research, and study the DSM-IV-TR are clinical, forensic, and neuro.

The DSM-IV-TR can be an interesting and fascinating book to read in terms of accumulating and increasing knowledge about "self." However, the volume does not have all the answers as the Bible claims to have. In the Old Testament, we read where God used a donkey to speak to a prophet.

Likewise, God can use whatever and whomever He wishes, whether it be philosophy, psychology, psychiatry, and so on. God knows how to communicate with us. All we have to do is to be open, ready, and willing to listen.

The Biblical View of Personality

People all over the world experience depression, despair, loneliness, and stress. But it does not have to be that way, at least not for those who are born-again, or saved. God's plan for us is to live a victorious life.

If we are not living a victorious life, it is not the fault of God or His Word. God is perfect. Since He and His Word are right one hundred percent of the time, the problem lies with us as it relates to our personalities. God knows and understands us because He created us. (Refer to Matthew 19:28 to learn how Jesus reassures us.)

The problem with the secular (or worldly) system is that people expect answers, choices, and solutions to every challenge they face. They can be sidetracked easily, choosing to go their own way, thus making their lives (and the lives of those around them) more challenging.

The Bible, on the other hand, presents everyone with only two choices: heaven or hell, yes or no, for God or against Him. In the next chapter, I will explain in greater detail psychology's view of man and how it identifies him.

Conclusion

Though the Bible may not contain the word *personality* in either the Old or New Testament, it covers much more ground than psychology ever did or could. Psychology does not deal with many of the basic issues of one's life, such as compassion, grace, mercy, sin nature, and so on.

The Word of God gives us a clear picture of mankind and his nature. Psychology for the most part focuses only on "self," whereas the Bible encourages us to work as a team. We are told to encourage one another, pray for one another, and love one another.

Chapter Nine

Psychology: Can It Be Trusted?

A False Gospel

Psychobabble

Introduction

What is psychobabble? The dictionary defines the term as "writing or talk using jargon from psychiatry or psychotherapy without particular accuracy or relevance." In other words, it is using language that is loaded with psychological terminology. Allow me to mention a few observations that apply to many individuals as it relates to psychobabble:

1. People all over the world use psychobabble because they have convinced themselves that they are experts in the field of psychology. Few people like to admit that they do not know everything about everyone. The phrase "too many chiefs and not enough Indians" certainly applies here.
2. Family members rarely seek the aid of a counselor or therapist for fear that family issues might be exposed. In many cultures, both Eastern and Western, advice or counseling typically comes from parents, grandparents, or family elders, such as aunts, uncles, or older siblings.

3. Many professing Christian counselors claim authority and knowledge over God's Word. This is dangerous territory, for absolutely nothing and no one supersedes the Bible as the final authority on every subject. In the Word of God, we read, "Many are called, but few are chosen" (Matthew 22:14), and we also discover what the Lord Jesus Himself will say one day to false, professing believers: "I never knew you; depart from Me" (Matthew 7:23). It is not just the knowledge we claim but the action we follow and practice that matters in God's eyes (see Matthew 7:16).

A rude awakening is in store for many individuals. Hearing the Lord say, "I never knew you," is a frightful and unimaginable prospect, but it is also unnecessary. Each one of us has the same opportunity to receive God's offer of salvation to all who accept His Son as Savior.

Let's detour briefly and talk about psychotherapy—broadly defined as a "talking treatment in which a trained person deliberately establishes a professional relationship with a patient for the purpose of relieving symptoms" (Kaplan & Sadock, 89). In Western culture, especially in America, the practice of psychotherapy is "diverse, widespread, respected, ingrained, and assumed to be efficacious" (Almy & Almy, 94).

The major problem with psychology (counseling and/or psychotherapy) is that no single method or style is universally accepted. Over four hundred different types of therapies are in use, and one can only imagine the confusion that abounds at the uncertainty of not knowing which therapy works best for whom.

In the secular world, especially when it comes to psychology, truth becomes relative, whereas from a biblical standpoint, truth is abstract. Therapists in the field of psychology tend to be subjective, or biased; the Word of God, on the other hand, presents the truth clearly and objectively.

Another weakness with psychology is that it tends to operate in the gray area if and when it is perceived that the need or situation warrants it. On the opposite spectrum, the Word of God neither mentions nor supports any gray areas. Here are some examples that prove the point:

1. Our communication is to be either "yes" or "no."
2. We either love and serve God or we do not.
3. We are to be either "hot" or "cold."
4. Our final destiny is either "heaven" or "hell."
5. We are either "of this world" or we "belong to God."
6. We are either "for God" or "against Him."
7. We are either "saved" or we are "not saved."

How Psychology Sees Mankind

Psychology views human nature as basically "good," which is quite the opposite of God's perspective (see Romans 3:23). Psychology emphasizes human growth and potential; in other words, the buck stops with mankind and not with God. Psychology puts self on a pedestal and gives justifiable excuses for wrongful (sinful) behavior.

Psychology does not always teach the individual to accept personal accountability or responsibility. But God holds everyone personally accountable, as we will all give an account one day for all we say and do. The secular world focuses on intelligence, whereas the Word of God emphasizes wisdom. In other words, the worldly system dwells primarily on head issues, whereas the Word of God accentuates matters of the heart.

The following Bible verses illustrate the significance of focusing on concerns of the heart:

- "Keep your heart with all diligence, for out of it spring the issues of life" (Proverbs 4:23).
- "Man looks at the outward appearance, but the Lord looks at the heart" (1 Samuel 16:7).

- "Out of the abundance of the heart the mouth speaks" (Matthew 12:34; Luke 6:45).

Psychology encourages mankind to "look out for number one" and tends to see man apart from God. The secular system generally has no illumination of God's Word; therefore, it is obligated to develop its own system of philosophy and values for handling human beings and their problems in this life.

To understand further how God's Word disagrees with psychology and its system, let us observe a key verse that deals with this issue. Speaking through the prophet Isaiah, God warns: "'Woe to the rebellious children,' says the Lord, 'who take counsel, but not of Me, and who devise plans, but not of My Spirit, that they may add sin to sin'" (30:1).

The Lord clearly expects us to approach Him with our counseling needs: "Come to Me, all you who labor and are heavy laden, and I will give you rest" (Matthew 11:28). When we seek secular counselors, we are only adding "sin to sin," not to mention that we have chosen a rebellious system over God's way.

Psychology's fundamental focus on self is so strong that self eventually can become a god. The Bible, on the other hand, encourages us to die to self, which means our old self is crucified with Christ when we accept Him as our personal Lord and Savior.

Psychology delves into one's history and uses past experiences to justify present behavior. God neither remembers nor resurrects our forgiven past: "As far as the east is from the west, so far has He removed our transgressions from us" (Psalm 103:12).

Psychology not only recommends but also insists that we get in touch with our feelings in order to "keep it real." Anyone who refuses to do so is supposedly in denial. From a psychology standpoint, feelings can become a god. The Bible, on the other hand, encourages and expects us to focus on the Lord instead of on our own feelings and to walk in His Spirit.

Psychology gives man false hope. Psychologists see themselves as "experts in the field." They don't mind inferring their superiority simply because you sought their counsel. From a biblical viewpoint, both the counselor and the counselee are equal before the cross; no one is above the other.

If psychology disagrees so much with the Bible, why do many Christians accept it and even choose to see a psychologist rather than a Christian counselor or pastor? One reason may be that many of the primary psychological theories embrace some biblical truth. In other words, it is like a counterfeit that almost looks like the real thing. However, some commonalities do exist between psychology and the Bible:

- Psychologists (behaviorists) talk about "rewards and punishment," and so does the Bible as it relates to "sowing and reaping" (Galatians 6:7).
- Cognitive psychologists focus on "cognitions," otherwise referred to as "thoughts." The Bible also refers to thoughts: "As [a man] thinks in his heart, so is he" (Proverbs 23:7; also see Philippians 4:8).
- Psychologists encourage a twelve-step therapy that focuses primarily on "group interaction." Likewise, the Bible encourages believers to follow the "one-another" principle: pray for one another; encourage one another; confess faults to one another; and so on.

From these examples (and many more), one can only imagine how misleading and confusing it can be when the fields of psychology and theology try to work together. The truth is, the view of mankind from a psychological standpoint is inaccurate and incomplete and tends to be subjective (biased) in nature.

How God Sees Mankind

God's perspective of His highest creation is paramount and should be the only viewpoint that matters. The logic behind this statement is simple: God is always right, and He shows no partiality toward anyone, regardless of age, ethnicity, gender, race, and such like.

Our view of ourselves should not matter as much as how God sees us, for we can be biased in our judgment. For instance, it's easy for us to present ourselves more spiritual than we actually are. The same holds true with regard to how others view us. Those who love us tend to cover for us, making it easy for us to maintain a "holier-than-thou" attitude.

Pride and self-righteousness can cause a person to elevate himself above others. Many think so highly of themselves as to place themselves on pedestals. Self-confidence may be considered an asset in the secular world, but it amounts to little in God's kingdom. Regardless of how we elevate and esteem our own uprightness, the Word of God declares, "All our righteousness are like filthy rags" (Isaiah 64:6). We are by nature sinful and rebellious people. The Bible declares that there is not even one righteous person in the whole world: "There is none righteous, no, not one" (Romans 3:20).

Consider some additional Scripture passages that address human nature. In the book of Romans we read, "All have sinned and fall short of the glory of God" (3:23). God speaks clearly about our sin nature, and yet He loves us so much He gave us His best. As sinners, we are spiritually dead (Ephesians 2:1); slaves to sin (John 8:34); enemies to God (Colossians 1:21); separated from God (Isaiah 59:2); and under God's condemnation (John 3:18).

Christianity in general and Christ in particular are awesome and unique in that God loves us so much He sacrificed His only begotten Son for us (John 3:16). Jesus, being the Son of Man on Earth, was obedient to the will of His heavenly Father, surrendering Himself to death on the cross for lost humanity.

We are a rebellious and sinful people who do not deserve such a heavenly and loving sacrifice, but such is His grace and mercy. Someone has defined grace as receiving what we do not deserve and mercy as *not receiving* what we *do* deserve.

Despite our sin nature, God views mankind as precious and special. After all, He created us in His own image. Though we choose to go our own ways (mostly for selfish reasons), He is always ready and willing to forgive and accept us back into fellowship with Him. God puts our past behind us, unlike psychology, which is bent on delving into and dwelling on it repeatedly. We can be thankful for God's great grace and mercy.

A question many Christians ponder is, how can a loving, gracious, and merciful God send people to hell? The simple answer is that God is also just. Because He is holy and righteous, He must judge us because of our sin and rebellion and not because we are human beings.

Humanistic psychologists, like Dr. Carl Rogers, emphasize the nobility of man to such an extent that they idealize his goodness: Since man is so good in his nature, why should he go to hell? But eternity deals with the choices we make (as in salvation) and does not focus on any other aspect of life, whether it is education, experience, goodness, money, power, or status.

Too many Christian psychologists (an oxymoron, in my opinion) side with the humanistic psychologists when they focus on the goodness and nobility of man. In the process, they put aside the biblical emphasis on humility—seeing mankind as God sees him.

Their view of man's nature comes from secular psychology and definitely not from the Word of God. These counselors and therapists, who identify themselves as Christian psychologists, are only hurting themselves in the long run by joining hands with the worldly system and not standing up for the Word of God.

Conclusion

It is crucial for us to know our natural state, which is sinful, and to realize how incapable we are of altering it in our own strength and wisdom. We must trust God to help us make the necessary changes in our lives. Ask the Lord in prayer to reveal those areas that need to be reformed in your life. Then, as you humble yourself and are honest and open about your sins, God will guide you in the right direction.

Myths of Psychology

Introduction

It might be wise to begin this section by describing psychology; it is generally defined as the "scientific study of behavior and mental processes" (Pastorino & Portillo, 2006). These authors further explain that "behavior includes: action, feelings, and biological states, and mental process include: problem-solving, intelligence, and memory," to name a few.

Psychology is derived from two Latin words: *psyche*, meaning "soul," and *logos*, meaning "knowledge." Therefore, psychology is the study of the soul. It focuses on the mind as well as on behavior.

The mind encompasses emotions, sensations, and thoughts. Mind and behavior are examined separately because only behavior can be measured directly. On the other hand, neither the mind nor its individual components or elements can be quantified. In order for something to be measured, it must be observed in a systematic fashion.

Psychology is perceived as a science; however, it is not considered to be a *pure* science, such as biology, chemistry, physics, and so on. A growing interest in the study of psychology has spawned the publication of a plethora of self-help books. In fact, these volumes seem to outnumber Christian inspirational books that offer help based on sound doctrine. I have found that many self-help books contain hidden new-age ideas and concepts contrary to the Word of God.

In his book *Why Christians Cannot Trust Psychology*, Dr. Ed Bulkley exposes six myths about psychology:

Myth #1: Psychology is Scientific

Many integrationists believe psychology is truly a science. In my opinion, psychology cannot be considered as a pure or natural science. It can, however, be viewed as a social science. Examples of natural or pure science include the study of biology, chemistry, mathematics, physics, and so on.

The problem with most scientific studies is that they cannot guarantee the same results on a consistent basis; in other words, what is true today may not be true tomorrow. For something to be scientific, it must have a guarantee of consistency—events have to follow some sort of lawful order. A good example would be "the sun rises in the east." We know that to be true; we can bank on the sun always rising in the east, and therefore, we have a guarantee of that happening.

We also note that scientists tend to disagree with one another, thus creating inconsistencies, not to mention ongoing confusion and debate that is open for argument and discussion.

For something to be deemed scientific, it must follow a four-step process:

1. Observation of events
2. Collection of data
3. Creation of a hypothesis

4. Testing of the hypothesis by repeated observation and controlled experiments

Psychology does not always follow this process; therefore, it lacks credibility of being scientific. A well-known psychologist and Christian author, Dr. Larry Crabb, agrees that psychology cannot be classified as science. He writes:

> Many admit now that the scientific research method is inherently inadequate for the job of defining truth. Science can provide neither proof nor meaning. In another paper, I pointed out that modern philosophers of science confess the incurable impotency of science to ever say anything conclusively. Science can assess probability but can take us no further.
> To reach certainty demands that we go beyond (not deny) reason and exercise faith. Humanistic optimism that man is sufficient to solve his problems has crumbled under the weight of science's inability to clearly assert that any single proposition is true. We need proven universals. Science cannot provide them. We must, in faith reach beyond ourselves to get what we need.

The problem with psychology is that it rarely deals with facts. Instead, it focuses on subjective opinions and interpretations, which means it can be biased.

Now let us examine how the Bible addresses this issue. In the book of Romans, we read:

> Since the creation of the world, His invisible attributes are clearly seen, being understood by the things that are made, even His eternal power and Godhead, so that they are without excuse, because, although they knew God, they did not glorify Him as God, nor were thankful, but

became futile in their thoughts, and their foolish hearts were darkened.

Professing to be wise, they became fools, and changed the glory of the incorruptible God into an image made like corruptible God into an image made like corruptible man—and birds and four-footed animals and creeping things (1:20-23).

Myth #2: Psychology is Effective

A well-known Christian counselor and author, Dr. Gary Collins, lists five major reasons why psychology produces disappointing results:

1. Unrealistic expectations by counselees
2. Inaccurate assumptions about the ability of psychology to explain human behavior
3. Wrong motivations for seeking counsel
4. Unfounded faith in psychology "experts"
5. Undelivered promises by the "experts" (Collins, 1988)

The points mentioned above can apply to any counseling situation, whether secular or Christian. Those who seek counsel often assume the counselor is there to solve all their problems. But this is not necessarily true because there are two ways to look at the situation: (1) to rely solely on the counselor's education, experience, expertise, knowledge, and training; and (2) to look at the counselor's openness and willingness to change.

Figuratively speaking, it is like taking the horse to the water but not being able to make it drink. The water here represents the counselor and his or her education, experience, expertise, knowledge, and training. And the horse represents the counselee having to make some choices.

There seems to be some sort of cognitive dissonance occurring, mostly on the part of the counselee. On one hand, many counselors, psychiatrists, and psychologists portray themselves as problem solvers, sending counselees a false message that they can and will resolve all of their problems. For this reason, when a person volunteers to go for counseling, his or her expectations may be too high. Then when a counselor fails to meet those expectations, the counselee is even more disappointed. It is possible and likely that these counselors, psychiatrists, and psychologists are portraying and advertising themselves inaccurately.

Dr. Bulkley further adds that "psychology is not only relatively ineffective in changing thought and behavior patterns, but in many cases it is also actually harmful to its clients" (Bulkley, 1988). Since a secular counseling system does not support biblical or Christian counseling, it sends the discouraging message to Christian counselors that they are neither trained nor educated to deal with serious problems.

Because of existing beliefs in the presumed effectiveness of psychology, many Christian colleges and universities now offer psychology degrees, merging psychology and theology, which is what the integrationists desire.

The field of psychology and psychiatry can be confusing and complicated. For example, it began with just three schools of thought:

1. Psychoanalysis, founded by Sigmund Freud
2. Behaviorism, founded by John Watson
3. Humanism, founded by two prominent and well-known individuals, Carl Rogers and Abraham Maslow

Many other schools of thought followed, including: behavioral, cognitive, cognitive-behavioral, existential, gestalt, and so forth. We now have at least four hundred different kinds of therapies, with several different schools within each major group.

For example, those who follow Freud are known as neo-Freudians, which includes Karen Horney, Erik Erikson, Carl Jung, Alfred Adler, and others. Each one of these neo-Freudians has his or her own pattern for explaining human behavior. As you can see, this system of schools and more schools within the main school can be complicated and confusing.

But that is not the case when it comes to biblical, or Christian, counseling. Even though the Bible was written thousands of years ago, it is still relevant, and those who choose to believe it can trust God with any personal or social issues because it is His Word. Every principle in the Bible was inspired by the Holy Spirit and is applicable to every human need.

I am not proposing that we forsake other valid fields. For example, if someone needs medication or surgery, he or she should seek appropriate consultation in order to address that particular condition. I mentioned earlier that God can use whomever and whatever He chooses to make a point and to effect positive and productive change in us, even if it involves a medical doctor, psychiatrist, pastor, or psychologist.

Speaking about the simplicity of the counseling process, Dr. Bulkley highlights some essential qualifications for a competent counselor. He states that for a counselor to be considered skilled, he or she "must have an extensive knowledge of the Scriptures (Romans 15:14), a good measure of divine wisdom (Colossians 3:16), goodness (1 Peter 5:5), an ability to relate to others (Colossians 4:6), the ability to communicate (Titus 2:8), and a genuine desire to help others (1 Thessalonians 5:14)."

A word of caution to a Christian counselee: Before choosing to see a therapist, question his or her counseling philosophy. Any areas that contradict the Word of God should raise red flags in your mind. The decision of who to follow must be considered wisely, for our choices come with consequences.

In Mark's gospel we read: "All too well you reject the commandment of God, that you may keep your tradition" (7:9). This passage is well stated and speaks for itself.

Myth #3: Psychology is Motivated by Compassion

In this category, we will examine and discuss monetary concerns, as there seems to be a direct correlation between the amount of money one pays and the level of compassion he or she receives.

From a biblical standpoint, this is bogus, for the best things in life, including compassion, are still free (see Chapter 12). Some people do believe, however, that the level of consideration they receive from the church is directly related to the amount of money they place in the offering plate. But that is not the case, nor should it ever be that way.

Some would rather talk with a psychologist or a psychiatrist because they are convinced that these counselors are motivated by compassion and also because they are not there to judge and condemn. But at the same time, the counselees are not recognizing the exorbitant fees these counselors charge. Therapy can be very expensive in the long run.

But when it comes to giving or investing in the Lord's work, people often complain that all the church wants from parishioners is their money. People have a tendency to think of pastors as wealthy, living in large houses, driving luxury automobiles, and taking expensive vacations regularly.

But they fail to see the bigger picture. Many pastors' salaries are at the low end of the professional pay scale. Few really "make it big." Despite the money factor, a godly pastor's desire and goal is to help parishioners by teaching sound biblical doctrines and by showing genuine compassion.

A fifty-five-minute session with a psychiatrist can cost ninety dollars or more, and a fifty-five-minute session with a psychologist can run at least sixty dollars. But when a parishioner sees a pastor for counseling, he or she often expects the session to be gratis. Even if some counselees are willing to pay a clergyman for his time, they usually contribute a small amount. Plus, the counseling session may stretch beyond an hour. Yet the parishioners are receiving godly wisdom and instruction—something a psychologist or a psychiatrist may not be equipped or choose to offer.

There seems to be so much attention on the field of psychology in general and on psychologists in particular. The questions to ask are, "Does psychology have all the answers we need or are seeking? If psychology does have all the answers for everyone, why is there so much trouble in the world, such as high divorce rates, people being fired or laid off from their jobs, domestic abuse, and other problems?"

In addition, some individuals who have received numerous sessions of counseling either from a psychologist or a psychiatrist are still suffering. The treatment never seems to end.

I am not saying that psychology or psychiatry is all bad. These professionals are known to effect some helpful changes, but in my opinion, they fail to solve man's spiritual problems. I believe God has provided solutions to all our problems in His Word, the Bible.

Once again, let us examine Dr. Gary Collin's evaluation of the psychotherapeutic industry, which he calls "the selling of therapy." He states, "Most therapists probably haven't even noticed what they are doing." They convince people subtly that their lives could be better, that therapy would help them, and that a "few more sessions" would be a wise investment in their future happiness and stability.

Soon, people who aren't sick are willing to pay to "get better." In Isaiah, we read, "Why do you spend money for what is not bread, and your wages for what does not satisfy?" (Isaiah 55:2).

Myth #4: Psychological Labels

Two psychiatrists once ran into each other, and one of them wanted to know if they might play a round of golf. The other replied that he could not play because he was on call to talk to a "schizophrenic."

It is sad that in today's society many individuals are given labels to describe their behavior instead of being addressed by name. The Bible says we are created in God's image and that we are uniquely and wonderfully made. Labeling an individual is not only wrong; it also creates confusion and may eventually lead to compounded emotional and mental stress.

Some believe in labeling because they claim it helps us understand who we are and makes it easier for us to manage our disorders. A major problem with this approach is that it tends to ignore the sin issue. Many behaviors that are placed under the genre of "mental illness" provide lame excuses for sinful behavior. In other words, nearly every mental illness is justified in a medical fashion, and the concept of sin and sinful behavior is never taken into consideration.

Dr. Thomas Szasz, a well-known psychiatrist and Christian author, once stated, "It is customary to define psychiatry as a medical specialty concerned with the study, diagnosis, and treatment of mental illness. This is a worthless and misleading definition. Mental illness is a myth" (Szasz, 1987).

Another problem with labeling is that it can lead to victimization. When an individual chooses to accept a label, he or she is being pigeonholed, such as: "I am an alcoholic," "I am a codependent," and so on. This sort of thinking and labeling can be debilitating and ongoing.

However, once a person confesses and accepts responsibility for his past and then repents and makes changes, he can rejoice in who he can become in the present. In the book of 2 Corinthians we read: "If anyone is in Christ, he is a new creation; old things have passed away, behold, all things have become new" (5:17). When God forgives us, He wipes the slate clean, and we are no longer slaves to our past. Everything is forgiven and forgotten.

So far, we have looked at problems associated with labeling from a psychological perspective. However, Dr. Bulkley has suggested five labels from the biblical standpoint. He further adds that these biblical labels have been known to set millions of people free from any bondage to the past or the present.

1. *Child of God.* When an individual confesses, repents, and accepts Jesus Christ as his personal Lord and Savior, he becomes a child of God. In the gospel of John we read: "But as many as received Him, to them He gave the right to become children of God, to those who believe in His name" (1:12). Paul emphasizes this truth in Romans: "For as many as are led by the Spirit of God, these are sons of God" (8:14).

2. *Redeemed.* An individual who has been redeemed is no longer a slave to his past; the chains of bondage are broken, and he can live with peace and joy, knowing he has been redeemed. What a wonderful place to be. The prophet Isaiah declared: "I, even I, am He who comforts you. Who are you that you should be afraid of a man who will die, And of the son of a man who will be made like grass?" (51:12).

3. *Forgiven.* As mentioned earlier, when we accept Jesus as our personal Lord and Savior, God will forgive all of our sins from our birth until the day we accept Him. He will continue to forgive future sins as they are confessed, except there will be consequences to bear.

   The psalmist David spoke of the Lord as One "who forgives all your iniquities, who heals all your diseases" (Psalm 103:3). We need not fear or worry about who we once were because God can and will cleanse all of our sins and freely forgive us.

   In 1 John we read, "If we confess our sins, He is faithful and just to forgive us our sins and to cleanse us from all unrighteousness" (1:9). A strong correlation exists between forgiveness and healing. Genuine healing begins when we learn to accept God's love and forgiveness.

4. *New Creation*. Can God transform an individual from a tormenting past? Absolutely. Consider the apostle Paul and who he was before his conversion and where God took him following his Damascus Road experience. We read in the Bible that Paul, who was originally named Saul, was a high-ranking Roman soldier who tortured and killed many Christians, including men, women, and children.

   Paul committed such atrocities that he actually labeled himself a "chief of sinners" (1 Timothy 1:15). Yet when Jesus saved him, he wrote under the anointing of the Holy Spirit: "If anyone is in Christ, he is a new creation; old things have passed away; behold, all things have become new" (2 Corinthians 5:17).

   The problem with secular therapy/treatment is that it cannot guarantee the transformation process that only the Holy Spirit can produce. Someone once said, "Do not expect from man that which only God can provide." A good example is "true love." Only God's love is pure and unconditional.

5. *Victor*. We live in an age of victimization; many of are victims to one thing or another, and it is because of sin and the depraved world in which we live. Sometimes it is because of our own bad choices; at other times, we are victimized because of what others do to us (an alcoholic or abusive father, mother, or spouse; an angry or violent husband or wife; and so on).

   It is a comfort to know that God cares for us and understands what each one of us endures. We cannot transform ourselves in our own strength. Therefore, we must learn to trust God and cast all our burdens upon Him, for He not only understands, He also can deliver us from all bondage so we can truly be free and start living a victorious life.

   In his first letter to the Corinthian church, the apostle Paul wrote: "Do you not know that the unrighteous will not inherit the kingdom of God? Do not be deceived. Neither fornicators, nor idolaters, nor adulterers, nor homosexuals, nor sodomites, nor thieves, nor covetous, nor drunkards, nor revilers, nor extortioners will inherit the kingdom of God. And such were some of you. But you were washed . . ." (1 Corinthians 6:9-11).

Myth #5: Psychology is Trustworthy

When it comes to trust, it is evident that only God and His Word are reliable. The Bible declares: "Let God be true but every man a liar" (Romans 3:4). One cannot put his or her trust in both God and psychology. The Bible addresses this issue clearly:

1. We are told that "no one can serve two masters" (Matthew 6:24).
2. The Bible warns us not to be "unequally yoked together with unbelievers" (2 Corinthians 6:14).
3. The Bible asks us to "Choose for yourselves this day whom you will serve" (Joshua 24:15).

When something is consistent, it becomes easy to trust. God's Word, the Bible, is unswerving; we can depend on it the same today as when it was written thousands of years ago.

This is not the case with psychology and psychiatry. We have already established that the field of psychology includes many schools of thought, each of which has numerous sub-schools. And each of these has its own psychologist, and each psychologist has his or her own theory for explaining human behavior.

Most psychology textbooks report that as many as four hundred psychological theories are in existence. With so many philosophies offering so many different treatment plans, it becomes difficult to trust all these therapies and therapists. Each method of treatment may offer some good, but none can be trusted in its entirety. Only God's Word repeatedly stands the test, from the beginning of time to eternity.

Some exceptions apply to things that are physical in nature (ailments, diseases, injuries, and remedies). Medical problems require medical attention. Certain mental issues (mood disorders, schizophrenia, etc.) also need professional attention. The Bible is not against medical doctors, diagnoses, and treatments. Where medication is necessary, one must use it properly. Yet one must not ignore the power of prayer. The Bible strongly encourages us to "pray without ceasing" (1 Thessalonians 5:17), we are told to "call upon the Lord in the day of trouble" (Psalm 50:15), and we are encouraged to request prayer in times of sickness (James 5:14).

One cannot put his or her full trust in psychology as well as in the Bible. God's Word warns us that we cannot "serve two masters" (Matthew 6:24). Water and oil do not mix. Light and darkness are incompatible. Likewise, God and secular theology, such as psychology, do not go hand in hand. In this vein, the apostle Paul issued a stern warning to the Corinthian believers and to us: "Do not be unequally yoked together with unbelievers. For what fellowship has righteousness with lawlessness? And what communication has light with darkness? (2 Corinthians 6:14).

Another issue has to do with defining the word *abnormal*. No psychology textbook dares to define the term, because there is no such thing as abnormal—what is normal for one person may not be normal for another. One also must consider who is doing the judging and on what authority? Therefore, psychology cannot be trusted when it comes to identifying behavior that is normal or abnormal.

On the contrary, the Bible speaks clearly with regard to sin, and its summation is applicable to everyone. It is easier to admit we have sinned than to say we are normal or abnormal. In Paul's letter to the Galatians we read, "I marvel that you are turning away so soon from Him who called you in the grace of Christ, to a different gospel" (1:6).

Myth #6: Psychology Can Heal the Past

Many psychological theories heavily emphasize the "past." In other words, we humans are captives of our past.

Psychologists and even many Christian writers use the phrase "adult children." This refers to adults who were hurt in their youth either by divorce or emotional or physical abuse, which interrupted their maturing process. In order to deal with those issues in the present, they must revisit their past so healing may take place. One can argue that such therapeutic measures may help make changes.

However, when God forgives, He also forgets. God does not dwell on our past. Jesus said, "Whoever desires to come after Me, let him deny himself, and take up his cross, and follow Me" (Mark 8:34). In the book of Psalms we read, "As far as the East is from the West, so far has He removed our transgressions from us" (103:12).

Sigmund Freud, a psychoanalyst, considered to be the father of modern psychology, strongly emphasized the past. Using a technique called hypnosis, he made his clients deal with their past by recalling repressed memories—memories that have been repressed (ignored) since their childhood. Freud stressed the significance of the unconscious—that which "lies beneath the surface level." *Conscious* is defined as "being aware of one's self and the environment at all times possible." Freud's goal was to bring to light what was hidden, or making the unconscious events conscious. And he did this by hypnotizing people and helping them deal with the repressed memories so that when the past was brought to light, it became easier to deal with and thus brought closure.

According to Dr. Bulkley, there are at least three weaknesses with the healing-of-memories theory. First, the theory itself is unproven. There is neither solid scientific nor scriptural evidence for such a practice. On the contrary, the Bible encourages us to look forward: "Brethren, I do not count myself to have apprehended, but one thing I do, forgetting those things which are behind and reaching forward to those things which are ahead" (Philippians 3:13).

God offers us His grace and forgiveness, which are sufficient to heal our memories, regardless of how damaging they may be. When the apostle Paul complained about a thorn in his flesh, God gently reminded him, "My grace is sufficient for you" (2 Corinthians 12:9).

When individuals choose to return to their past, there is always a possibility of reigniting hatred, bitterness, and unforgiveness that God has already dealt with and reopening wounds Jesus Christ has already healed. The question is, "Do we really need to revisit the pain of the past when God has already covered it and wants us to move on?" Genuine peace comes only when we surrender our anxieties and worries (especially those from the past) to our Lord and learn to forgive and forget as He does.

Dr. Bulkley cites a second weakness to the healing-of-memories theory: Memories can be inaccurate and selective. For example, one can fabricate, distort, add, or delete memories, and thus lose touch with reality. Any of these aberrations has the potential to cause incalculable harm.

Much contemporary research focuses on what is known as the "false memory syndrome." When an individual loses touch with reality and with God, he or she is vulnerable to becoming a victim of cultic and occultic practices, which are actually influenced by Satan. Country singer Aaron Tippen once said, "If you don't stand for something, you will fall for anything." There is much truth in that statement.

Dr. Bulkley says the third weakness of the healing-of-memories theory is that it spotlights the counselee (his suffering and his past) instead of emphasizing the God of healing, His power, and a glorious future in Christ. Unlike psychology, the Bible draws the attention away from self and onto God.

The Bible does mention memories, but none of the passages refer to their healing. Likewise, the words *imagine* and *imagination* are also found in the Bible, yet none of the references are connected to the healing of memories.

On one hand, the Scriptures encourage us to remember God (see Psalm 78 and Psalm 143). On the other hand, we also read that King David pleaded with God not to remember his past. In Psalm 25:7 we read, "Do not remember the sins of my youth, nor my transgressions; according to Your mercy remember me, for your goodness' sake, O Lord."

In Psalm 42:6 we read, "O my God, my soul is cast down within me; therefore, I will remember You." Clearly, the focus is on remembering God and not on recalling one's painful past. The apostle Paul reminds us how he dealt with this issue: "Forgetting those things which are behind and reaching forward to those things which are ahead . . ." (Philippians 3:13).

Conclusion

Psychology is not all bad. It does offer some good insights into human behavior. Psychology is more of a descriptive science in that it can help us understand why we behave a certain way, and it does describe our behavior. But because it avoids the spiritual aspect, it is powerless to deal with sin.

In the Bible, we read that God once used a donkey to speak to a prophet. Likewise, God can and will use whatever He feels necessary to teach us a lesson, whether it be family, friends, nature, philosophy, relatives, or even psychology. It is not what we use as much as how we use it that matters.

Having examined the six myths (or lies) of psychology, one can clearly see how the science can be misleading and confusing. Psychology cannot solve all of man's problems. It can only leave an individual confused, empty, and even lonely.

Since psychology does not take into consideration one's spiritual life, it is reasonable to assume that it does not have all the answers one needs in order to understand the self, the sin nature, God, salvation, redemption, and so forth. Jesus came to offer peace, healing, and eternal life through salvation. "I have come that they may have life, and that they may have it more abundantly" (John 10:10).

Chapter Ten

Integration

Merging Psychology and Theology

Introduction

Many Christian counselors, church leaders, and pastors fall into the trap of trying to integrate psychology and theology. Those who combine or mix these two studies are known as integrationists. But the Bible tells us we "cannot serve two masters." By attempting to do so, we cannot be one hundred percent loyal to either and will always be compromising between the two.

Some people lack confidence in the ways of the Lord. Besides, psychology *sells* because it tends to tell counselees what they want to hear. Since psychology sidesteps the sin factor, it generally encourages and puffs up, and of course, that is what many people desire.

Two well-known authors on the subject of psychology and theology note that more and more, "Psychologists are lecturing at Bible conferences. Increasingly our society is looking to psychology to shed new light on the problems of human existence" (Carter and Narramose, 1979).

Psychology versus Christianity

Is psychology needed today? Should it be part of biblical counseling? My personal answer to both questions is an emphatic no.

Let us look at how the apostle Paul counseled people in his day. We find a good example in the book of Colossians: "Him we preach, warning every man and teaching every man in all wisdom, that we may present every man perfect in Christ Jesus" (1:28). Later in Colossians, Paul sternly warns his readers to be wary of charlatans: "Beware lest anyone cheat you through philosophy and empty deceit, according to the tradition of men, according to the basic principles of the world, and not according to Christ" (2:8). Based on the apostle's appraisal, we conclude that we can find all the answers we need in Jesus Christ.

Sigmund Freud is considered to be the father, but not the founder, of psychology. The truth is, "psychology has its roots in ancient philosophers like Socrates, Aristotle, and Plato" (Wommack, 2011). None of these individuals was a godly man because they were not considered to be worshippers of the true and loving God, as most philosophers of those days worshipped multiple pagan gods. Nor could Freud be thought of as godly. His research and study focused primarily on an obsession with sex, and much of man's problems relates to his inability to control the sex drive.

Herein lays the problem with the individuals mentioned above and many other philosophers: their foundations are askew. And if the foundation or root is corrupt, it can produce nothing good. Jesus explained this law of nature (see Matthew 7:17-18). If its foundation is weak, a house will collapse, and if a tree's root (or seed) is bad, the fruit also will be bad. Since the root of psychology is corrupt, the fruit it produces cannot be good. Yet many churches and ministries hire and maintain psychologists and/or psychiatrists on staff in salaried positions with full benefits.

How did Jesus handle people's issues or problems? Through the power of the Holy Spirit, He met the needs of everyone who came to Him for help. As His followers in faith, we are equipped to do the same. After all, He promised to send us the Holy Spirit—also referred to in Scripture as the Holy Ghost and Comforter. (Refer to John 14:16 and John 16:7 regarding Jesus' promise.)

Does the Word of God provide enough information on every subject? No, it does not. For instance, the Bible does not list any mathematical formulae, laws of gravity, geographic locations, or underwater species (marine life). It says nothing about biology, chemistry, and such alike. Take note, however, that none of these studies deals with essential spiritual truths as the Bible does.

Because of their supreme importance, spiritual truths (as they relate to God) take precedence over every other discipline. The Bible may not deal with natural, physical, or social sciences, but its claims are far more significant and life altering (refer to 2 Timothy 3:16-17).

So should we integrate psychology with Christianity? Despite the fact that I earned a doctorate degree in Counseling Psychology and taught various psychology-related courses at a college level, my answer to that question is no. Personally, any time I need advice, feedback, or suggestions, I go straight to the Bible where I find direction, guidance, and wisdom.

Psychology versus the Church

Does psychology belong in the church? I have concluded that psychology has no place in the church. The sad truth is, psychology is not only creeping into the church, it is also assuming the *role* of the church in modern Christianity as well as in society. The reasons for this shift may include the following:

1. Few pastors are educated and/or trained in understanding human behavior.
2. Many pastors drive the sheep away from God.
3. Spiritual damage is being inflicted from within the church.
4. More and more Christian counselors and therapists are beginning to esteem psychology and are integrating it with the Word of God.

The Word of God is known to convict, whereas psychology's goal is to make people feel good, without bringing the accountability factor (sowing what we reap) into the equation (see Galatians 6:7).

In order for an individual to integrate psychology and theology, he or she must believe that the Word of God does not answer all of life's quandaries. When that is true, one is apt to place psychology in the seat of authority. The Christian psychologist is obligated to decide whether or not the Word of God offers a solution for any challenge or problem.

An integrationist may want to know what psychology has to say about a particular issue. For a genuine believer, the order of questioning must be reversed. The first question we should ask is, "What does God say about this situation?" without focusing on any psychological evidence or empirical research.

The issue here is not what seems logical or appears to work. The real concern must be: What is the truth from God's perspective? God often works in ways that contradicts man's thinking in terms of evidence, logic, research, and such.

God is not subject to human reasoning; instead, we are subject to His reasoning. God made this clear when He said, "My thoughts are not your thoughts, nor are your ways My ways" (Isaiah 55:8). Psychology and theology cannot coexist, just as you cannot have both "heads" and "tails" at the same time.

Where should Christians turn for counsel? Christians need to realize that psychology does not provide any new techniques that are not already mentioned or revealed in the Word of God. One author states, "The burden of proof, however, does not lie with the biblical counselor, but with the integrationist" (Bulkley, 1988). So to answer that question, a believer should go to the Word of God and to a certified or licensed counselor who encourages, promotes, and provides biblical (nouthetic) counseling. Psychology neither encourages nor advocates a fear of the Lord; therefore, it is void of wisdom.

The Bible declares, "The fear of the Lord is the beginning of wisdom" (Proverbs 9:10; Psalm 111:10). Psychology says that every human consists of only body and soul, whereas the Bible teaches that every person is comprised of body, soul, and spirit.

Psychology and biblical teaching are miles apart; they are as diverse as night and day. Some examples of their adversity include but are not limited to such subjects as eternity, the Holy Spirit, prayer, seeking God, seeking truth, self-esteem versus a broken and contrite spirit, etc. In each of these areas of life, one can find extremes on both ends of the spectrum when comparing the roles of psychology and theology.

It is time for the church to wake up and deal with the love affair it has with Christian psychology. Sir Francis Bacon, a famous British philosopher, once said, "God hath this attribute, that He is a jealous God; and therefore, His worship and religion, will endure no mixture, nor partner."

The Bible warns us to beware of those who come in sheep's clothing (Matthew 7:15). Too many professing Christians masquerade as shepherds and counselors/therapists. These are the "ravening wolves" about whom the apostle Paul warned so long ago.

The Bible tells us, "Satan himself transforms himself into an angel of light. Therefore, it is no great thing if His ministers also transform themselves into ministers of righteousness, whose end will be according to their works" (2 Corinthians 11:14-15). This passage of Scripture refers to many counselors and even to some preachers.

Blaise Pascal, a well-known French mathematician and physicist, once said, "Unless one loves truth, he is unlikely to know it." There are professing Christians who say they love Jesus, yet they do not love the truth.

Mere lip service to the truth reaps serious consequences. If it is not confessed and repented for, God will give us our heart's desire, just as He allowed Saul to be the king when Israel wanted to be like other nations. As a result, the nation's spiritual problems soon began.

The bottom-line is simply this: psychology has no place in the church, and it must not be integrated with the Word of God. The apostle Paul wrote about a time when people would have itching ears, meaning, they would replace sound doctrine with false teachings and false teachers.

To conclude this section, consider the apostle's question to the Galatians: "Have I therefore become your enemy because I tell you the truth?" (4:16) The only thing we can do with the truth is accept it and not try to hide or run from it. It always finds its way back and catches us off guard.

Psychology versus the Bible

In this section, we will compare psychology and the Word of God in relation to some key issues, including the Bible, God, the Holy Spirit, hope, love, mankind, man's nature, self, self-esteem, and sin. Please keep in mind that when I mention the term *psychology*, I am referring primarily to the three most influential schools of thought:

1. Psychoanalysis, represented by Sigmund Freud, Carl Jung, Alfred Adler, etc.
2. Behaviorism, represented by John Watson, B. F. Skinner, Edward L. Thorndike, etc.
3. Humanism, represented by Carl Rogers, Abraham Maslow, Rollo May, etc.

Since this is neither an academic dictionary nor a psychology textbook, I will not go into great detail regarding each psychologist. However, I will point out a few key comparisons between the Bible and psychology; enough to help the reader see with certainty that, unlike psychology, the Bible shows genuine care, concern, and love for each individual.

The following list describes the biblical approach to various terms and concepts as opposed to psychology's assessment of each subject. One might title this section, "The Word of God versus the Words of Men" or "Wisdom versus Foolishness."

God: all-knowing, all-powerful, everywhere present, wise, holy, and loving,
   Versus a god that is either nonexistent or plays a minor role, if any.

The Word of God: the Bible, God's written Word (2 Timothy 3:16-17),
   Versus the words of men and the norms of society.

Jesus: Son of God, Son of Man, part of the Holy Trinity, Lord and Savior, loving, kind, compassionate, graceful, merciful, and forgiving,
   Versus either a nonexistent savior or one who plays a minor role, if any.

Holy Spirit: third person of the Holy Trinity, leads us into all truth, sharper than a two-edged sword dividing even the soul from spirit,
   Versus a denial that the Holy Spirit exists.

Mankind: created in God's image, consisting of body, soul, and spirit (1 Thessalonians 5:23), precious in God's sight,
   Versus the idea that man is a creature of evolution, made up of body, mind, personality, and soul.

Man's Nature: essentially sinful, responsible for his sin, a spiritual being,
   Versus the belief that man is not responsible for his actions, not a sinner, is essentially good, a social animal, a god in his own universe.

Self: loving self is mankind's problem, offered to drink the waters of life freely, commanded to deny self and take up the cross,

Versus the view that loving self is mankind's solution, water of life comes with a price, encouraged to celebrate self.

Self-Esteem: the Bible urges us to humble ourselves, treat others better than ourselves, and maintain a broken and contrite spirit,
> Versus self-esteem being elevated to "pedestal status," humility is discouraged, and being proud of oneself is promoted.

Sin: everyone is a sinner, individuals are to confess, repent, and ask for forgiveness for their sins,
> Versus everyone being considered a victim; therefore, there is no need to confess and repent, and counselees are led to blame either their past and/or others for their problems.

Love: Understanding that God loves everyone, sent His Son Jesus to die for sins, and offers mankind an eternal destiny,
> Versus man being encouraged to love himself, look out for number one, and disregard the thought of an eternal destiny.

Hope: found in Christ, through Him man promised an eternal destiny,
> Versus man being offered no hope for eternity; all hope rests in man's hands.

Behavior: bad behavior flows out of a sinful heart, it exists because man's heart is deceitful and desperately wicked (Jeremiah 17:9), rebellious, bad personal choices,
> Versus culture, environment, past, power drive, and sex being seen as contributing factors to behavior patterns.

Fear of God: fear of the Lord is the beginning of wisdom (Psalm 111:10),
> Versus no counsel to fear the Lord at any time.

Goal/Priority: seek first the kingdom of God (Matthew 6:33) and glorify God,
> Versus seeking God and His kingdom never advised or promoted, being able to adjust to fellow man is primary goal.

Counseling: warned against seeking counsel among the ungodly (Psalm 1:1),
Versus encouragement to seek counsel from the ungodly.

The Danger of Integration

The idea of integrating psychology with Christian biblical counseling is wrong. I can think of at least two reasons (there may be more) why anyone would want to integrate these two fields:

1. Some people are not convinced that the Word of God can solve all of man's problems in life.
2. Others are curious enough to try something new in an effort to solve mankind's problems.

When we turn away from the Word of God and lean toward the words of men, we are entertaining and inviting a "corrupt mind," and in doing so, we run the risk of losing our identity in Christ.

We are living in an age (end-times) when conflict, emotional and mental strain, and stress abound. Many people prefer to seek instant relief, and psychology seems to promise that immediate solution.

We must avoid the concept of integration because it does not mix with the Bible. Instead, it relies on human reasoning as opposed to God's revelation. It has little or no spiritual and theological base or foundation and fails to accept and recognize the importance and value of God's Word for everyday living.

Conclusion

Some Christian integrationists lean on the field of psychology for several reasons:

1. Many integrationists believe the Bible does not cover or include human problems; they conclude that the Bible was

not written as a self-help or question-answer format covering every possible human condition.
2. Others argue that the Bible is not an appropriate substitute for a counseling textbook, which seems to offer counseling techniques or problem-solving techniques.
3. There are those who strongly believe that the Bible was not written to address contemporary issues, such as which college to attend, what person to marry, or which automobile to buy. The reason why the Bible does not give these kinds of specifics is because God wants us to be responsible and use our minds, common sense, experience, and wisdom by exercising free will.

God created us as human beings and not as robots. As humans, we exercise the right to think, feel, act, decide, and so on. Dr. Bulkley points out that the Bible presents life principles which, if followed, will provide the answers for every human problem.

I also believe that integrating psychology with biblical counseling is unscriptural and ungodly. Enough evidence and facts have been presented to confirm and justify this opinion and also in defense of Christ-centered counseling.

The Bible is inspired by almighty God, whereas psychology was invented by sinful men. Integrating these two fields is out of the question because they represent two contradictory views on basic tenets, such as God, the Bible, eternity, man, sin, salvation, and so on. Too many churches, Christian colleges, seminaries, counselors, and pastors have compromised God's Word by adopting and yielding to integration and eventually supporting the integrationists.

Rev. Raja Sekhar Vemuri, Ph.D., Th.D.

Christian Counseling

Introduction

There is a difference between biblical and Christian counseling. Though Christian counseling seems to incorporate psychology with theology (the Word of God), not all Christian counselors try to blend the two.

One author states that, "Denver Seminary, Talbot Seminary, Trinity Evangelical Divinity School, Liberty University, Moody Bible Institute, Fuller Theological Seminary, and a host of other Christian schools are convinced that psychology and the Bible must be integrated in counseling if the church is to remain relevant to our contemporary culture" (Bulkley, 93).

I prefer the practice of biblical counseling, also sometimes referred to as nouthetic counseling. The word *nouthetic* comes from the Greek term *noutheteo*, meaning, "to admonish or warn." It is a form of counseling that uses biblical principles to treat psychological problems and views and treats psychological disorders as spiritual problems. Nouthetic counseling was developed by Jay E. Adams and was introduced in 1970 in his book *Competent To Counsel*.

Many different counseling terms are in use today, including the following:

- biblical counseling
- Christian counseling
- Christian psychology
- nouthetic counseling
- religious counseling

Personally, I prefer to use the term *Christ-centered counseling*, which adheres strictly to the Word of God to treat all psychology-related problems.

One may ask if psychology is even needed today. In biblical times, psychologists were nonexistent, yet counseling needs were met. Since the apostle Paul wrote thirteen epistles, which accounts for almost one-half of the New Testament, let us examine how he counseled people in his day.

First, he encouraged his readers to trust Jesus and warned them to beware of "hollow and deceptive" teaching (see Colossians 1:28; 2:8). In his second letter to the Corinthians, Paul explained how a person can experience genuine change: the Holy Spirit must act on his or her heart, resulting in the formation of a "new creation" (5:17).

Biblical Foundation for Counseling

People expect to receive the best and the most for what they pay. A well-known expression in this regard says, "I want to get my money's worth." The hourly counseling fee with most licensed professional counselors (LPC) at a doctorate level begins at about $75. Christian counselors, Christian psychologists, and so on, do not and cannot always guarantee to offer counsel that is strictly scriptural.

There seems to be a universal confusion about Christian counseling in today's church. Many counselors and psychologists claim to be Christians and their counseling methods to be biblical. The truth is, these so-called Christian counselors use secular psychological theories of human behavior rather than depending and relying on God's Word.

With so much confusion and misrepresentation in the name of Christian or biblical counseling, how can we know what to look for and whom to believe? If a counselor, minister, or pastor is offering genuine scriptural counseling, look for the following clear and specific signs:

1. First, determine the counselor's stand regarding the absolute sovereignty of God. A biblical counselor must uphold the sovereign power of God. He or she must believe that God created all things and knows everything: "Known to God

from eternity are all His works" (Acts 15:18). Because He is sovereign, God has the ability to change and heal people.
2. The counselor must believe in John 14:6: "[Jesus said,] I am the way, the truth, and the life. No one comes to the Father except through Me." Jesus is the answer to every problem we humans face (See 2 Peter 1:3; Hebrews 2:17-18; 4:14-16 for further assurance and confirmation.)
3. A biblical counselor must believe in the ultimate authority of the Scriptures. The Bible, we are told, "is God's inspired, infallible, and inerrant Word to man" (Chung, 2011). (Refer to 2 Timothy 3:16.)

Authors Walter and Stephanie Chung add three more characteristics (or signs) of genuine biblical counseling: redemption-oriented, church accountability, and Bible-defined competence.

It is one thing to have the knowledge of Scripture (a head issue) and yet another thing to have conviction (a heart issue) that God's Word is sufficient enough to handle all our needs. In this context, the saying, "garbage-in and garbage-out," means secular counseling can only lead to a secular gospel, which always focuses on self and is not of God. The focus at all times should be on God and not on man, as John the Baptist confirmed when he said of Jesus, "He must increase, but I must decrease" (John 3:30).

God's Way for Lasting Change

Psychology to a lesser extent may bring about some changes or improvement. However, these changes or improvements can be temporary, not to mention that they rely on human strength and wisdom to achieve them. If we rely on our own strength and wisdom, what is the meaning of 2 Corinthians 5:17: "If anyone is in Christ, he is a new creation; old things have passed away; behold, all things have become new"?

On the flip side, let us look at what God has promised in order to help us change for the better. In the book of Ezekiel we read: "Then I will give them one heart, and I will put a new spirit within them, and take the stony heart out of their flesh, and give them a heart of flesh" (11:19). Contrary to secular counseling, the Word of God not only offers wisdom, it also promises to make the change permanent through the power of the Holy Spirit. Of course, we may choose to rebel against any such advice or comfort He so freely provides.

The Ezekiel 11 passage quoted above describes total (not partial or temporary) transformation. Psychology can offer only a short-lived treatment, if at all. However, the Bible provides genuine hope and offers a lasting change, provided we believe and stick to it. If psychology has all the answers, Christ's resurrection was in vain.

What does the Bible say about a lasting change in our lives? There are certain steps we can take to bring about a permanent transformation. A majority of the content material that follows is based on 2 Timothy 3:16-17: "All Scripture *is* given by inspiration of God, and *is* profitable for doctrine, for reproof, for correction, for instruction in righteousness, that the man of God may be complete, thoroughly equipped for every good work" (emphasis added).

- ▶ The first step deals with the issue of "correction." What are we correcting? Anything that is an error or false teaching. In other words, we are correcting (replacing or substituting) false teaching, irrational thoughts, wrong ideas, etc. with that which is of God. Change does not come easy because we are by nature creatures of habit, and habits are hard to break.

Correction starts when an individual accepts Jesus Christ as his or her Lord and Savior. Genuine change or correction can be experienced only when an individual is born-again. A counselor often tries to help the counselee change outward behavior by addressing symptoms; however, the Holy Spirit effects inward transformation.

- ▶ The second step focuses on the Holy Spirit, whom the Bible refers to as the Comforter. Some people try to change by pushing their limits in the flesh. If one depends on his own strength and wisdom, he will fail. Genuine change comes from the Holy Spirit at work in us and not by our own effort (see 2 Corinthians 3:18).

An individual experiences genuine change as he maintains a deep and intimate relationship with God. The more time he spends reading God's Word and in prayer, the more he will begin to understand His love, grace, mercy, and will.

Change does not happen overnight, and there are no shortcuts. We may sin from time to time, and until we are delivered from it, we need to follow 1 John 1:9: "If we confess our sins, He is faithful and just to forgive us our sins and to cleanse us from all unrighteousness."

- ▶ Step 3 deals with teaching ourselves and following what is right before God. This step focuses on a struggle with two natures: the old and the new. The apostle Paul explains this tug-of-war in his letter to the Romans: "For the good that I will to do, I do not do; but the evil I will not to do, that I practice" (7:19).

We must learn to "die to self" daily. The old nature looks for complaints and excuses, but the new nature focuses on being right before God, and there is no room for excuses. The old nature focuses on "earthly things" (Philippians 3:19), whereas the new nature dwells on the matters of truth, because only "the truth shall set us free" (John 8:32).

- ▶ The fourth step spotlights integrity. It is crucial that we live honest lives: "He who walks with integrity walks securely" (Proverbs 10:9). We are to examine our thoughts and learn to search our hearts. King David understood the importance of this step: "Search me, O God, and know my heart; Try me, and know my anxieties; And see if there is any wicked way in me, And lead me in the way everlasting" (Psalm 139:23-24).

- Step five focuses on motivation. Change for many people comes through guilt (pressure) or because of selfish desires. For instance, a smoker who feels guilty may consider buying a "nicotine patch" to help him break the habit. It seems to work for awhile, and then he is back at his old habits again. But why? The patch was bought as a result of feeling guilty and not because of a desire for genuine change. Remember: Satan condemns, but God convicts.

Change for selfish reasons is often short-lived because the motivation behind that kind of improvement is the acceptance of others as opposed to a true, inward change wrought by the Holy Spirit. If you want to be wise, learn to fear God (see Psalm 111:10).

- Step six confronts sin head-on. There is a saying: "When you are right, you are right; and when you are wrong, you are wrong." When dealing with the truth, there are no shortcuts. Truth must be told, dealt with, received, followed, and shared.

Confronting sin does not mean rebuking someone else. Rather, we must examine our own hearts. Some people are quick to judge others, and one way they do this is by telling them why and how they have sinned. The Bible calls this hypocrisy (see Matthew 7:5).

If the Lord directs us to confront (or rebuke) a sin in others' lives, we must do so at the right time and then only in love. We all know the story of David and his lust for Bathsheba, which led him eventually to kill her husband, Uriah. Nathan confronted David about his sin (see 2 Samuel 12:7, 9). David received Nathan's rebuke as though it came from God because he loved God and was referred to as a man after God's own heart. After he received the rebuke, David immediately repented.

Any person who truly wants to change will receive rebuke with thankfulness because it will make him or her a better child of God. Psalm 141:5 confirms David's willingness to receive Nathan's rebuke.

- ▶ The seventh step deals with spiritual transparency. An X-ray reveals what is put in front of it. In a sense, there is also a spiritual X-ray. According to the Bible, the tongue represents one's heart and soul. Jesus made this clear in Luke's gospel (see 6:45).

Another Scripture passage that emphasizes the tongue is James 3:2-12. Here the writer tells us that in order to control our lives we must learn to control our tongues. I have observed how the tongue can affect an individual in almost every area of life: career, employment, friendships, marriages, and so on.

- ▶ Step number eight in our journey toward lasting change focuses on sound doctrine—what we trust in and obey. What we believe is crucial because our faith influences both our thoughts and our actions. We may not be what we eat, but we surely are what we believe.

Any person who professes to be born-again should have a thorough working knowledge of the Word of God. This familiarity will not only help him live a better life spiritually, it will also help him teach others who may be confused about what the Bible says regarding important issues of life.

Dr. Bulkley points out that "spiritual growth, developing maturity in Christ, and personal change require accurate doctrine" (Bulkley, 93). Another benefit of knowing the Bible is that God often speaks to us through His Word.

The Change Process, Utilizing God's Power

The God of the Bible is all-powerful (omnipotent): "God has spoken once, twice I have heard this: that power belongs to God" (Psalm 62:11). I know from experience that God's power can work in our lives, not every now and then but daily.

In today's world, "most people want to succeed in some area: business, family, relationships, music, athletics, politics, education, etc." (Pratte, 2005). While their intentions may be good, the motivation behind their pursuits may be self-centered and not necessarily Christ-centered. God promised Joshua that he too could succeed in life if he learned how to serve God (see Joshua 1:7-8).

We can apply God's power (His blessings) to keep our change process positive, productive, and perhaps long lasting. But what power does God make available to us so we can accept, believe, receive, and put it in action? We can have the power:

- To know and believe the truth (Romans 1:16; 10:17)
- To become a child of God (John 1:12)
- To resist the Devil (James 4:7)
- To overcome every temptation (1 Corinthians 10:13)
- To withstand hardship and suffering (Romans 8:31-39)
- To confess our faults to one another (James 5:16)
- To serve and teach others (2 Timothy 2:2)
- To receive eternal life (John 3:16).

The Bible also tells us which methods to use in order to experience and receive all God has for us. These methods include but are not limited to: His love, His Word, His nature, His precious blood, His children (other believers), and so on. God changes our lives by His power. Because of that, we are no longer the same; we are "new creatures," ready and willing to serve Him and others.

Conclusion

Chapters 9 and 10 have given some important insight and knowledge about psychology, along with its lies, misconceptions, and myths. With this new understanding, perhaps those who have been leaning toward psychology and its so-called expertise will reconsider and redirect their path toward biblical or Christ-centered counseling.

It is one thing to want to define psychology in terms of what it teaches; it is another thing to trust in it without realizing the spiritual damage it can do. One author notes:

> When the whole counsel of God is not taught, the portion of truth that is taught may be emphasized to the point where error creeps in. The Bible is a book of history, a book of prophecy, a book of promise to help in time of need, and the book on soul-winning; but it is so much more than that: It is the book of life (Solomon, 1993).

So true. The Bible speaks truth, and truth can stand on its own. One cannot say that for psychology.

The Bible has all the answers and solutions we need, with the exception of physical and/or medical needs, such as diagnoses, surgeries, and prescription medications.

The Bible encourages us to "seek first the kingdom of God and His righteousness" (Matthew 6:33) and leave the rest in His hands by trusting Him. We are to always do the best we know how, as unto the Lord. We develop patience by waiting on the Lord and whatever He has for us, which we need to receive with thanksgiving, even if it may not go the way we prefer or want.

Chapter Eleven

The Accountability Factor

Sin and Its Consequences

Introduction

This chapter focuses on the principle of sowing and reaping. There is much confusion about forgiveness and its relation to sin and its consequences. Many individuals have asked me to explain why a forgiving God would actually take time to teach us lessons, all in the name of correction and discipline.

It is true that God forgives each time we ask. But He is also a holy, just, and righteous God who deals with sin however He deems appropriate. He does everything in our best interest because He loves us.

The following Scripture verses pertain to the issues of sin, consequences, and forgiveness. Refer to these passages for a greater understanding of the topic: Proverbs 3:12; Matthew 18:21-22; Galatians 6:7; and Hebrews 12:6-7.

We live in a world laden with chaos, distress, emotional turmoil, fear, and temptations. I can think of at least two steps you must follow in dealing with ungodly influences:

1. Go before the Lord in prayer, confess, and repent. Just as King David did time and time again, you can plead for God's

forgiveness, grace, and mercy. David asked the Lord to search his heart and to cleanse him (see Psalm 139:23-24).

2. Choose prayer partners—individuals you can trust and with whom you can share your heart's desire as well as your thoughts. Select partners who show genuine compassion and love, people who will not judge you once the truth is revealed.

Your prayer team might include a spouse, children, parents, grandparents, pastor, friends, employer, colleagues, and extended family members, such as siblings, aunts, cousins, and uncles.

It is always good to have a brother or sister in the Lord to whom you can be accountable when you are faced with temptations. Sadly, that was not the case during King David's temptation and ultimate sin with Bathsheba. He was alone when Satan tempted him with her physical beauty, and he allowed lust to get the upper hand (see 2 Samuel 11).

Though the incident with Bathsheba appears to have been "of the flesh," it actually involved much more than that. The apostle Paul confirmed this fact in his epistle to the Ephesians: "We do not wrestle against flesh and blood, but against principalities, against powers, against the rulers of the darkness of this age, against spiritual hosts of wickedness in the heavenly places" (6:12).

Having a Christian accountability partner has many advantages and benefits. The following biblical activities will help you focus on the "one another" factor:

- Confess faults to one another
- Pray for one another
- Encourage one another
- Love one another
- Learn from and teach one other (see Proverbs 27:17)

Sowing and Reaping

Present circumstances are often the result of past thoughts and actions. Likewise, today's thoughts and actions are seeds you are sowing for a future harvest. As a matter of fact, one's entire life operates on the principles of accountability and sowing and reaping. That being true, you must know, learn, and understand these codes.

We tend to lose sight of the principle of sowing and reaping, inevitably either blaming God or Satan for our sins. The truth is, we are to blame ourselves and must be held accountable for the choices and decisions we make, all in the name of exercising free will.

Regardless of what may or may not happen to us, three characters—God, Satan, and self—play major roles in our lives, albeit in different proportions. Of course, other performers also play significant parts. These include family members, friends, extended relatives, church family, coworkers, and even strangers. I group all of these in the "self category," which I will explain later.

As we examine each of these three characters, we will discover how they influence our day-to-day life. Knowing this information will help us understand the principles of accountability and sowing and reaping.

1. God

Few people consider that what is happening presently in their life may be the result of God's plan and will for them at that moment.

Job is an excellent example. Though he feared and loved God, Job suffered persecution, testing, trials, and tribulations. He lost his children, property, and his health. Even his character was questioned.

Job had done nothing wrong, yet he suffered unjustly because God allowed it as a way of making Satan understand that Job would trust God regardless of what happened. In Job 19, we read Job's statement of faith in his Redeemer: "For I know that my Redeemer lives, And He shall stand at last on the earth; And after my skin is destroyed, this I know, That in my flesh I shall see God" (vv. 25-26). God is known to take matters into His own hands to shape us into better persons.

2. Satan

Many churches inadvertently teach their members to blame Satan for unrighteousness instead of taking personal responsibility for their sins. That is a cop-out.

The Bible cautions us to "be sober, be vigilant; because your adversary the devil walks about like a roaring lion, seeking whom he may devour" (1 Peter 5:8). This Scripture verse is often misquoted and taken out of its proper context.

I believe the only way anything adverse can happen to us is for God to allow it (as in Job's case) or we choose to yield to Satan for whatever reasons. Yet Satan can do nothing on his own. Either God gives him permission or we surrender to him out of temptation or selfish desires. Satan tried three times to undermine Jesus' authority and power in the wilderness. However, Jesus firmly resisted and prevailed. By quoting the Scriptures, He put Satan in his place (see Matthew 4:1-11).

Assume for a moment that Satan is free to do whatever he pleases. Even then, God provides a solution: "No temptation has overtaken you except such as is common to man; but God is faithful, who will not allow you to be tempted beyond what you are able, but with the temptation will also make the way of escape, that you may be able to bear it" (1 Corinthians 10:13).

In addition to the promise quoted above, God equips us with the authority and power to rebuke the Devil: "Resist the devil and he will flee from you" (James 4:7). The question remains: Do you want to resist, or do you want to surrender?

We need to realize that God not only knows the number of hairs on your head (Matthew 10:30; Luke 12:7), He also has full knowledge of everything and everyone (see Matthew 10:29).

3. Self

God not only provides a way out of every situation, He has promised never to give us more than we can handle. We have also established that we have God-given authority and power to rebuke and resist our adversary, Satan. What then is the problem?

The difficulty lies within ourselves. No need to complain, blame God, or credit Satan for every misstep. As stated earlier, Satan is helpless to do anything on his own unless either God permits it or we allow it.

In the book of Romans, the apostle Paul challenges us in the form of a question: "If God is for us, who can be against us?" (8:31). Once again, we are primarily to blame for our struggles. Yet in the long run, our free will somehow becomes part of God's will.

As a way of explanation, consider the following principles of sowing and reaping:

   1. *We sow what we reap* (see Galatians 6:7). This is similar to the concept of "an eye for an eye and a tooth for a tooth." This is how it works: If you sow gossip, you will reap gossip; if you bad-mouth someone, someone is apt to slander you. If you sow generosity, you will reap the rewards of that giving.

   Our present set of circumstances is often a collection (or sum) of all we have said and done in the past. Likewise, what we sow today will affect the future. We are responsible for our actions, deeds, and thoughts. No point in blaming God, Satan, or anyone else, and no point in presenting lame excuses or trying to find an easy way out.

We are cautioned not to follow the eye-for-an-eye concept, but God is free to practice it if He so chooses. Being God, He is always right and knows what He is doing with both the saved and the unsaved. God said to Moses, "I will have mercy on whomever I will have mercy, and I will have compassion on whomever I will have compassion" (Romans 9:15).

2. *A harvest is inevitable.* Each time you sow, you surely will reap. And the harvest's productivity is entirely up to the Lord. For instance, your pastor sows precious seed each time he declares God's Word; the result of that preaching—the lives transformed and matured—is the work of Holy Spirit.

3. *Productivity may vary.* The output resulting from the sowing and the reaping likely will not be in equal proportions. In fact, you may reap more than you sowed. In the book of Matthew, we read, "But others [seeds] fell on good ground and yielded a crop: some a hundredfold, some sixty, some thirty" (13:8).

4. *You reap proportionally to how you sow.* You determine the outcome of the harvest at the time of planting, which means you likely will reap in proportion to what you plant. Scripture verses that confirm this concept are 2 Corinthians 9:6-11 and Psalm 126:5-6.

5. *You sow in faith and in patience* (refer to James 5:7-8). For instance, you are led to witness to an unsaved loved one—a spouse, parent, child, grandparent, or sibling. You do your best to exhibit patience and maintain your faith that someday that individual will come to the saving grace and knowledge of Jesus Christ.

6. *Sometimes you sow and someone else reaps.* This works for the positive as well as the negative. On the positive side, a wealthy person dies and leaves his or her inheritance for you to reap based on what he or she has sown. On the negative side, a

child dies (auto accident, AIDS, gunshot, war, etc.) as a result of what someone else sows (see John 4:37-38).

7. *You may sow in secret and yet reap openly and publicly.* For instance, you pray and sometimes fast, seeking God's will for others. These persons may not even know you are interceding for them, but our heavenly Father knows and sees it (see Matthew 6:4).

8. *You reap later than you sow.* Seeds often take time to be harvested. We may work two or three weeks before receiving our wages. Neither successful nor disastrous marriages happen overnight. In other words, reaping does not always take place immediately. There is a time and season for everything (see Ecclesiastes 3:1).

9. *You may not reap in kind what you sow.* It is possible that you will reap the opposite of what you sow. The prophet Jeremiah confirms this principle: "They have sown wheat but reaped thorns" (Jeremiah 12:13).

For instance, parents may do everything in their power to set their children on the right path. Yet a rebellious child can choose the company of wayward peers and may even become involved in criminal activities. In other words, an enemy can destroy the good we have sown.

Our Treasure and Our Heart

The human heart is an important and interesting issue that God takes seriously. To underscore its significance, take a few minutes to examine some Scripture verses that should convince even doubters and skeptics. Read 1 Samuel 16:7; Psalm 101:5; and Proverbs 4:23; 6:18.

From God's perspective, the heart is the core of our being. When a person is born again, God gives him or her a new heart (2 Corinthians 5:17).

Occasionally, we hear someone try to justify a barb or sharp retort by giving the excuse, "I was just kidding." They usually say that only after discovering that what they said was hurtful or offensive, and instead of apologizing, they offer that pretext. Whether they were kidding or not is between them and God, but the Bible reveals the wellspring out of which our conversations flow: "Out of the abundance of the heart the mouth speaks" (Matthew 12:34; Luke 6:45).

A direct correlation exists between one's heart and those things he or she values. If you want to read a person's heart, discover and understand his or her treasure. I once heard someone say we are known by the company we keep. This is another way of saying, "Show me your friends and I will tell you the type of person you are." Likewise, show me what you treasure, and I will tell you the condition of your heart.

As believers in Christ, we must ask ourselves what we prize and if it lines up with the Word of God. Our heart affects, controls, and influences our very lives; in other words, it is the driving force behind our attitudes, thoughts, actions, and words. In addition to the treasure, the heart is also closely related to the mind, where thoughts originate.

Speaking of thoughts, the apostle Paul cautioned the Corinthian believers to bring "every thought into captivity to the obedience of Christ" (2 Corinthians 10:5). This Scripture verse is a companion to Philippians 4:8, which in essence encourages us to think only about what is good and of God. Positive, productive, and godly thoughts will shape our heart's affections and desires.

Though the entire Bible is precious, I tend to read certain books, including the Psalms, again and again. One of my favorite passages is Psalm 119:11, which focuses on the heart: "Your Word I have hidden in my heart, that I might not sin against You."

Treasures can vary from person to person and can include such things as assets, career, education, financial status, gadgets, home, material possessions, money, power, status, and wealth (which seems to be the common denominator for many). Speaking about money, one author strongly suggests that every Christian get to know five Bible verses that have revolutionized his financial life: Proverbs 22:7; Malachi 3:10; Acts 20:35; Philippians 4:19; and 1 Timothy 6:10 (Lotich, 2008).

We must be careful where we lay our treasures here on Earth. Matthew 6, which focuses primarily on our relationship with God the Father, describes some of the benefits of laying up of treasures in heaven (6:19-21). In that chapter, Jesus explains that a person's heart follows what he treasures. As His disciples, our hearts should cherish Jesus, who is the real treasure.

Conclusion

A foolproof measure of what one treasures is the amount of effort, energy, money, resources, and time he or she spends on particular endeavors. These factors are clear indicators of where one's heart is focused. Likewise, if we treasure our faith and love for God, we will plant God's Word into our hearts and invest in His kingdom. The stronger our faith, the more we talk about God, His love, and His Word.

Chapter Twelve

The Best Things in Life are Still Free

Areas to Focus On

Introduction

This chapter defines eleven attributes or actions that can bring happiness, joy, and peace in our lives and in the lives of those who cross our paths directly and indirectly. Each of these attributes can and will produce positive and productive change, but just imagine the level of maturity possible if we were to make all eleven a major part of our day-to-day living.

The good news is that they are all free; there is no price tag attached, nor should there be. Though some people abuse or misuse to con, control, dominate, or manipulate to get what they need or want, the best things in life will always be free.

We tend to use these attributes to earn some trust, but keep in mind it is easy to be hurt by those we trust and to hurt those who trust us. God desires that we use these traits to make a difference in our lives and not to use them to benefit us in a manner that does not honor God.

Compassion

The term *compassion* is subject to individual interpretation. Personally, I define it as showing empathy, sympathy, and having pity. We serve a God who is full of compassion (Psalm 86:15; Lamentations 3:22).

Jesus demonstrated compassion so often that even death, evil spirits, and nature were motivated and moved by it. Jesus took on all of His Father's attributes, character, and nature, especially compassion, forgiveness, and love. The Bible says Jesus was moved with compassion with regard to feeding the hungry, healing a leprous man, restoring paralyzed individuals, raising Jairus' daughter and Lazarus from the dead, and weeping at the tomb of His good friend Lazarus.

To show genuine compassion means to love someone sincerely. Jesus defined the two greatest commands as loving "the Lord your God with all your heart, with all your soul, and with all your mind" and loving "your neighbor as yourself" (Matthew 22:37-40). That is how important it is to practice compassion. And showing compassion has many spiritual benefits:

- It helps build patience.
- It demonstrates genuine care and concern.
- It shows true love and spiritual maturity.

Simply put, compassion goes beyond words.

Encouragement

Encouragement, also referred to as edification or exhortation, means to build or lift someone up. Almost all of us need to be encouraged from time to time. It does not take much to become discouraged, especially in these last days when persecutions, stress, tests, trials, and tribulations abound.

In his letter to the Christians in Rome, the apostle Paul lists encouragement as one of the spiritual gifts: "Having then gifts differing according to the grace that is given to us, let us use them: . . . he who exhorts [encourages], in exhortation; he who gives, with liberality; he who leads, with diligence; he who shows mercy, with cheerfulness" (12:6-8).

Encouragement comes to us by many different avenues:

- remembering God's faithfulness
- the examples of others
- words spoken by others
- recognizing the eternal destiny and hope offered by God
- through God's creation (animal and human)
- God's nature (forests, mountains, seas, etc.)

Prior to leaving the earth, Jesus promised to send another Helper or Comforter (speaking of the Holy Spirit). Along with directing us into all truth (John 14:16, 26; 15:26), encouragement is one of His many works.

Encouragement is an important tool that can be used in numerous settings. It is beneficial in counseling, discipleship, mentoring, parenting, preaching, teaching, and so on. With proper encouragement, an individual may change his or her thought processes and begin to make decisions that are acceptable to God.

When we encourage others, we are also helping them reinforce their faith. The Bible gives an example of a man named Barnabas, who was described as "the son of encouragement" (Acts 4:36). Barnabas exhorted the believers to continue in their faith and in the grace of God (see Acts 13:43).

In Acts 15, we learn about a disagreement that arose between the apostle Paul and his ministry partner, Barnabas. The dispute was over a young man named John Mark (John called Mark) and his involvement in their ministry. John Mark had deserted Paul and Barnabas earlier, which discouraged Paul from taking him with them. But Barnabas opted in favor of including John Mark in the ministry (Acts 15:36-41). Barnabas encouraged Paul to give John Mark a second chance, and the Scripture tells us that John Mark proved himself faithful.

Faith

What is faith? The Bible defines the concept perfectly: "Faith is the substance of things hoped for, the evidence of things not seen" (Hebrews 11:1). Faith is essential and plays a pivotal role in our relationship with God.

We are lost without faith because "without faith, it is impossible to please God" (Hebrews 11:6). Whatever we try to do in our own strength and wisdom may fall short because it lacks the spiritual dimension and element of relying on God. In John's gospel, we read, "Without Me, you can do nothing" (14:5).

In our tendency toward perfectionism, we have a propensity to beat up on ourselves when we "drop the ball." Each time we fail and fall, we doubt ourselves and wonder if we had maintained enough faith.

But how much is *enough* faith? By whose standards is it judged as lacking or sufficient? What does God say about it? How much faith does He expect from us? Actually, we do not need an abundance of faith (even though it would be nice). Jesus answered this concern when He said: "If you have faith as a mustard seed, you can say to this mountain, move from here to there, and it will move" (Matthew 17:20; Luke 17:7).

Where does faith originate? It must come from God. It is not innate, nor is it something we can buy, borrow, or sell. We do not create or conjure faith, nor can we achieve or attain it by reading about it. Simply put, faith is a gift from God (Ephesians 2:8-9).

God gives faith to those who are open to receive it and have a desire to seek it. It is not given because we deserve it, earned it, or asked for it. We are not worthy of it, and yet God gives it as a free gift. Faith also "comes by hearing and hearing by the Word of God" (Romans 10:17).

Why should we have faith? Because God expects us to be faithful as He is faithful. Faith also sets apart those who belong to Him as opposed to those who do not. For instance, an individual who does not believe in or care about God has no need to be faithful other than believe in his or her own strength and wisdom.

Faith pleases God and brings us closer to Him. The closer and more intimate we are with God, the more He can use us to bless others. It is an awesome thing to be used of God. Faith along with hope and love can help us get there.

Forgiveness

The dictionary defines *forgiveness* as "the act of excusing a mistake or offense; compassionate feelings that support a willingness to forgive." Some synonyms for forgiveness are *benignity*, *kindness*, *mercifulness*, *mercy*, and *pardon*.

When we forgive others (and even ourselves), we let go of all anger, bitterness, and resentment. Forgiveness can be classified in two categories: God's forgiveness and human forgiveness. God takes the issue of forgiveness personal.

In the chapter on prayer, I mentioned that unforgiveness is one of the key reasons why God may not answer our prayers. It is a serious spiritual offense that hinders many areas of our lives, including blessings, spiritual maturity, and God's will, to name a few.

Forgiveness is difficult for most of us. Everyone has his or her own reasons for withholding pardon, but I believe pride or self-righteousness is why most people opt not to forgive. Other reasons may include abuse, betrayal, fear, guilt, rejection, self-defense, and so on.

Extending clemency is a choice we must exercise and is not just a "state of being or mind." God expects us to choose to forgive. In fact, we are commanded to bear "with one another, and [forgive] one another" (Colossians 3:13). The Bible also instructs us to forgive just as the Lord has forgiven us. This reminds me of Jesus' instruction to His twelve disciples: "Freely you have received, freely give" (Matthew 10:8).

Another element—forgetting—is closely associated or partnered with forgiveness. Some people profess to have dismissed a grievance, yet they do not let it go because they choose to remember it. As children of the Most High, forgiving and forgetting should be our desire and goal. Another way of saying it is "Let go, and let God."

Forgiveness is complete only when we turn loose of the matter for good and allow no arguments, emotions, or feelings to bring it back to our remembrance. If we continue to ruminate on the issue, we have not really forgiven to begin with.

Corrie Ten Boom, a Christian woman who survived a Nazi concentration camp during the Holocaust, once said, "Forgiveness is setting a prisoner free, and realizing the prisoner is you." Wow! That is a profound statement. But forgiveness does not always come at a moment's notice. It is generally a slow, time-consuming, action-oriented process.

The Bible contains numerous verses on forgiveness, but the one to which I most closely relate is Jesus' answer to Simon Peter's question: "'Lord, how often shall my brother sin against me and I forgive him? Up to seven times?' Jesus said to him, 'I do not say to you, up to seven times, but up to seventy times seven'" (Matthew 18:21-22).

I believe forgiveness elicits at least two important blessings: freedom and healing. These benefits are so awesome and far-reaching that they are worth forgiving anyone of anything. Choosing not to forgive does us more harm spiritually than the other person because it ruins our daily relationship and walk with God, which in turn affects every other aspect of our lives.

To conclude this section, consider an important encouragement and instruction from the Lord Himself regarding His position on forgiving others: "Leave your gift there before the altar, and go your way. First be reconciled to your brother, and then come and offer your gift" (Matthew 5:24; Mark 11:25).

Grace

Grace, a characteristic of God's awesome nature, is mentioned about 170 times in the Bible. The dictionary defines the term as "the free and unmerited favor or beneficence of God; God's grace is manifested in the salvation of sinners." According to one author, "True grace is given freely, liberally, personally, voluntarily, and cheerfully. Grace is the unmerited, undeserved, unpaid, unexpected, unselfish, non-owned, non-compulsive, non-pressured favor of God" (Weber, 2008). God gives us grace, and we in turn share that grace with others. As we have received the gift, we give it freely: "Freely you have received, freely give" (Matthew 10:8).

Giving is a major component of grace. When we are led to give and when we choose to give, we must make sure it is done unexpectedly and unselfishly. In other words, we give unconditionally, which is how we show the attributes of our Savior in our giving. It is always a great feeling and a true joy when we give.

In the book of Acts we read, "It is more blessed to give than to receive" (20:35). We should never grandstand our giving (Matthew 6:3). I mentioned earlier that much of how we share and show grace is in giving. Giving what? Whatever we can afford and whatever the need may be at the time.

You may have heard the expression that the Old Testament fulfills the law and the New Testament is bound by grace. That is true because Jesus made that possible for us by reconciling the lost and sinful humanity to God. Without God's grace, no one would be able to live in eternity with Him.

In his gospel account, John helps us understand the concept of law and grace: "The law was given through Moses, but grace and truth came through Jesus Christ" (1:17). But that does not mean we forsake and ignore the law. We are thankful for grace, but we also accept and respect the law, which Jesus speaks clearly about in the gospel of Matthew: "Do not think that I came to destroy the Law or the Prophets. I did not come to destroy but to fulfill" (5:17). Jesus' action of fulfilling the law is grace. Grace may have overtaken law, but that does not mean we can live our lives any way we please. Absolutely not!

Grace and faith are the two requirements in our salvation: "By grace you have been saved through faith, and that not of yourselves; it is the gift of God" (Ephesians 2:8). It is evident that God's grace makes our salvation possible.

We are what we are and who we are only by God's grace. In his first letter to the church in Corinth, the apostle Paul testified to this truth: "But by the grace of God, I am what I am, and His grace toward me was not in vain" (1 Corinthians 15:10).

Hope

The dictionary defines *hope* as "the general feeling that something desired will be fulfilled; someone (or something) on which expectations are centered; a specific instance of feeling hopeful."

Hope is one of the three Christian virtues mentioned by the apostle Paul as he concluded his extraordinary dissertation on love: "And now abide faith, hope, love, these three; but the greatest of these is love" (1 Corinthians 13:13).

Most people perceive hope to be the same as wishful thinking as in, "I hope this or that will come through or happen." However, the Bible does not defend or support the wishful thinking concept or idea as its own. The biblical concept and meaning of hope is completely different.

In the English language, the word *hope* communicates an element of doubt. For instance, "I hope the weather holds tomorrow so I can play a round of golf." However, the biblical interpretation of the word conveys confidence, leaving no room for uncertainty. Hope from a biblical viewpoint conveys reality or truth as opposed to its secular (worldly) counterpart, which expresses reservation and wishful thinking. We put our hope (confidence) in Jesus, meaning, we believe (by faith) that God always keeps His promises.

As born-again believers, our hope is in eternal life, as confirmed in John's gospel: "Most assuredly, I say to you, he who believes in Me has everlasting life" (6:47). When we accept Jesus as our Lord and Savior, we have confidence that we will go to heaven and be with the Lord: "We are confident, yes, well pleased rather to be absent from the body and to be present with the Lord" (2 Corinthians 5:8). As a Christian, I have no need to say, "I *hope* I will make it to heaven," as this statement expresses doubt.

How do we develop hope? In other words, what is our source? Our hope is in Christ and everything about Him. Simply put, our hope is anchored in trusting Jesus—His faithfulness, love, sacrifice, grace, mercy, crucifixion, and resurrection.

Listening

Paying attention involves two components: hearing and listening. We listen to God, and we listen to people. But this section emphasizes the privilege and opportunities we have of actually hearing God. We can do that by tuning in to His still voice as we read His Word, study His nature, listen to the teachings of others, and so on.

A fine line marks the difference between hearing and listening. It is possible to hear while multitasking, whereas truly listening to someone or something requires our undivided attention.

Most of us have heard the expression: "In one ear and out the other." At times, we are exposed to hearing two things at the same time. One example would be an airport terminal, where we hear two people conversing in the seat next to us, yet we also hear the ongoing flight announcements and instructions.

Listening is an art. Unfortunately, not everyone has mastered it, and because of that, they are apt to miss out on the details, both spiritually and personally. God said, "Whoever listens to me will dwell safely and will be secure, without fear of evil" (Proverbs 1:33).

In the New Testament, Jesus addressed the topic as He challenged and questioned the Jews: "Why do you not understand My speech? Because you are not able to listen to My Word?" (John 8:43). Much can be gained when we learn to listen, and much can be lost when we refuse the discipline of listening to God.

So how can we listen to God? We can learn to hear the Father effectively and efficiently by following a few principles:

1. Learn to be quiet and still. The Lord Himself said, "Be still, and know that I am God" (Psalm 46:10). He commands and encourages us to be still. We can learn much when we are still and patient.
2. Read the Bible. God is known to speak to us through His Word.
3. Pray. Communicating with God is another way of knowing Him and His will. Prayer begins with conversation, maintaining an open line of communication with God.
4. Avoid distractions. Each time you pray or read the Word, you need to be in a quiet place away from all interruptions.

5. Examine your heart. Since listening to God involves both heart and mind, you must search your heart to make sure you have a "broken and contrite heart" (Psalm 51:17).
6. Examine your thoughts to make sure they are focused. Meditate on what is good, as encouraged by the apostle Paul (Philippians 4:8).
7. Obey God by learning to listen to Him. But hearing God's voice is not as easy as it sounds. For instance, our world is filled with chaos, noise, and voices that bombard us from every direction: cell and home phones, the Internet (YouTube), radio, television, and street clamor and clatter.
8. Start each day by spending quality time with the Lord. Invite Him to direct the rest of your day. King David followed this principle: "Cause me to hear Your loving kindness in the morning, for in You do I trust" (Psalm 143:8).

Seeking God's direction each morning is one of the wisest things you can ever do. In the book of Lamentations we read, "They [mercies] are new every morning" (3:23). Morning may not be suitable for everyone. Personally, I prefer to begin and end the day with prayer and reading the Word.

Maintain the right heart attitude. Our list thus far has included learning to be quiet or still, reading the Word, spending quality time with God in the morning, and so on. But listening to God is difficult when our attitudes are not right. Some obstacles that may hinder our hearing God include: busyness, pride, selfishness, anger, bitterness, hostility, unforgiveness, envy, greed, jealousy, and lust.

We must learn to be obedient, be ready and willing to serve, and walk in God's will. By doing so, we can begin to hear Him and thus receive His instruction. Prevention is always better than cure. Learning to do what is right the first time may prevent headaches and heartaches. We can start with listening.

Love

Earlier, I cited three Christian virtues the apostle Paul mentioned in his first letter to the Corinthians: "And now abide faith, hope, love, these three; but the greatest of these is love" (13:13). Jesus spoke of two great commandments (Matthew 22:37-40) in which love is the common denominator. The key salvation verse, John 3:16, hinges on the word *love*.

The English word *love* has many different connotations, giving people the option of using it wherever they see fit. For instance, some pet owners use the word *love* when referring to their furry and feathered friends: "I love my dog or my cat. I love my parakeet." Yet during worship service at church, we also say, "I love Jesus."

If the pet owner happens to be a believer, the word *love* should have a different meaning or value. How can someone love his pet and God the same way? The term *love* is expressed differently for different purposes. Love for some means giving; for others it may have sexual and romantic implications.

This section focuses on God's love. How does the Bible describe (or portray) God's love toward us? God loves us so much He sacrificed His own Son, Jesus, for us. And Jesus loved us so much He willingly went to the cross for us.

The gospel of Luke paints a clear picture of God's precious love, even for one soul: "There will be more joy in heaven over one sinner who repents than over ninety-nine just persons" (15:7). Peter confirms Luke's statement: "The Lord is . . . not willing that any should perish but that all should come to repentance" (2 Peter 3:9).

The Bible describes God's love as beyond measure, eternal, forgiving, impartial, inexhaustible, pure, sacrificial, and unchanging. We know of God's many attributes, such as faithfulness, grace, kindness, mercy, and so on. But when it comes to love, the word doesn't just describe Him; it identifies Him. God is love (1 John 4:16).

I have a precious, special-needs daughter, and as a parent, I love her dearly and want only the best for her. I am always there for her and am eager and quick to forgive her each time the opportunity arises. If we can love our children so much, how much more does God, our heavenly Father, love us?

A Scripture verse from the gospel of Luke brings God's love for us up close and personal: "Are not five sparrows sold for two copper coins? And not one of them is forgotten before God. But the very hairs of your head are all numbered. Do not fear therefore, you are of more value than many sparrows" (12:6-7).

God loves everyone equally and shows no partiality. He loves all of us, but some of us choose not to reciprocate His love. And yet He offers His gift of love and salvation freely to everyone, even to those who choose to follow an ungodly path. This truth was addressed in the gospel of Matthew: "He makes His sun rise on the evil and on the good, and sends rain on the just and on the unjust" (5:45). It is not God's nature to show partiality (Acts 10:34). He is no respecter of persons.

At the beginning of this chapter, I mentioned the two greatest commandments that share love as the common denominator. Jesus made it clear that our most important responsibility in life is to love God, and the best way to show our love for Him is to obey His commandments. Jesus Himself said, "If you love Me, keep My commandments" (John 14:15).

The apostle Paul stressed the importance of love and boldly declared that love is the greatest of all spiritual gifts. It even takes precedence over faith. He stated this truth distinctly in the beautiful passage in his first letter to the people of Corinth (13:4-8, 13).

Mercy

Mercy is defined as "a disposition to be kind and forgiving; the feeling that motivates compassion; something for which to be thankful; showing great kindness."

How do we differentiate mercy from grace? Mercy and grace are opposites. When you show mercy, you are withholding just or deserved punishment, whereas grace is receiving unmerited favor.

A pastor friend described grace and mercy with the following equations:

- grace = receiving what we *do not* deserve
- mercy = not receiving what we *do* deserve

I could not have said it any better.

God's Word has much to say about mercy. In fact, the word appears about 262 times in the King James Version. The concordance supports this claim where we find several pages consisting of several hundred verses.

Imagine committing a crime. Then, as you stand before the judge awaiting your punishment, he announces that you do not have to serve any time because you are being shown mercy. King David puts it well: "He has not dealt with us according to our sins, nor punished us according to our iniquities" (Psalm 103:10).

Mercy is definitely one attribute (besides love) that comes to mind when describing God. Mercy is the word used most often to reveal God's nature, as we read, "God, who is rich in mercy" (Ephesians 2:4). Why is mercy so important? Because through mercy we are forgiven, and our heavenly Father is all about forgiveness.

We must express our thanks for the grace and mercy God extends toward us. However, it is also important that we realize and acknowledge that

God is holy, just, righteous, and sovereign. He clearly teaches that mankind will not go unpunished for its sins (Numbers 32:23; Jeremiah 21:14).

Some people take God's mercy for granted, even complaining when they are disciplined. We actually have no right to whine or offer excuses when we receive just punishment or discipline (see Lamentations 3:39; Hebrews 2:2).

All of us go through times and seasons when we may not feel or sense God's grace, love, or mercy. Yet God does not change; He is still merciful even when we are not aware of it. He declares His own immutability: "For I am the Lord, I do not change" (Malachi 3:6).

God extends His mercy because of His nature and not because we are worthy. Some people consider themselves to be righteous and therefore expect to be awarded and rewarded. The prophet Isaiah knew something that can put self-righteous individuals in their place: "All our righteousnesses are like filthy rags" (64:6). Proud people do not experience God's mercy (the Pharisees and Sadducees, for example).

This is why God has a right to extend His mercy whenever, however, and to whomever He chooses: "I will have mercy on whomever I will have mercy, and I will have compassion on whomever I will have compassion" (Romans 9:15).

Tolerance

The dictionary defines *tolerance* as "willingness to recognize and respect the beliefs or practices of others; allowing some freedom to move within limits." But this thing called tolerance is getting ugly and out of control in our world. Certain aspects of life are in direct violation of God's laws and what He stands for. Consider, for instance, abortion, adultery, fornication, homosexuality, and the like; yet the world demands that we be tolerant and stop being judgmental.

Since the world is Satan's domain, he does his best to convince every individual to act, believe, think, tolerate, and even accept anything that displeases or opposes God.

As mentioned earlier in this text, Satan has no power over believers unless God grants him permission or we allow him access into our lives. Satan does have a rather large audience on which to prey. Even Christians are sometimes pressured into tolerating ungodly principles. When we take a stand against evil, we are often accused of discrimination and being judgmental.

It is time for Christians to stand up and speak in favor of what is right before God. Why not? People of other religions and cultures, such as Hindus and Muslims, are vocal about their biases. We don't need to be harsh, hostile, or judgmental. We can leave that to God. The Lord Himself said, "Vengeance is Mine, I will repay, says the Lord" (Deuteronomy 32:35; Romans 12:19; Hebrews 10:30).

I am not here to judge anyone lest I be judged. To those whose lifestyle is not acceptable and pleasing to God, my message is, I may not agree with or approve of your particular choices. However, I am willing to share God's love and truth with you, if you allow me to do so.

The ability to tolerate that which is not of God is a hard-won virtue. In the Western World, especially in the United States of America, the Constitution gives each individual the right to believe and practice whatever he or she feels is right. These rights include First Amendment free speech, the right to an opinion, separation of church and state, and so on.

As an American citizen, I consider it an honor and privilege to call this great and blessed nation my home. I thank God for allowing me to live in a country where I am free to believe and practice Christianity (worship Jesus) without serious consequences, unlike Christians in many Muslim nations where persecutions await them at every corner.

But with freedom comes accountability and responsibility. When we begin to abuse and misuse our liberty, we are only asking for trouble, both spiritual and otherwise. Slowly and surely, people from other cultures and religions are incorporating their beliefs and expecting Americans to tolerate them. Sadly, many of us are giving in to their deception.

This nation, I am told, was founded on godly principles, by founding fathers who were all men of faith. But it seems we have drifted so far away from God that nearly anything is permissible in today's society. As Aaron Tippen, a country singer, once said, "If you don't stand for something, you will fall for anything." We can see the reality of this statement everywhere.

On one hand, godly principles are being compromised in areas such as adultery, idolatry, removing the Ten Commandments from government facilities, and eliminating public prayer. On the other hand, Hindu temples and Muslim mosques are springing up in many of the major metropolitan cities. So much for religious freedom and tolerance. God's grace and mercy is running thin, and He will judge what needs to be judged in due time.

God is truth (John 14:6), and anyone who tolerates what is not of God is simply rejecting the truth. It is one thing for unsaved people to tolerate whatever works for them, but the sad thing is, "53% of Bible-believing conservative Christian adults do not believe in absolute truth" (George Barna Survey).

To an unbeliever, truth is relative, whereas for a saved person, truth is abstract, and there is no room to bargain, compromise, or negotiate. Anyone who does not believe in absolute truth tends to tolerate secular principles, concepts, and ideology. When we tolerate sin, it not only undermines our faith, it also hurts others as well as ourselves.

Tolerating anything that is not of God has its own negative effects and outcomes. For instance, our relationship with Jesus Christ, who is the truth, is severed, since truth and tolerance cannot coexist. A person must choose one or the other. Tolerating sin also affects one's understanding of the Holy Scriptures, which is also truth (John 17:17).

Allowing sin to go uncontested affects the way we apply and handle our freedom, love, and worship. We are free to compromise to sin and the sin nature, but doing so inevitably distorts our ability to love God and others because God is love. Plus we are not able to worship as unto the Lord, for we are commanded to worship Him in spirit and in truth (John 4:23-24). The bottom line: Tolerance interferes with anything that defends and stands for the truth.

What does the Bible say about tolerance? The word *tolerance* appears infrequently in the Bible. In each instance where it is mentioned, there is no suggestion that we tolerate sin. On the contrary, the word *tolerate* was used in defense of condemning sin and not supporting it. Then why should we?

Understanding

Understanding others falls under the category of "interpersonal relations" or "social skills." My father—a wise man—once told me that we can't give what we don't have. I believe that is true. For instance, how can we get along with and understand others when we don't fully know their identity? Believers especially need to know who they are in Christ.

Understanding is a weighty word. Many relationships become strained or estranged because of a lack of understanding. In our homes, during counseling sessions, and on television we often hear the phrase, "He or she does not understand me."

The more we understand ourselves, the better we are able to present ourselves to others as it relates to our attitude, attributes, and character. The more we understand one another, the less misunderstandings will occur. I personally would rather have an argument (disagreement) with full understanding than to have a healthy discussion with no understanding, purely out of obligation.

Though understanding is important, the Bible teaches that other things, such as love, obedience, and trust, are more important. Yet without understanding, we don't always know what we want, how we feel, or what is wrong with us.

Our thoughts, desires, and goals tend to fluctuate, so in the process, we become confused. Some individuals' minds and thoughts are like dry leaves; they can blow in any direction at any time.

Trying to understand others can be difficult for many people, but a much bigger problem is that many (even saved individuals) do not desire or take the time to understand God. King David wrote, "The Lord looks down from heaven upon the children of men to see if there are any who understand, who seek God. They have all turned aside" (Psalm 14:2-3).

The Bible is filled with information about people skills or interpersonal relations. It says enough to make us better people, starting with spiritual maturity. Much of Jesus' and His apostles' teachings, as well as the five poetical or wisdom books, deal with these issues in great detail.

God's Word teaches everything we need to know about our enemies, friendships, and other relationships, including parents, children, husbands, wives, friends, family, and coworkers. The best instructions with regard to interpersonal relations come from the two commandments Jesus labeled as "the greatest" (Mark 12:29-31). Both of these commandments focus on love, which is the most important attribute to help us understand God and others. In order to understand others better, we must learn to show both empathy and sympathy.

Empathy is the ability to enter into another's feelings or situation. Sympathy, on the other hand, is the ability to feel sorry and also to be able to share the feelings of others.

One way we can make the concepts of empathy and sympathy work effectively and efficiently is to follow the Golden Rule, spoken by Jesus: "Just as you want men to do to you, you also do to them likewise" (Luke 6:31). If everyone were to apply this principle, the world would be a much better place in which to live and learn.

Interaction between two individuals should be mutual and reciprocal, following a give-and-take policy. No one should be giving or receiving one hundred percent of the time. For instance, if you want to be loved, you must give love. If you wish to be respected, you must respect others. If you want to be accepted, learn to accept others. You don't have to agree with them on every point, but you can still respect their opinions, because Jesus died for them too.

Please keep in mind that the give-and-take principle applies only to those things that are God-approved. For instance, if someone hates you, love him or her in return because that is what Jesus did. The principle of an "eye for an eye and a tooth for a tooth" is not of God (Matthew 5:38-40).

Good news! Someone understands us completely: "Great is our Lord, and mighty in power; His understanding is infinite" (Psalm 147:5). The best way to understand ourselves is to know and learn to understand God and His ways.

Conclusion

This chapter has discussed eleven characteristics or actions that can make a significant difference in our lives. In fact, by developing and practicing these traits we can become emotionally mature, mentally strong, and spiritually wise, not to mention many other benefits.

Do not rule out anything just because it sounds simple. I have learned that the simple things are often the most profound. Friendships and relationships sometimes fail and fall because of the simple things. We tend to argue and fight over trite matters that carry little significance.

Let us set aside quality time to get to know God, our heavenly Father, and His nature by reading His Word and praying. He is faithful and is known to keep His promises. As we draw close to Him, He will draw close to us (James 4:8). The more we understand God, the better we will be able to get along with others and ourselves.

Chapter Thirteen

The Conclusion

Telling Yourself the Truth

Introduction

What does it take to be free and serve God? To be set free, one has to be born again, and that can only happen when he or she believes in Jesus Christ. To serve God, we must pursue nothing but the truth, and the Bible declares that God is truth (John 14:6). The Lord Jesus Himself said, "You shall know the truth, and the truth shall make you free" (John 8:32).

Truth is powerful, so powerful that it stands on its own. It needs no witness, will survive on any terms, and cannot be destroyed or concealed.

We cannot run from truth. The only smart way to deal with and handle it is to simply accept it. In other words, one must deal with the truth the best way we know how and move on.

The more honest and forthright we are, the less accountable we will be. My heart's desire is that this book will encourage you to attain more emotional maturity, mental stability, and spiritual wisdom than you presently possess.

We can never say, "Enough is enough," when it comes to intelligence, knowledge, wisdom, and spiritual development. There is always room for growth, more than enough to learn, and plenty to teach. That is what life should be all about: forever learning and teaching. The best way we can do that is by being humble.

Most of us can pinpoint areas of our lives where we would like to see adjustments. Those desired changes are different for each one of us, but some possibilities include attitude, beliefs, career, destiny, education, finances, friendships, goals, honesty, love, relationships, and so on. And yet few people end up making changes. Why?

Change does not come easy for many people. We are creatures of habit, and habits are difficult to break. But deep down, anyone with a clear conscience knows a change must take place if he or she is to be whole. Change happens when disbelief (misbelief) or erroneous thinking is replaced with truth.

God loves us, and He wants us to be happy. However, there are right and wrong ways of obtaining happiness. Of course, we want to find it the way God intended, as His ways are right and true. Authors Backus and Chopian (2000) define three steps to becoming the happy persons we were meant to be:

1. Locate our misbeliefs.
2. Remove them.
3. Replace misbeliefs with the truth.

An example of erroneous thinking would be, *I am a loser, and no one cares.* Substitute this kind of thinking with *I am someone special, and God cares for me.* Applying truth will help you adapt to whatever comes your way.

Examining Our Heart

I said this earlier in this text, but I will say it again: God sees heart issues as precious, and so should we. I have always believed that anything that is worth mentioning once is definitely worth mentioning twice, and, of course, in God's case, there is never a limit, because He is worthy of our attention, praise, and worship.

How we speak and what we say has everything to do with the condition of our heart. Jesus said it is not what goes into the mouth that defiles a man, but what comes out of the mouth. "But those things which proceed out of the mouth come from the heart, and they defile a man" (Matthew 15:11, 18; also see Matthew 12:34 and Luke 6:45).

Just as a tree is recognized by its fruit, a person is known by the type of fruit he or she bears. When you sow good seeds, you reap good produce; likewise, when you sow bad seeds, you will reap bad fruit (see Matthew 7:16, 20).

We are identified (or known) by the fruit we produce, and when we only act holy on the surface, we become examples of the Scripture that talks about "wolves in sheep's clothing" (Matthew 7:15). From a biblical sense, the heart refers to our attitudes, character, feelings, motives, thoughts, and so on.

A wise man once told me that people by nature tend to speak their minds when they are angry, drunk, hungry, or sleep deprived. I am not sure if this is totally true, but I have heard many people speak the truth (telling it like it is) under each of these conditions; therefore, it must carry some validity.

Let us develop the habit of searching our hearts regularly as King David did. In the book of Psalms we read: "Search me, O God, and know my heart" (139:23). A similar verse states the action this way: "Examine me, O Lord, and prove me; try my mind and my heart" (Psalm 26:2).

David understood the importance of the heart. This is probably why he was known as "a man after God's own heart," despite all he did as it relates to Bathsheba and her husband, Uriah.

King Solomon, David's son and heir to the throne, made a wise statement when he said, "The heart of the righteous studies how to answer" (Proverbs 15:28). As children of God, we must learn to build and keep our foundation strong in order to withstand any calamities and obstacles that come across our paths. A clean and pure heart will produce godly and healthy thoughts, which in turn will help us become positive and productive individuals who are ready and willing to serve God and others.

Examining Our Thoughts

In one sense, it all boils down to two areas of our lives that we must guard carefully: our heart (matter) and our mind (thoughts). Mind refers to logic—what makes sense—and the heart refers to matter.

Experience, intelligence, and knowledge deal more with the mind, whereas wisdom is closely related to the heart. Intelligence can come from education, experience, listening, and reading, but wisdom comes from God.

In the beginning of this section, I mentioned that mind and matter are extremely important components of who we are. Please don't misunderstand me; many other aspects of our lives are equally important. Consider, for instance, one's character (as in personality) and the all-important development of the fruit of the Spirit (Galatians 5:22-23).

I also mentioned earlier the strong correlation between our thoughts and our heart, meaning, our thoughts determine our heart. In his letter to the believers at Corinth, the apostle Paul encouraged his readers to "bring every thought into captivity to the obedience of Christ" (2 Corinthians 10:5).

What does it mean to take your thoughts captive? I believe it has to be about disciplining yourself to think only those things that are within God's boundaries and standards. Simply put, that is any thought that is acceptable to God. Once again, the apostle Paul encourages his audience, this time the Philippians, to think only those thoughts that are admirable, noble, true, and of a good report (see Philippians 4:8).

During the years I have done biblical counseling for individuals, marriages, and families, I have encouraged each participant to maintain a private journal. The plan is to record every thought accurately and as it comes. Then, at the end of each day, the counselees are to listen or read what has been recorded throughout the day. As they read or listen, they must pay attention to anything that is negative or ungodly, such as anger, bitterness, envy, gossip, greed, jealous, lust, pride, self-centered, unforgiveness, and so on. Finally, they are urged to ask God to forgive them, to bless everyone they have sinned against, and to give them an opportunity to make it right. The goal is to have a clear conscience before God and others.

We need to monitor our thoughts closely, and ask ourselves, "Does this thought please God, or does it only please me?" Cognitive psychologists use the term *automatic thought stopping*. Each time a negative thought enters our mind, we immediately stop it by replacing (or substituting) it with a good or positive thought.

Try practicing automatic thought stopping on the following negative thoughts, except replace them with language from the Word of God:

- "*I can't do that, because I am a loser.*" Replace this negative thought with, "*I can do all things through Christ who strengthens me*" (Philippians 4:13). *According to God and His Word, I am not a loser.*
- "*I am worthless; no one cares for or loves me.*" Substitute the prophet Jeremiah's encouraging statement: "*Yes, I have loved you with an everlasting love*" (31:3). When it comes to love, there is always that

great salvation Scripture, John 3:16, which is well known to both the saved and unsaved.

Thoughts are nothing but ideas that reveal how we feel and what we think. However, if we dwell on a thought long enough, it has the potential of becoming action. We are not only accountable for what we do, but also for the thoughts that produced the action.

For instance, a student receives a bad grade and, because of that, harbors negative thoughts toward the professor. The professor has no knowledge of the student's views, so he has not sinned against the professor. If the student is a believer, he or she can confess those thoughts to the Lord, ask for forgiveness, genuinely repent, and move on.

It is not sinful to have thoughts that are evil or negative. After all, we are human beings, and each time we go through personal stress, we tend to divert our thoughts in a direction that may not always be pleasing to God. However, sin becomes part of the equation when we act on an ungodly thought. Let us not forget that "whatever a man sows, that he will also reap" (Galatians 6:7). There is no shortcut to repentance. Simply admit the sin and move on.

How do we make our thoughts captive to Christ? One author answers this question with this solution: "First, we must give our lives to Jesus; second, we need to read and memorize God's Word in order to fill our minds with this truth; and third, we monitor our thought life" (Marks, 2011).

So monitor your thoughts, record them, make a spiritual assessment, and think twice before you speak. Actions actually do speak louder than words, and words, once spoken, cannot be retrieved. Let's bring our thoughts into captivity.

Ready and Willing to Serve God and Others

How can we serve others? The best way to serve others is to learn how to serve God. In order to serve, we must have a servant's attitude and heart. We have been slaves to sin and our sin nature. Let us turn that around and become slaves to God. We can become slaves to God and His Word by becoming "servants of righteousness" (Romans 6:18).

When an individual accepts Jesus Christ as his personal Lord and Savior, he becomes God's child and a servant. As such, he must learn how best to serve God and others. The apostle Paul's statement to the Romans will help us understand the concept of servanthood more clearly: "Present your bodies as a living sacrifice, holy, acceptable to God, which is your reasonable service" (Romans 12:1).

In his gospel, the apostle John gives us a perfect example of serving others performed by the Lord Himself. As Jesus washed His disciple's feet, He said, "If I then, your Lord and Teacher, have washed your feet, you also ought to wash one another's feet. For I have given you an example, that you should do as I have done to you" (John 13:14-15).

This Scripture helps us understand the importance the Lord placed on serving others. One of the best ways we can serve others is to put aside our own selfish desires and focus on meeting the needs of those the Lord brings across our path. One author notes, "To serve God is to serve others and is the greatest form of charity: the pure love of Christ" (Bruner, 2011).

A genuine sacrifice made as unto the Lord never hurts anyone. There will always be people who refuse to serve others, and the Lord surely has serious consequences in store for those individuals (Matthew 25:41-46). One Christian author wrote:

> Our Lord and Savior set a superlative example of serving others during His brief three-year ministry. A study of the

life of Christ will reveal a character unconcerned with the serving of self.

Jesus took advantage of every opportunity to instill this same trait in His disciples. Christ wanted His disciples to understand that they must learn to think little of serving self and much of serving others (Waters, 91).

Keep in mind that serving others includes family (spouse, children), parents, siblings, the body of Christ, friends, relatives, acquaintances, strangers, church leaders, our community, and so on.

In how many ways can we serve others? We can serve by donating funds to kingdom endeavors and to the needy; by encouraging, fasting, giving tithes and offerings, mourning with those who grieve, serving children, the elderly, homeless, orphans, and widows; sharing our experience, knowledge, skills, and talents; visiting hospitals, nursing homes, and shut-ins; volunteering in our community, and so on.

But it begins with serving our own family. We must do whatever necessary to minister to members of our own household. This service may include cleaning, encouraging, fasting (if permitted medically), listening, loving, praying, teaching, working, and so on. Everything must and should start at home. We should make our home a sweet home in which to learn, live, and love.

Conclusion

Each chapter in this book has included an introduction and a conclusion. However, this conclusion is more than a mere summation, as in all the other chapters. Rather, it is a conclusion to the closing remarks of each chapter.

I sincerely apologize for any content you may have considered redundant. I repeated some emphases only because of their importance and because I felt it was necessary and worth restating.

Once again, I will explain and reiterate some important and thought-provoking facts, precautions, and gentle warnings as they relate to God, Satan, and self. Consider these facts as food for thought.

God

Let us come to a realization and understanding of the nature and character of God. Whether we like or not, accept it or not, understand it or not, God is who He says He is, and we accept Him by faith and not by logic.

God is love; God is Truth; God is always right; God is always on time; God does not discriminate; God shows no partiality; God is forgiving; God is holy, just, and righteous; God wants the best for us; and God gives us all a free will.

Satan

Satan cannot do anything on his own terms. Either God gives him permission or we allow him access into our lives, which we do by choosing to yield to his temptations. He will try his best to tempt us and is known to plant fear and guilt if we let him. He likes to condemn and desires that we walk away from God. Without God's permission and our cooperation, Satan is powerless.

Mankind

We are created in God's image. God loves and cares for us. Jesus died for us by sacrificing His own life. God gave us the authority to rebuke and resist the Devil. Let us get our priorities right and straight, meaning, God comes first, and then spouse, children, parents, siblings, career, and so on.

Remember to use the following phrases regularly:

- How can I serve you?
- I am sorry.
- I will pray for you.
- Please forgive me.
- Thank you.

General

The words of wisdom listed below are from personal experience as well as from others dealing with similar issues as it concerns day-to-day activities in the areas of behavior, communication, judging, and thoughts:

1. Focus on forgiveness. Just because someone says or does something to offend us does not mean we are free to hold grudges against that person. We can be thankful for the good others do, and yet when offenses come, we should be quick to forgive and move on.
2. Encourage others, and entertain good and positive thoughts. Work toward maintaining a broken and contrite spirit. Let us keep our heart clean, clear, and pure.
3. Do not dwell on the past. The only thing we can do with the past is learn from it and not keep bringing it up repeatedly. God does not remind us of our past, and neither should we.
4. Be thankful, even when it is difficult. Let us not use our own logic and reasoning in trying to analyze or question God. God expects us to trust Him without any doubt or reservations.
5. Work diligently to maintain a clear conscience at all times. As long as there is breath and a clear conscience, there is hope. Hope for change and a better tomorrow. Become a new person who God can call one of His own.

Closing Remarks

I have been a born-again Christian for over twenty-six years. During that time, I have seen many people (beginning with myself), both the saved and unsaved, who have used God, His name, and His nature for personal gain, power, and status. I also have heard Christians abuse and misuse biblical or spiritual terminology, such as amen, hallelujah, praise the Lord, etc.

I am not proud of many things I have said and done to hurt and offend others, particularly my siblings and my brothers and sisters in the Lord. But God, by His grace and mercy, has delivered me. I am thankful for His love and forgiveness. I will end this book with this personal note.

I Once Used God.
Now He is Using Me.

Salvation

Introduction

This section contains some information about salvation that I hope will remove any confusion you may have about the meaning of this experience and what it stands for. Some people, including some Christians, do not understand the concept of salvation.

I would like to explain three things concerning salvation: (1) some thoughts regarding the term *denomination*, (2) the correct terminology to be used for salvation, and (3) information about the salvation process.

First, after having read the entire Bible cover to cover at least twice, I have found that the word *denomination* is mentioned nowhere in the Scriptures. Therefore, I conclude that the word *denomination* is not a biblical concept.

The denominational concept is purely the creation of men. I personally do not believe in denominations. Rather, I prefer the term *nondenominational*. I am comfortable worshipping in any church that believes, follows, preaches, and teaches only the Word of God, without adding or deleting from it as they see fit.

Second, I know many individuals who profess to be Christians. I also have known those who could not explain the meaning behind John 3:3, 7: "Unless one is born again, he cannot see the kingdom of God . . . Do not marvel that I said to you, 'You must be born again.'"

The Bible mentions at least five terms that can be used interchangeably, which means they have the same spiritual connotation. Any individual who accepts Jesus Christ as his personal Lord and Savior can call or identify himself as a believer, born-again, a child of God, or saved. All these individuals are brothers and sisters in the Lord. Examine the scriptural references for these four terms (italics have been added for emphasis):

- Believer

"And *believers* were increasingly added to the Lord, multitudes of both men and women" (Acts 5:14).

"Let no one despise your youth, but be an example to the *believers* in word, in conduct, in love, in spirit, in faith, in purity" (1 Timothy 4:12).

- Born-Again

"Jesus answered and said to him, 'Most assuredly, I say to you, unless one is *born-again*, he cannot see the kingdom of God. Do not marvel that I said to you, you must be *born-again*'" (John 3:3, 7).

- Child of God

"But as many as received Him, to them He gave the right to become *children of God*, to those who believe in His name" (John 1:12).

- Saved

"Whoever calls on the name of the Lord shall be *saved*" (Acts 2:21; Romans 10:13).

- New Creature in Christ

"Therefore, if anyone is in Christ, he is a *new creation*; old things have passed away; behold, all things have become new" (2 Corinthians 5:17).

After accepting Jesus Christ as personal Lord and Savior, a person may identify himself with any of these five titles. My wife told me she was born into a Catholic family. But since accepting Jesus Christ as her personal Lord and Savior, she now refers to herself as born-again or saved and not as a born-again Catholic.

I was born into a Hindu family. When I accepted Jesus Christ as my personal Lord and Savior, I also began referring to myself as born-again or saved. There is no other choice or way because I am not a Hindu anymore. Those who come from other belief systems, cultures, faiths, and religions, upon accepting Jesus Christ, must call themselves something—but what? Born-again!

Having read my thoughts on the subject (based on the Bible), decide for yourself if you still wish to hold to the denominational concept or be open and willing to be identified according to what the Bible recommends. Of course, all this depends on your acceptance of Jesus Christ as your personal Lord and Savior.

And third, the Bible makes it clear that in order to be born-again or saved, we must follow only two requirements: "If you confess with your mouth the Lord Jesus and believe in your heart that God has raised Him from the dead, you will be saved" (Romans 10:9).

My sincere desire, hope, and prayer is that anyone who does not know Jesus Christ as his or her Lord and Savior will come to Him in childlike faith and become born-again or saved.

The Four Spiritual Laws

During my undergraduate years, when I was still a Hindu, a pastor approached me and asked if he might share with me the Four Spiritual Laws. I told him I was not aware of those laws, but I was interested to know about them. He shared them with me, and I liked them.

The Four Spiritual Laws explain, in brief, about God's love, our sinful nature, Jesus presented as the Savior, and our need to confess, repent, and accept Jesus Christ as our personal Lord and Savior.

I understand there are many versions or ways of interpreting the Four Spiritual Laws. However, the meaning, as it relates to God, Jesus, and mankind, is the same in all interpretations.

1. God loves us, and He created us so that we can know Him personally.
    God's love. John 3:16
    God's plan. John 17:3

2. Man by nature is sinful and therefore separated from God. Because of this separation, we cannot know Him personally or experience His love.
    Man is sinful. Romans 3:23
    Man is separated. Romans 6:23

3. Jesus Christ is God's only provision for our sins. Only through Jesus can we know God personally as well as experience His love.
    He died in our place. Romans 5:8
    He rose from the dead. 1 Corinthians 15:3-6
    He is the only way to God. John 14:6

4. The above three points state facts about God, Jesus, and man. All we have thus far is head knowledge, and it is not enough just to know the facts. In order for these truths to come to pass, we must accept and receive Jesus Christ as Lord and Savior.

- We must receive Christ. John 1:12
- We receive Christ through faith. Ephesians 2:8-9
- We receive Christ by personal invitation. Revelation 3:20

So there they are, the Four Spiritual Laws. Based on the Scripture verses provided, there is no room for any confusion. Everything seems to be clear in terms of where they stand as it relates to God, Jesus, and man (Global Media Outreach, 2011). All that is left for us to do is make a personal choice (or decision) based on faith and not on feeling.

A Model Salvation Prayer

When an individual is ready to accept Jesus as his or her personal Lord and Savior, God will give him or her the words to say in prayer, and those words will agree with their spirit.

But the most important thing to remember is that whatever a person confesses with his mouth and believes in his heart, he must make sure he wholeheartedly means when he prays.

Here is a model salvation prayer:

> Dear God,
>
> I am a sinner and have lived a sinful life. I am not proud of the things I have said, nor am I proud of my actions. I have offended not only You but also many others, including my family, friends, strangers, and acquaintances. I have lived a selfish life and cared only for myself.
>
> Please forgive me of my sins. I believe that Jesus died on the cross for my sins, and I believe that only through Him can my sins be forgiven. I now confess with my mouth and believe in my heart that Jesus is Lord and Savior, and I am ready to accept Jesus as my personal Lord and Savior.

Please come into my heart and life and help me live a godly life. I want to surrender my all to You, and I want to live for You and serve You and others. Please use me in your kingdom.

Thank You for accepting me as Your child. I ask and pray this in Jesus' precious and mighty name.

Amen.

A Final Note

This book presents facts about God, Jesus, the Holy Spirit, Satan, and mankind. I strongly suggest that you carefully examine and search the evidence presented in each chapter and concentrate on the content of this evidence while keeping an open mind concerning each area and topic.

All the evidence, facts, and opinions presented in this book point in only one direction: toward Jesus Christ, who is the truth as it relates to God. The Lord Jesus Himself made a compelling statement that is an appropriate conclusion to this book: "You shall know the truth, and the truth shall make you free" (John 8:32).

I pray that you will seek and find the truth as it relates to God and that you will choose to accept it.

In Jesus' Love and Service,

Raj
A Servant at Heart

Bibliography

Albert, Barb and Empson, Lila. *100 Answers to 100 Questions about prayer.* Lake Mary, Fla.: Christian Life, 2008.

Allport, Gordon. Attitudes: In C. Murchison (Ed): *A Handbook of Social Psychology.* (pp. 798-844). Worcester, MA: Clark University Press.

Almy, Gary and Almy, Carol. *Addicted to Recovery: Exposing the False Gospel of Psychotherapy.* Eugene, Ore.: Harvest House Publishers, 1994.

Arch, David. "The Conscience." www.askapastor.org, 1999.

Backus, William and Chapian, Marie. *Telling Yourself the Truth.* Minneapolis, MN: Bethany House Publishers, 2000.

Bacon, Sir Francis. British Philosopher.

Barna, George. *What Americans Believes: An Annual Survey of Values and Religious Views in the United States of America.* Gospel Light Publications, 1991.

Beck, Aaron T. Cognitive Therapist.

Boa, Kenneth. "Time Management." www.bible.org, 2005.

Brott, Rich. "8 Kingdom Principles of Sowing and Reaping." www.richbrott.com, 2007.

Bruner, Rachel. "15 Ways To Serve God and Others." http://www.lds.about.com, 2011.

Bulkley, Ed. *Why Christians Can't Trust Psychology.* Eugene, OR: Harvest House Publishers, 1993.

Carter, John and Narramore, Bruce. *The Integration of Psychology and Theology.* Grand Rapids, MI: The Zondervan Corporation, 1979.

Cherry, Kendra. "What is Personality?" http.//psychology.about.com, 2011.

Chung, Walter and Chung, Stephanie. *In Search of Genuine Biblical Counseling.* The Rebuilder's Ministry, 2011.

Church, Melissa. *Old Testament God Vs. A New Testament God.* San Antonio, TX: Verse-By-Verse Ministry, 2007.

Collins, Gary. *Can You Trust Psychology?* Downers Grove, IL: Intervarsity Press, 1988.

Crabb, Larry. *Basic Principles of Biblical Counseling.* Grand Rapids, MI: The Zondervan Corporation, 1975.

Dawes, Robyn and Smith, T.L. Attitude and Opinion Measurement. In G. Lindzey and E. Aronson (Eds): *The Handbook of Social Psychology.* (Vol. 1, pp. 509-566). New York, NY: Random House.

Descartes, Rene. French Philosopher.

DSM-IV-TR. *Diagnostic and Statistical Manual of Mental Disorders*, 4th Edition. Washington, D.C. American Psychiatric Association, 2000.

Efron, Ron P. and Efron, Pat P. *Letting Go of Anger.* Oakland, CA: New Harbinger Publications, Inc.

Fairchild, Mary. "Biblical Names of God." http://www.christianity.about.com/namesofgod, 2011.

Fairchild, Mary. "20 Bible Facts About God." http://www.christianity.about.com/biblefactsgod, 2011.

Fowler, Ray. "You Shall Not Bear False Witness." http://www.rayfowler.org, 2011.

Gandhi, Mohandas, K. Indian Civil Rights Activist, Freedom Fighter, Peace Activist, Father of the Indian Independence Movement.

Ganz, Richard. Psychobabble: *The Failure Of Modern Psychology and the Biblical Alternative*. Wheaton, IL: Crossway Books, 1993.

Global Media Outreach. "The Four Spiritual Laws." http://www.4laws.com/englishkgp/, 2011.

Graham, Ron. "Sowing and Reaping: A Simple Life Principle." www.simplybible.com, 2011.

Holy Bible. New King James Version (NKJV). Nashville, TN: Thomas Nelson, Inc.

Houdman, Michael S. *Got Questions: Bible Questions Answered*. Enumclaw, WA: Pleasant Word, 2009.

Houdman, Michael S. "What Does the Bible Say About Attitude?" www.gotquestions.org, 2009.

Jewell, Elizabeth J. *The Oxford Desk Dictionary and Thesaurus*. New York, NY: Spark Publishing.

Kalat, James W. *Introduction to Psychology*. Belmont, CA: Wadsworth/Thomas Learning, Inc.

Kaplan, H and Sadock, B. *Comprehensive Textbook of Psychiatry*, 5th Edition. Baltimore, MD: Williams and Wilkins, 1989.

Kraft, Krishana. "Bowing to Convenience." http://www.boundless.org, 2005.

Kruis, John G. *Quick Scripture Reference for Counseling*. Grand Rapids, MI: Baker Books, 2000.

Likert, Rensis, American Educator and Organizational Psychologist.

Lotich, Robert. "5 Bible Verses About Money Every Christian Should Know." http://www.christianpf.com, 2008.

Marks, Elizabeth. *Bring Every Thought Captive*. Think On It Bible Ministries, Inc., 2011.

Melton, James L. "Is It Right To Judge?" www.biblebelievers.com, 1999.

Merton, Thomas. Author, Roman Catholic Writer, Social Critic, and Spiritual Guide.

Miller, Betty. "What Does the Bible Say About Lying?" Dewey, AZ: www.bible.com, 1995.

Moore, Tom. "Attitudes to Develop." www.preachersfiles.com, 2011.

Online Article. "How To Change Your Attitude." www.Net BibleStudy.com, 2011.

Online Article. "Names of God: 21 Names of God and Their Meaning." Torrance, CA: www.rose-publishing.com, 2003.

Online Article. "Personality Disorders." http://www.mentalhealth.org/UK, 2011.

Online Article. "The Weak Conscience." www.weakconscience.com, 2011.

Online Article. "What Does the Bible Say About Judging?" www.getchristiananswers.com, 2008.

Pascal, Blaise. French Mathematician and Physicist.

Pastorino, Ellen and Doyle-Portillo, Susan. *What Is Psychology?* Belmont, CA: Wadsworth, 2006.

Perryman, Mark. "Are You Serving a God of Convenience?" http://www.sermoncentral.com, 2005.

Perryman, Mark. *Sermons on Evangelism: The Lost.* Springfield, MO: Assembly of God, 2005.

Peterson, Eugene H. *Three-Way Concordance: Word, Phrase, and Synonym.* Colorado Springs, CO: Nav Press, 2006.

Pratt, David E. "You Can Serve God Successfully: God's Power Can Work In Your Life." www.gospelway.com, 2005.

Ravenhill, Leonard. *The Taming of the Tongue.* Lindale, TX: www.ravenhill.org., 1994.

Rhodes, Ron. *Find It Fast in the Bible*: A Quick Topical Reference. Eugene, OR: Harvest House Publishers, 2000.

Robbins, Dale A. "Check Your Attitude." Grass Valley, CA: www.victorious.org, 1994.

Ross, Steven. "Different Types of Conscience." Richmond, IN: www.lecf.com, 2010.

Ryckman, Richard M. *Theories of Personality.* Belmont, CA: Wadsworth/Thomas Learning, 2000.

Seneca, Lucius A. Roman Stoic Philosopher.

Scott, Mike. *What Does the Bible Say About Our Conscience?: Is It Always a Safe Guide?* www.scripturessay.com, 2010.

Socrates. The Greek Philosopher.

Solomon, Charles. *Handbook for Christ-Centered Counseling.* Sevierville, TN: Solomon Publications, 1993.

Szasz, Thomas. *The Myth of Psychotherapy.* Syracuse, NY: Syracuse University Press, 1987.

Taylor, Paul S. *Lust: What Does The Bible Say?: The Naked Truth About Lust.* Gilbert, AZ: Eden Communications, 2001.

The Bible Promise Book. One Thousand Promises From God's Word. Uhrichsville, OH: Barbour Publishing, Inc.

The Merriam-Webster Dictionary. Springfield, MA: Merriam-Webster, Inc., 2005.

The Open Bible: Expanded Edition. New King James Version (NKJV). Nashville, TN: Thomas Nelson Publishers, 1982.

The Oxford Desk Dictionary and Thesaurus, 2nd Edition. New York, NY: Spark Publishing, 2007.

The Ultimate A To Z Resource. What Does the Bible Say About . . . . Nashville, TN: Thomas Nelson Publishers, 2001.

Tippen, Aaron. Country Singer and Songwriter.

Vemuri, Raj. *From Hinduism To Christ: A Former Hindu Brahmin Looks At World Religions and the Powerful Truths of the Christian Faith.* Enumclaw, WA: Pleasant Word, 2010.

Waters, Mike. *Spreading the Word.* Vol. 3, No. 8., 1991.

Weber, Owen. "What Does the Bible Say About Grace?" Christian Data Resources. www.christiandataresources.com, 2008.

Wilkerson, David. *Roving Eyes.* New York, NY: World Challenge Pulpit Series, 1988.

Wilson, Neil S. *The Handbook of Bible Application.* Carol Stream, IL: Tyndale Book Publishers, 2000.

Wommack, Andrew. "Psychology vs. Christianity." Andrew Womack Ministries. Colorado Springs, CO: http://www.awmi.net, 2011.

Wright, Gary D. "The Principle of Sowing and Reaping." http://lifesongchurch.wordpress.com, 2008.

Reference from the Holy Bible

<u>OLD TESTAMENT</u>

Genesis 1:1
Genesis 2:7
Genesis 15:13-16
Exodus 10:3
Exodus 20:16-17
Leviticus 19:2, 16
Leviticus 27:30
Numbers 18:26
Deuteronomy 4:31
Deuteronomy 7:9
Deuteronomy 14:22-23
Deuteronomy 16:17
Deuteronomy 32:4, 20, 35
Joshua 24:15, 20
1 Samuel 8:5, 8
1 Samuel 16:7
2 Samuel 11
2 Samuel 24:10, 14
Nehemiah 9:17
Job 26:14
Psalm 1:1
Psalm 9:12
Psalm 11:7
Psalm 14:2, 31
Psalm 25:7-8
Psalm 31:5

Genesis 1:26-27
Genesis 4:6
Genesis 18:14
Exodus 14:13
Exodus 34:6
Leviticus 20:26
Numbers 14:18
Numbers 32:23
Deuteronomy 6:4
Deuteronomy 8:18
Deuteronomy 15:13-14
Deuteronomy 24:19
Joshua 1:7-8
Ruth 2:6
1 Samuel 15:23, 29
2 Samuel 7:22
2 Samuel 12:7, 9
2 Chronicles 31:5
Job 19:25-26
Job 31:1, 11
Psalm 5:9
Psalm 10:4, 7
Psalm 12:3
Psalm 19:9
Psalm 26:2
Psalm 34:5-6, 9, 18

Psalm 36:1, 9
Psalm 46:1, 10
Psalm 51:10, 17
Psalm 66:18
Psalm 86:15
Psalm 90:2, 10
Psalm 102:25-27
Psalm 108:4
Psalm 111:10
Psalm 116:12
Psalm 120:2
Psalm 126:5-6
Psalm 135:16-18
Psalm 141:5
Psalm 145:3, 8
Proverbs 1:33
Proverbs 3:21-26, 34
Proverbs 6:6-8, 16-19
Proverbs 8:13
Proverbs 10:9, 31
Proverbs 12:15, 17
Proverbs 13:3, 22
Proverbs 15:4, 22, 26
Proverbs 16:5, 18, 25
Proverbs 18:2, 8, 13, 21
Proverbs 21:5, 13, 20
Proverbs 23:2, 7, 20-21
Proverbs 26:17, 20
Proverbs 28:7
Ecclesiastes 1:18
Ecclesiastes 3:1-8
Ecclesiastes 5:2
Isaiah 1:18
Isaiah 8:20
Isaiah 14:12-15
Isaiah 40:13-14, 18-26

Psalm 37:21, 30
Psalm 50:10-12, 15
Psalm 62:11
Psalm 78:56
Psalm 89:1-8
Psalm 101:5
Psalm 103:3, 8, 10, 12
Psalm 109:2, 8-18
Psalm 115:5-6, 8
Psalm 119:11, 137
Psalm 122:6
Psalm 130:4
Psalm 139:2-14, 23-24
Psalm 143:8
Psalm 147:5
Proverbs 3:5-7, 12, 19
Proverbs 4:23
Proverbs 6:20-21, 25-26
Proverbs 9:10
Proverbs 11:2, 13
Proverbs 12:18, 20, 22
Proverbs 14:12
Proverbs 15:28, 31, 32
Proverbs 17:4, 20
Proverbs 19:9, 17
Proverbs 22:7
Proverbs 25:15, 23
Proverbs 27:17
Proverbs 29:23, 25
Ecclesiastes 2:3
Ecclesiastes 4:4
Ecclesiastes 12:13-14
Isaiah 2:12
Isaiah 13:11
Isaiah 30:1
Isaiah 41:3

Isaiah 45:5
Isaiah 51:12
Isaiah 59:2
Isaiah 64:6
Jeremiah 7:19
Jeremiah 10:10
Jeremiah 17:9-10
Jeremiah 22:9
Jeremiah 29:7, 11
Jeremiah 33:3
Ezekiel 3:7
Ezekiel 18:23
Daniel 9:2-5, 7, 9
Hosea 4:6
Micah 7:8-20
Malachi 3:6, 8-19

Isaiah 46:9-11
Isaiah 55:2, 8-9
Isaiah 60:19
Jeremiah 5:1
Jeremiah 9:5-6, 23
Jeremiah 12:13
Jeremiah 21:14
Jeremiah 23:24
Jeremiah 31:3, 34
Lamentations 3:22-23, 39
Ezekiel 11:19
Ezekiel 28:17
Daniel 9:15-19, 24-25
Amos 5:14-15
Zechariah 7:5

NEW TESTAMENT

Matthew 4:1-11
Matthew 5:28, 33-40
Matthew 6:24, 33-34
Matthew 7:16-18, 20, 23
Matthew 9:13
Matthew 11:28-29
Matthew 13:8
Matthew 17:18, 20-21
Matthew 19:16-23
Matthew 22:14, 18
Matthew 23:23, 28
Matthew 28:19-20
Mark 7:9, 21-23
Mark 9:24
Mark 11:1, 23-25
Luke 2:37
Luke 6:31, 35-38, 45

Matthew 5:3, 9-15, 17, 24
Matthew 6:2-4, 7, 9-15; 19-21
Matthew 7:1, 5, 8, 15
Matthew 8:20
Matthew 10:8, 28-30, 34-35
Matthew 12:7, 30, 34
Matthew 15:11, 18
Matthew 18:21-22
Matthew 21:12, 22
Matthew 22:37-40
Matthew 25:14-30, 41-46
Mark 4:40
Mark 8:34, 38
Mark 10:18, 21
Mark 12:29-31, 41-44
Luke 5:33
Luke 8:17

Luke 9:23
Luke 12:6-7, 15, 48
Luke 16:23
Luke 18:18-23
Luke 22:42
John 1:12, 17-18
John 3:3-18, 30
John 6:47
John 8:7, 32, 34
John 10:30
John 13:5, 14-15
John 15:7, 26
John 17:3, 17
Acts 4:12, 36
Acts 10:34-35
Acts 14:23
Acts 16:18
Acts 20:35
Romans 1:16, 18, 20-32
Romans 3:20, 23
Romans 6:18, 23
Romans 8:1, 5, 13
Romans 9:1, 14-19
Romans 12:1-3
Romans 14:11-12
1 Corinthians 5:12-13
1 Corinthians 6:19-20
1 Corinthians 8:2, 4
1 Corinthians 10:13
1 Corinthians 12:14-22
1 Corinthians 15:3-6, 10
2 Corinthians 1:12
2 Corinthians 5:8, 17
2 Corinthians 8:9
2 Corinthians 10:3, 5
2 Corinthians 12:9

Luke 11:1, 9-10
Luke 15:7, 11-32
Luke 17:7
Luke 19:23
Luke 24:39
John 2:15
John 4:23-24, 37-38
John 7:24
John 8:36, 43-44
John 12:43
John 14:5-6, 15-16, 26
John 16:7
Acts 2:21
Acts 5:14
Acts 13:3, 43
Acts 15:18, 36-41
Acts 17:25
Acts 24:16
Romans 2:15
Romans 5:8, 17
Romans 7:19
Romans 8:14, 28, 31-39
Romans 9: 11, 13, 17
Romans 12:8, 12, 19
Romans 15:14
1 Corinthians 6:1-5, 9-11,
1 Corinthians 7:1-5, 8-9
1 Corinthians 9:22
1 Corinthians 11:31
1 Corinthians 13:4-8, 13
1 Corinthians 16:2
2 Corinthians 3:5, 18
2 Corinthians 6:14
2 Corinthians 9:6-11, 15
2 Corinthians 11:14-15
2 Corinthians 13:4

Galatians 1:6
Galatians 4:16
Galatians 6:1-3
Ephesians 1:14
Ephesians 4:5, 14-15
Ephesians 5:1, 5, 15
Ephesians 6:12
Philippians 2:3, 5-8
Philippians 4:6, 8, 13, 19
Colossians 2:8
Colossians 4:2,6
1 Thessalonians 5:12-24
2 Thessalonians 3:2
1 Timothy 2:1, 2, 5, 9-10
1 Timothy 5:12-13
2 Timothy 1:3
2 Timothy 3:5, 8, 16-17
Titus 1:1-2, 15
Hebrews 2:2, 17-18
Hebrews 4:14-16
Hebrews 10:30
Hebrews 12:6-7
James 1:5-8, 17
James 2:20
James 4:3, 6-8, 10, 14, 17
1 Peter 1:15
1 Peter 3:7, 12
2 Peter 1:3
1 John 1:5, 9
1 John 3:4, 22
1 John 5:14
Revelation 19:6
Revelation 22:7, 13

Galatians 3:20
Galatians 5:6, 22-23
Galatians 6:7, 9
Ephesians 2:1, 4, 8-9
Ephesians 4:22, 25-32
Ephesians 5:16, 22-24
Philippians 1:19, 27
Philippians 3:13, 19
Colossians 1:16, 21, 28
Colossians 3:8, 13, 16
1 Thessalonians 1:7
2 Thessalonians 2:3
1 Timothy 1:5, 15, 17
1 Timothy 4:2, 12
1 Timothy 6:10, 16-17
2 Timothy 2:2
2 Timothy 4:3-4, 16
Titus 2:8
Hebrews 3:8, 12-13, 15
Hebrews 9:14, 27
Hebrews 11:1,6
Hebrews 13:5-6, 8
James 1:19, 22, 26-27
James 3:2-12, 16-17
James 5:7, 14, 16
1 Peter 2:1, 23
1 Peter 5:5-6, 8, 10
2 Peter 3:9, 16
1 John 2:16
1 John 4:1, 10, 16
Revelations 3:15-16, 19-20
Revelation 21:8

My Testimony

I am the youngest of eight children (four girls and four boys) born into a Hindu Brahmin family. I was blessed to have been born into a family where there was so much love, affection, understanding, support, compassion, and tolerance. In my family, there was always plenty of unconditional love to go around.

I currently reside in Florida with my wife and daughter. During my early years, I failed the seventh, tenth, and twelfth grades of my schooling. Thus, I was considered to be the brown sheep of my family. Later in life, I earned three doctoral degrees. Some folks have asked me why I needed all of these degrees. It is because of the people I love.

I have never shown any interest in education. However, from the young age of ten or so, I had tremendous knowledge about many Hindu gods and goddesses. I was very knowledgeable in Hindu epics, such as *Ramayana*, *Mahabharatha*, and *Bhagawad-Gita*. There was a time I wanted to be a religious person within the Hindu tradition.

I was not a good son, not a good brother, not a good neighbor, and not a good student. I have sinned against holy God and against so many people that I cannot even count or remember. My parents thought it would be best if I came to the United States and made some positive and productive changes.

I arrived in the United States in August of 1982, and for the next two years, I stayed with my brother and his family, pursuing an Associate Degree in Business Administration. I began to feel homesick and started to think about God, truth, life, and so on.

I could not pursue much because I was a guest in someone else's home and had to wait for an opportunity to be by myself in order to think freely. In the summer of 1984, I transferred to a four-year university in Michigan, which was a three-hour drive from my brother's house.

For the first time in my life, I was free to think, and that is what I began to do. At that time, a man of God (pastor) told me about a Christian program on television called the *700 Club*, hosted by televangelist Pat Robertson. I started to watch the show in June of 1985.

For the first three months of watching that show, nothing happened. Then, slowly and surely, I began to get hooked on watching the program, which ran from midnight until one a.m. I did not and could not understand why, being a Hindu Brahmin, I was so addicted to that show.

I was on a date with a close female friend on the night of January 12, 1986, and returned to the dorm one minute before midnight. As soon as I walked into my room, I turned on the television and switched to the *700 Club*. What happened next was history in the making.

Reverend Pat Robertson was delivering the following "word of knowledge": "There is a young man who just turned the television on, and this young man comes from the East. All of his life, he has been serving and worshipping numerous other gods. For the past three years, this young man has been searching for the truth."

As Mr. Robertson continued to speak, I felt a spiritual tug in my heart. I knew he was describing me exactly. Three things happened at that very moment: I began to cry; I began to shake and shiver; and I fell to the floor. Even though what was happening looked strange, I knew God was trying to get my attention.

I was confused and wanted to know what was going on. Pat Robertson continued: "Behold, today is the day of your salvation . . . seek Him while He may yet be found." I laid aside all my reasoning and accepted

Jesus Christ as my personal Lord and Savior at the midnight hour on January 13, 1986.

Many things happened right after I got saved: my girlfriend broke up with me; I failed six courses I was taking at the time; my GPA dropped to 1.45, and I was put under an academic probation for about a year. Nor could I explain my newfound faith to my brother and the rest of my family.

All this adversity drove me to thoughts of suicide. Three months after I was saved, I made three attempts to end my life, but none of them succeeded because God had other plans for me. His Word says, "Faithful is He who called you, who also will do it."

I decided to move on with my life. I got back on my feet and finished an undergraduate degree in marketing. My father passed away of cancer in 1996, and a few years later, I lost my mother, also to cancer. To honor both of my parents, I earned doctoral degrees, one for each parent.

I consider myself to be a blessed man to have had such loving, caring, and wonderful parents who always showed nothing but unconditional love. I am also blessed to have married a woman of God whom I consider my better half. This blessing continued when God gave us a beautiful angel, our daughter, who at birth was diagnosed with Down syndrome.

All I can say to the Lord Jesus is a big and heartfelt, "Thank You."

About the Author

Raj Vemuri was born into a large, well-educated family in India that belongs to the Hindu Brahmin caste. He came to the United States in the fall of 1982 to pursue higher education. At the same time, he was also searching for the truth as it related to God.

On January 13, 1986, at the midnight hour, he accepted Jesus Christ as his personal Lord and Savior. He has been serving the Lord ever since. His heart's desire is to fulfill God's perfect plan for his life. Raj lives in Florida with his wife and daughter.

Education

ThD in Restorative Justice, Therapon University, US Virgin Islands
PhD in Clinical Christian Counseling, Cornerstone University, Lake Charles LA
EdD in Counseling Psychology, Argosy University, Sarasota FL
MA in Counseling, Liberty University, Lynchburg VA
BBA in Marketing, Eastern Michigan University, Ypsilanti MI

Certifications

Belief Therapist, Therapon Institute, Marrero, LA
Marriage and Family Therapist, NCCA, Sarasota, FL
Professional Pastoral Therapist, NAFC, Beaumont, TX
Re-Entry Crisis Counselor, Therapon Institute, Marrero, LA
Substance Abuse and Addiction Therapist, NCCA, Sarasota, FL
Temperament Counselor, NCCA, Sarasota, FL

Licenses

Belief Therapist, Therapon Institute, Marrero LA
Clinical Christian Counselor, NCCA, Sarasota FL
Clinical Pastoral Counselor, NCCA, Sarasota FL

Ordination

Chaplain, Chaplain Fellowship Ministries, Temple, TX

Teaching Experience

Adjunct Instructor of Psychology, Tallahassee Community College, Tallahassee FL
Adjunct Instructor of Psychology, Caldwell College, Caldwell NJ
Adjunct Instructor of Psychology, Brookdale Community College, Lincroft NJ
Adjunct Instructor of Psychology, Essex County College, Newark NJ
Adjunct Instructor of Psychology, Middlesex County College, Edison NJ
Adjunct Instructor of Psychology, Fairleigh Dickinson University, Atlantic City NJ

Other Work Experience

ESE Teacher, Taylor County High School, Perry FL
Child Welfare Specialist, City of New York NY
Behavioral Healthcare Assistant, Mercy Medical Center, Rockville Center NY
Therapist Intern, Mind/Body Connection, King of Prussia PA
Therapist Intern, Salvation Army, Norristown PA

Speaking Engagements

Assembly of God: Full-Gospel Businessmen's Association, Kalamazoo MI
Baptist Church Rahamathnagar, Hyderabad, India
Center For Biblical Studies, Tallahassee FL
Cody Pentecostal Holiness Church, Monticello FL
Donald Memorial P.H. Church, Hyderabad, India
Energy Infratech Private Limited, Hyderabad, India
Living Waters, Hyderabad, India
New Light Church, Crawfordville FL
Tallavana Community Church, Havana FL

TV Appearance

700 Club, Shared Personal Testimony, Aired on Easter Sunday, 1987

Counseling Experience

Cody Pentecostal Holiness Church, Monticello FL
Faith Horizon Ministry, Thomasville GA
Tallavana Community Church, Havana FL

Published Author

From Hinduism to Christ: A Former Hindu Brahmin Looks at World Religions and the Powerful Truths of the Christian Faith, published by Pleasant Word, a Division of WinePress Group, 2010.

Abbreviations Explained

NAFC: National Association of Faith-Based Counselors
NCCA: National Christian Counselors Association
NCCC: National Conservative Christian Church

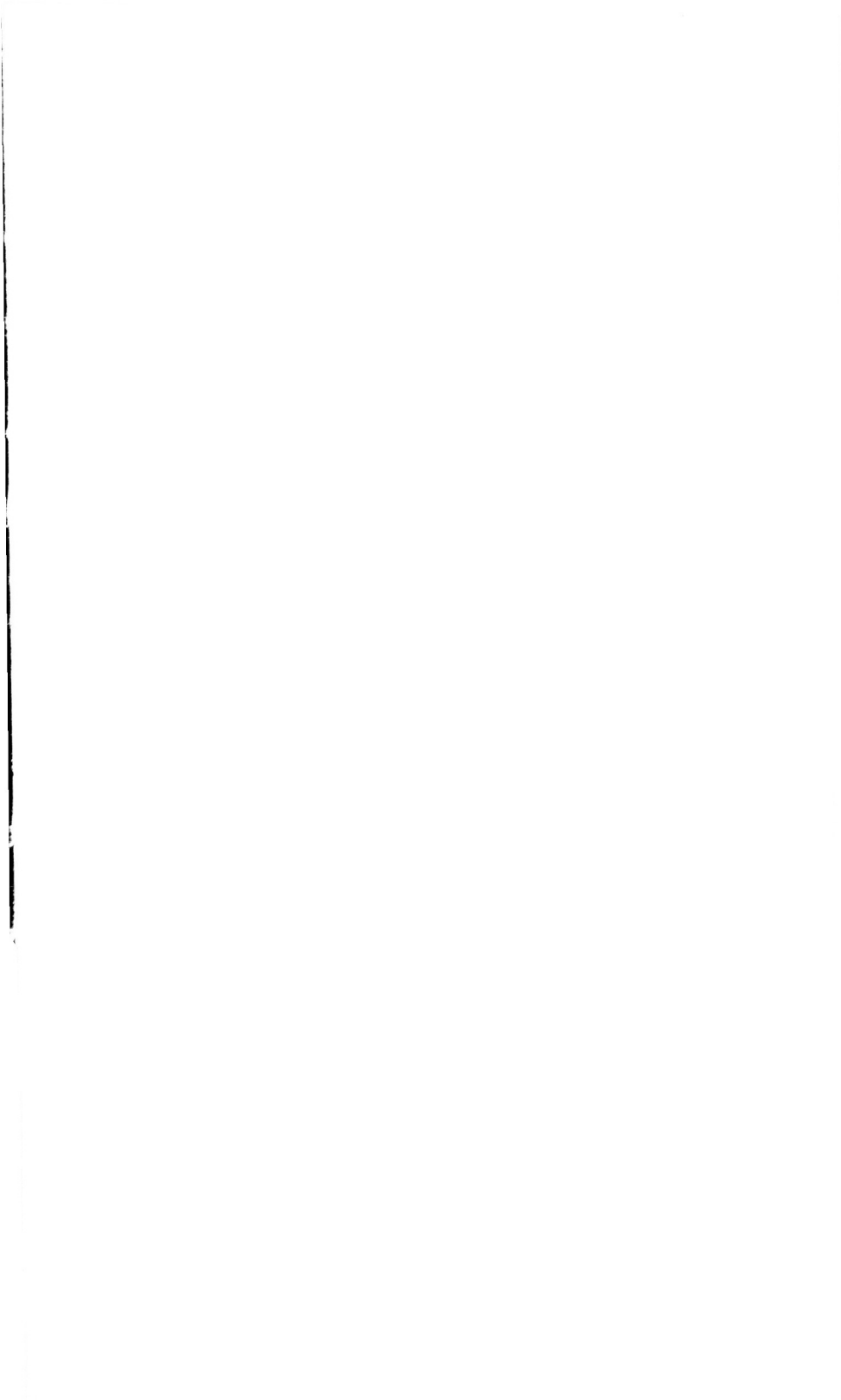